WHAT'S THE SCORE?

RED ⚡ LIGHTNING BOOKS

WHAT'S THE SCORE?

25 YEARS OF TEACHING WOMEN'S SPORTS HISTORY

BONNIE J. MORRIS

This book is a publication of

Red Lightning Books
1320 East 10th Street
Bloomington, Indiana 47405 USA

redlightningbooks.com

Manufactured in the United States of America

First printing 2022

Library of Congress Cataloging-in-Publication Data

Names: Morris, Bonnie J., author.
Title: What's the score? : 25 years of teaching women's
    sports history / Bonnie J. Morris.
Description: Bloomington, Indiana : Indiana University Press,
    [2022] | Includes bibliographical references and index.
Identifiers: LCCN 2021059718 (print) | LCCN 2021059719 (ebook) |
    ISBN 9781684351800 (hardback) | ISBN 9781684351817 (ebook)
Subjects: LCSH: Sports for women—History. | Sports—Sex differences. |
    Sex discrimination in sports. | Sexism in sports. | Morris, Bonnie J. |
    Women college teachers—United States—Biography.
Classification: LCC GV709 .M625 2022 (print) | LCC GV709
    (ebook) | DDC 796.082—dc23/eng/20220104
LC record available at https://lccn.loc.gov/2021059718
LC ebook record available at https://lccn.loc.gov/2021059719

For Christine Brennan, Billie Jean King,
Mariah Burton Nelson, and Patrick Nero
and
for the next generation of advocates:
Elana Meyers Taylor, Desi Carrasco, Layshia Clarendon,
Colleen Ryan, and my own brother, Coach John Morris.

And in loving memory of two athletic women,
Susan Vetter and Kathryn Dunn

CONTENTS

TIMELINE

101 TURNING POINTS IN WOMEN'S SPORTS HISTORY

Precolonial America Indigenous women of differing tribes are skilled at sports ranging from footraces, swimming, and wrestling to ball games, including lacrosse. White settlers are shocked to see women excel at what they consider "manly" pursuits—including leadership roles in tribal councils, peacemaking, conflict resolution, and diplomacy.

1780 Women are included in one of the first sports events of the new United States, horse races at the Hempstead Plains track on Long Island.

1866 Vassar College fields not one but two women's baseball teams.

1892 Senda Berenson introduces basketball with adapted rules to young women. The modified game soon moves from elite colleges to working-class women, who play at YWCA and YWHA gyms.

1895 Suffragist Frances Willard publishes *A Wheel Within a Wheel*, describing the independence and freedom she found by teaching herself to ride a bicycle at age fifty-three.

1896 The first intercollegiate women's basketball game, Stanford versus the University of California, is played with "half-court" rules before seven hundred female spectators at the Page Street Armory, with a final score of 2–1. Three years later, Stanford ends women's intercollegiate team sports "for the good of student's health" but also to end "unpleasant publicity accompanying the contests."

1896 The modern Olympics begin, banning women from competition just as they did during the first Greek games (although in ancient Greece, women caught watching were thrown off a cliff).

1900 Meeting in Paris, women join the modern Olympic Games in golf.

1904 The Fort Shaw Indian School sends the best women's basketball team in the United States to competition in western states; handily defeating all challengers, the players are also required to demonstrate their housekeeping skills while seated on display at the World's Fair in St. Louis.

1922 A Women's Olympics with twenty-two thousand spectators convenes in France, organized by Alice Milliat. Three more Women's Games are held: 1926 (Gothenburg, Sweden), 1930 (Prague, Czechoslovakia), and 1934 (London, England, with nineteen countries participating).

1922 Mrs. Herbert Hoover becomes head of the newly established women's division in the National Amateur Athletic Foundation, strongly opposing equal competition opportunities for girls and women out of concern pro competition will exploit and degrade women's athletics.

1926 Gertrude Ederle swims across the English Channel at age eighteen, returning home to a giant ticker-tape parade in New York City. (When nervous sponsors had begged her to come out of the water during a storm at sea, she famously responded, "What for?")

1927 Helen Wills, who wins eight women's singles championships at Wimbledon over six years, dares to predict that one day the best woman tennis player will beat a male player.

1928 Women are now permitted to compete at the Olympic Games; the sight of some exhausted female runners convinces officials to ban the women's eight-hundred-meter race until 1960.

1929 John Tunis publishes "Women and the Sport Business," praising noncompetitive playdays as more appropriate for women than the strenuous training required in elite public competition. He supports "idealists—who are anxious to keep the American girl from this commercialized competition, to safeguard her health by placing her athletic activities under the direction of properly qualified women supervisors."

1931 Seventeen-year-old southpaw Jackie Mitchell strikes out both Babe Ruth and Lou Gehrig in a possibly staged event, leading baseball commissioner Kenesaw Mountain Landis to ban women from baseball.

1932 Babe Didrikson emerges as the best female athlete of the twentieth century at the 1932 Olympic Games in Los Angeles. African Americans Louise Stokes and Tidye Pickett also qualify for the games but are banned from competing.

1936 Sportswriter Paul Gallico declares in *Vogue* magazine that "it is a lady's business to look beautiful. There are hardly any sports in which she seems able to do this. Ladies have no business playing squash, or any of the similar court games. They can't take it, or rather they can not take it gracefully."

1942–45 Japanese American women forcibly removed to internment relocation camps in the American West are permitted volleyball as recreation.

1943 Philip Wrigley starts the All-American Girls Professional Baseball League (AAGPBL), which lasts until 1954.

1948 At the first postwar Olympics (they were not held in 1940 or 1944), high jumper Alice Coachman becomes the first African American woman to win Olympic gold. Vicki Manalo Draves becomes the first Asian American (Filipina) to win Olympic gold and the first American woman to win two gold medals in diving.

1948 Patty Berg founds the Ladies Professional Golf Association.

1950 The US Lawn Tennis Association desegregates when Althea Gibson enters the US Open championship; by 1957, she is the top-ranked woman tennis player in the world.

1951 Janet Collins becomes the Metropolitan Opera's first African American ballerina, paving the way for future Black ballerinas, such as Misty Copeland.

1953–55 Toni Stone, Connie Morgan, and Mamie "Peanut" Johnson, barred from the all-White AAGPBL, make history as the only women to play baseball for the male Negro Leagues (on the Indianapolis Clowns and the Kansas City Monarchs). Much later, in 1997, when White player Ila Borders pitches a Minnesota Saints minor-league game, she is incorrectly reported to be the first woman to play professionally with men.

1953 The International Olympic Committee meets for a General Session meeting in Mexico City and recommends that women not be *excluded* from the Olympic Games—but specifies that they should be allowed to participate only in "suitable" sports.

1954 The Supreme Court decision in *Brown v. Board of Education* orders America's schools to integrate "with all deliberate speed." In response, the state of Virginia closes its public schools in various counties from 1956 to 1958, chartering White-only schools (as private institutions) and abandoning Black students. This time period with few or no organized Black schools has a huge impact on Black students' access to sports competition, college scouting, and state championships.

1958 Shirley "Cha Cha" Muldowney is the first woman to get a hot-rod license. She wins her first major drag race in 1971, later becoming the first person to win three National Hot Rod Association Top Fuel championships.

1959 Told that women may not compete in judo, Rusty Kanokogi wins the YMCA judo championship disguised as a man and is afterward stripped of her medal. She moves to Japan, becomes the first woman to earn a seventh-degree black belt, and in 1988 finally reaches her dream of introducing women's judo to the Olympics.

1960 At the Rome Olympic Games, Wilma Rudolph becomes the first American woman to win three gold medals at one Olympics. Coached by Ed Temple, the Tennessee Tigerbelles team, including

Willye White and Wyomia Tyus, ultimately bring home twenty-three Olympic medals and dozens of national championships to historically Black Tennessee State University.

1960 Earlene Brown becomes the first American woman to win an Olympic medal in shot put.

1964 After being the youngest swimmer to compete in the 1960 Rome Olympics, Donna de Varona wins two gold medals at the Tokyo Olympic Games. She becomes the first woman sportscaster for the Olympics.

1967 Kathrine Switzer enters the 1967 Boston Marathon under simply "K. Switzer" and is thrown out and disqualified, later succeeding in changing the rules forever so that all women may compete.

1967 Women elected to Congress are banned from using the congressional swimming pool and gym. Representatives Charlotte Reid (Illinois), Patsy Mink (Hawaii), and Catherine May (Washington) demand to enter the pool only to be told no—that congressmen prefer to swim naked. After the congresswomen protest, they are allowed to swim early each day, before the men arrive.

1970 Billie Jean King and Gladys Heldman form the Virginia Slims tournament for women's tennis in protest of the lower prize money given to women tennis champions.

1971–73 Girls gain the right to wear pants and sneakers to most American public schools, improving athletic participation and confidence.

1971 Australian Evonne Goolagong is ranked the number one tennis player in the world, in defiance of anti-Aboriginal racism, as well as sexism.

1972 Bernice Gera is the first female umpire in pro baseball, officiating a game on June 23, the same day that President Nixon signs Title IX into law.

1972 Women gain permission to run in the Boston Marathon.

1973 An audience of forty million fans watches Billie Jean King defeat Bobby Riggs in three straight sets on national television.

1973 Ann Meyers becomes the first woman to receive a basketball scholarship—and to play in the NBA.

1974 Girls are permitted in Little League baseball—however, not without harassment. Some team fathers demand that girls wear the athletic supporters required of boys.

1975 Junko Tabei of Japan becomes the first woman to climb Mount Everest.

1975 Martina Navratilova defects from Czechoslovakia to the United States and becomes the top-ranked US tennis player throughout the 1980s.

1976 Nadia Comăneci scores a perfect 10 at the Montreal Olympic Games, changing gymnastics forever. She and coach Béla Károlyi defect to the West; Károlyi's private gym in Texas becomes the top training facility for a generation of gold-medal American gymnasts, despite rumors of abuse.

1976 The Yale women's crew team stages a remarkable protest over the lack of a women's boathouse, entering the office of the Athletic Director and revealing "TITLE IX" written across their bare chests.

1976 "Boys' rules" finally replace eight years of "girls' rules" in basketball after varsity guard Victoria Ann Cape sues the Tennessee Secondary School Athletic Association.

1977 Janet Guthrie becomes the first woman race-car driver to compete in both the Indianapolis 500 and the Daytona 500.

1977 With support from Billie Jean King, Renée Richards becomes the first trans woman to play in a professional tennis tournament.

1978 As a journalist for *Sports Illustrated*, Melissa Ludtke wins equal access for women to enter men's team locker rooms for postgame interviews.

1982 The film *Personal Best* introduces the first mainstream script centered on lesbians in sports; the film also pays homage to the many American women and girls who, although beneficiaries of Title IX, lost their opportunity to compete on the global stage when the United States boycotted the 1980 Moscow Olympic Games. The film features cameos from many top track athletes.

1982 The Association for Intercollegiate Athletics for Women merges with the National Collegiate Athletic Association (NCAA) and goes bankrupt as more than 1,500 women athletic administrators lose their jobs. As schools combine their previously separate men's and women's athletic programs, salaries rise for men interested in coaching women's teams, but women are not similarly hired to coach men.

1982–89 Reebok, Nike, L.A. Gear, Adidas, Fila, and Asics manufacture their athletic shoes in South Korea, hiring local women and girls as a tightly controlled labor force. Professor Cynthia Enloe later takes on abusive labor practices in her essay "The Globetrotting Sneaker."

1984 Nawal El Moutawakel is the first Muslim woman to win gold as the Olympics permit women to compete in four-hundred-meter hurdles for the first time; Morocco's King Hassan II orders all Moroccan girls born that day to be named Nawal.

1984 American runner Joan Benoit wins the gold medal in the first year that women are permitted to compete in the Olympic Marathon.

1984 Due to the Olympic boycott against apartheid South Africa, White South African runner Zola Budd must compete as a member of the United Kingdom's team. The "barefoot runner" gains disfavor after American favorite Mary Decker trips on Budd's heels in a disputed incident watched by millions.

1985 Journalist Christine Brennan, after becoming the first woman sportswriter for the *Miami Herald*, becomes the first woman to cover DC's NFL team for the *Washington Post*.

1985 Libby Riddles is the first woman to win the 1,100-mile Iditarod dogsled race. The next year, the winner is also a woman, Susan Butcher, who ultimately claims five titles.

1987 The AAGPBL is inducted into the National Baseball Hall of Fame in Cooperstown, New York, inspiring director Penny Marshall to begin preparation for the hit film *A League of Their Own.*

1987 For the first time, a woman who is an athlete, not a swimsuit model, appears on the cover of *Sports Illustrated*: Jackie Joyner-Kersee.

1988 Evelyn Ashford is the first Black woman to carry the Olympic flag; skater Debi Thomas is the first Black woman to win any medal at the Winter Olympics. But a joint study between Wilson Sporting Goods Company and the Women's Sports Foundation, surveying five hundred families nationwide, finds that while Black and White girls are equally interested in sports, 33 percent of the Black girls concede that their families cannot afford the lessons or gear required for sports in their age group. The issue of cost is raised by 18 percent of the White girls in the survey.

1989 Native American artist and activist Charlene Teters arrives at the University of Illinois and begins an ongoing campaign to change the university's "Indian" mascot, Chief Illiniwek. The mascot is not retired from official halftime performances until 2007.

1994 The ladies' skating event at the Lillehammer Winter Olympics is overshadowed by an attack on favored skater Nancy Kerrigan. The suspect is soon identified as a former boyfriend of rival skater Tonya Harding, leading to vilification of Harding as "trash" and her eventual banning.

1995 Sheryl Swoopes is the first woman to have a signature basketball shoe marketed by Nike.

1996 At the Atlanta Olympics, Kerri Strug clinches the gold for the US women's gymnastics team by completing her routine and landing correctly—on a broken ankle. US women bring home the gold in basketball, paving the way for two pro leagues in 1997, the Women's National Basketball Association and the American Basketball League, as well as two memoirs of the winning gold-medal team, *Venus to the Hoop* and *Shooting from the Outside.*

1996 CBS Sports pulls golf commentator Ben Wright for remarks made over the previous year, such as "Lesbians in the sport hurt women's golf" and "Women are handicapped by big boobs. Their boobs get in the way."

1997 Violet Palmer and Dee Kantner become the first women referees in the NBA game. Kantner later becomes the first openly lesbian ref in pro basketball, and Palmer becomes the first woman to officiate in the NBA playoffs.

1998 The first US women's Olympic ice hockey team wins gold against rival Canada at the Winter Olympic Games in Nagano, Japan. The US men's team responds to its own defeat by going on a historic room-trashing rampage.

1999 The US women's soccer team wins the FIFA Women's World Cup. The image of Brandi Chastain rejoicing in her sports bra appears on magazine covers around the world.

2000 For the first time, a woman, Sandra Baldwin, is elected president of the US Olympic Committee.

2000 The Summer Olympics in Sydney, Australia, change many people's ideas of what a female competitor looks like, from champion Stacy Dragila in the first-ever women's pole vault event, to three-hundred-pound weight-lifting medalist Cheryl Haworth; to forty-year-old Dara Torres, who, as the oldest champion in swimming, earns two gold and three bronze medals. Cathy Freeman's gold-medal victory lap with the Aboriginal flag leads to new dialogue on Australia's historic mistreatment of the Aboriginal community.

2002 At the first Olympic women's bobsled event, Vonetta Flowers becomes the first African American woman to win gold in the Winter Olympic Games.

2002 The all-male Augusta National Golf Club faces pressure to admit women as members during its hosting of the Masters Tournament. It steadfastly refuses to change policy until August 20, 2012, when former secretary of state Condoleezza Rice is invited to become the first female member.

2002 At the Las Vegas Bowl, Katie Hnida becomes the first woman to play in an NCAA Division I-A football game.

2003 Golfer Annika Sörenstam enters the all-male PGA, shooting one over par. While she fails to make the cut the following day, she scores well above dozens of male competitors.

2003 On January 14, University of Tennessee's Pat Summitt becomes the first women's basketball coach to win eight hundred games, followed by another, University of Texas coach Jody Conradt, eight days later. By 2005, Summitt celebrates the most victories (880) of any coach in NCAA basketball history, shattering the record of University of North Carolina men's coach Dean Smith.

2003 Teresa Phillips of Tennessee State University becomes the first woman to coach a men's Division I basketball team.

2004 FIFA president Sepp Blatter creates an uproar by suggesting that women soccer players wear more revealing, "feminine" uniforms, such as "tighter shorts," to attract more viewers.

2004 Beach volleyball is added as a new and increasingly popular Olympic sport. American doubles players Misty May and Kerri Walsh win gold in 2004, 2008, and 2012.

2007 Aheda Zanetti designs the "burkini"—modest, all-covering swimwear for observant Muslim women and girls. Although intended to help accelerate the inclusion and acceptance of Muslim women in sports and encourage their employment as beach lifeguards in Australia, the appearance of the burkini creates backlash at some public pools and beaches. It is banned in France during the summer of 2016.

2008 The ITVS documentary film *Doping for Gold* reveals the extent to which the East German women's national and Olympic teams were heavily doped with experimental steroids, calling into question their dominance in the 1960s and 1970s.

2008 The NCAA recognizes the men's basketball double-double record (held by NBA all-star Tim Duncan) but does not keep statistics for the women's division. During the 2008 season, women's basketball fans watch Courtney Paris attain a record ninety double-doubles, surpassing Duncan's record of eighty-seven.

2009 Dee Mosbacher's film *Training Rules* examines the climate of homophobia in women's sports with an in-depth look at Penn State University coach Rene Portland, whose "no lesbians" policy for the women's basketball team was first publicized in a 1991 news feature.

2009 Celebrated women's basketball coach Kay Yow, who led the 1988 US women's basketball team to an Olympic gold medal and surpassed seven hundred wins in a thirty-eight-year career, dies of breast cancer. Dozens of cancer funds, game classics, ball courts, and Nike initiatives are named in Yow's honor, making breast cancer awareness a signature part of women's basketball. Male athletes break new ground by also donning pink uniforms to honor Yow and other women with cancer.

2009 Outstanding South African runner Caster Semenya is subjected to the first of many sex tests to prove she is female. She will be challenged and banned throughout her career.

2009 Kye Allums, a member of George Washington University's women's basketball team, comes out publicly about identifying as male—the first Division I college basketball player to become a trans man, supported by GWU's coach and university athletics program.

2012 Turkish columnist Yüksel Aytuğ publishes an article titled "Womanhood Is Dying at the Olympics," suggesting that female Olympic contestants should gain bonus points based on how feminine they look.

2012 For the first time, the United States sends more female than male athletes to the Olympics; Saudi Arabia, Brunei, and Qatar send their first female athletes; and women's boxing is introduced.

2014 FIFA lifts its longtime ban on Muslim women soccer players competing in headscarves. Women's ski jump is allowed at the Winter Olympics. Elana Meyers becomes the first American woman to earn three Olympic bobsled medals. She will become

the first woman to earn a spot as a pilot on the men's national
bobsled team.

2016 The Harvard men's soccer team is sidelined for the season after
it is revealed that players have rated the incoming women's
soccer team players in a sexually degrading "scouting report"
since 2012. They publish a public apology. The women's team
responds with an editorial in the *New York Times.*

2017 Former USA Gymnastics national team doctor Larry Nassar is
sentenced to 60 years in federal prison and, in 2018, an additional
175 years plus 40 to 125 years in Michigan state prisons, after
being charged with assaulting more than 250 girls since 1992.

2017 The NCAA requires all member schools to offer sexual violence
prevention training for athletes, coaches, and administrators.
(Earlier, in 2015, the fourteen-college Southeastern Conference
pledged to ban any transfer athlete with a history of sexual
misconduct.)

2017 Former Women's Football Alliance player Katie Sowers becomes
an assistant coach for the San Francisco 49ers.

2018 Serena Williams's "catsuit" is banned at the French Open, leading
to explosive debate over the strict dress standards applied to
women in the sport of tennis—and lingering racism as well.

2019 The World Surf League commits to equal prize money for male
and female contestants.

2019 Nike announces it is removing contract penalties for pregnant
athletes.

2019 All twenty-eight members of the US Women's National Team sue
the US Soccer Federation for gender discrimination and unequal
pay. US Soccer argues that biological differences are the reason
for different pay.

2019 After being banned from attending most live sports events since
Iran's Islamic Revolution in the late 1970s, Iranian women are at
last allowed to attend a FIFA soccer game at Tehran's Freedom
Stadium.

2020 Olympic ice hockey gold medalist Kendall Coyne Schofield becomes the first woman to broadcast men's pro hockey game coverage for the NHL's NBC affiliate.

2020 Sabrina Ionescu scores the most recorded points of any NCAA basketball player, male or female, just as the COVID-19 pandemic shuts down seasonal March Madness play and cancels the 2020 NCAA tournament. The Summer Olympic Games are postponed.

2021 The first full-time female referee in NFL history, Sarah Thomas, becomes the first woman to officiate at the Super Bowl. Due to COVID-19, the normally packed stadium is downsized to a limited, masked audience, but millions of viewers at home and abroad meet Thomas on-screen. In March 2021, the NFL names the first Black woman to its officiating staff, Maia Chaka.

WHAT'S THE SCORE?

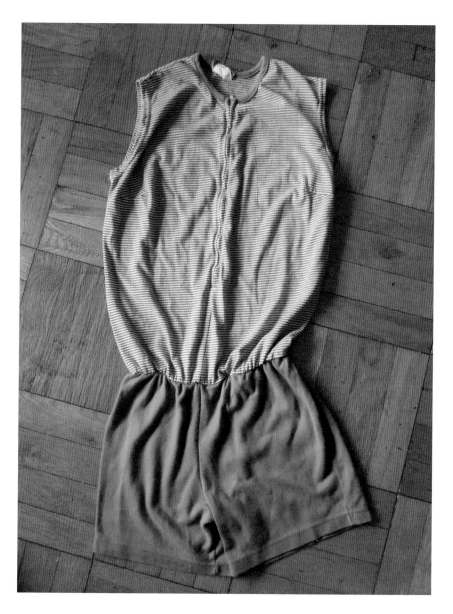

Fig. P.1 The author's ninth-grade gym suit, Western Junior High, Bethesda, Maryland, 1975. *Photo by the author.*

PROLOGUE

The Bus Ride before the Game—or, A Parable about
Our Low Expectations for Women's Sports Knowledge

Imagine, if you will, a father and son on a city bus. Or it might be grandfather and grandson; the boy is young, no more than six. They sit together near the front. At a bus stop, an older adult male steps on and, spying the pair, says to the young boy in a friendly tone, "Hiya, tiger! Who's your team in the World Series?" Shyly, the little boy whispers, "The Dodgers," and the two adult men, strangers mere seconds before, laugh together. A three-generational conversation about baseball has begun, initiating the youngest participant into a lifelong cozy world of man-talk about sports.

Familiar to most of us. Now, let's imagine a mother and daughter are on that bus, the six-year-old girl uncomfortable and itchy in her required school-uniform skirt. At a bus stop, an elderly woman gets on, sees the girl, and shouts, "Hey there, cub! Who ya favor for the Super Bowl?" Heads turn. *A crazy lady.* The mother covers her daughter with a protective arm. Passengers aren't acculturated to view this moment as three generations of athletic *women* or as a normal conversation bringing a strong girl into the fold. At best, the strange woman remains that: a stranger, socially marginal in her odd behavior. We still don't expect women to initiate, share, participate in, or pass along sports literacy. In other words, except on a few annual occasions, we don't expect women to know the score.

Very early in life, girls get left behind and left out of a swath of popular culture expected of most males. It's even considered "cute," or appropriately feminine, when a woman doesn't understand the rules of a game or what just happened on the field. Male companions interpret the action for her—or, intent on the outcome, the score, they explain what happened afterward.

Not knowing the score puts women and girls at a disadvantage. It extends to not knowing the score historically (who *were* the top women athletes of all time, and how many broke records set by men?) or financially (what *are* the salaries for the best women players in the world, and why doesn't the women's national soccer team earn as much as the men's?). Ignorance of the score is a social-justice disadvantage, too, as we seek ways to undo centuries of racism. Not knowing how long and how totally America's sports were segregated limits athletes' alliances now. Throughout Jim Crow segregation, many Black athletes' scores weren't even entered into official state statistics, making it impossible to be certain—and pass on—just who had the best season or set time-shattering record. To take the image of the bus ride further, we know that women athletes often endured long bus trips to away games, while better-funded men's teams flew and enjoyed nicer hotels. But we don't hear as much from the Black women who always rode in the back of the bus—or how Black women athletes, denied beds at Whites-only motels on the road, slept on the hard seats of their own team buses on nights before away games.

As a women's history professor, I was already keeping score of how far women had come, how well or poorly we were doing, and how far we had to go. Too many of my own students started college not knowing when women won the right to vote; year after year, this never changed. Among the many student athletes I taught, more than half were female, but none could name five female athletes who had won gold at the Olympics. None had heard of an African American woman named Toni Stone, who had played pro baseball alongside men in the Negro Leagues; no White students knew about segregated baseball, for that matter. Though many of my students in Washington, DC, were pursuing careers in government or were interns on Capitol Hill, they were unfamiliar with Title IX law and with past rules that kept congresswomen from using the sports club available to male elected representatives.

But I hadn't learned any of that, either, in high school, dressed in my sagging one-piece gym suit (see fig. P.1). As a young girl, I would not have had an answer for which team I favored even if Toni Stone herself had boarded my bus in LA and challenged me to a friendly woman-to-woman conversation about sports. We had all been left out of sports literacy, not encouraged to learn the names of Black or White sports heroines, and allowed to feel it didn't matter whether we were ignorant in this area.

There was a score to settle, and I invented a class to launch the conversation. The class was called Athletics and Gender. I taught it for twenty-five years.

I went to the men's basketball game tonight. The bleachers were packed. Most of the women's basketball team were seated together right in front of me. And one of those women stood up and yelled to the sold-out crowd, "Why don't you guys come to the girls' games?"

—FROM MY JOURNAL, SPRING OF 1997

INTRODUCTION

Nothing Better to Do on a Friday Night?

Why is a course called Athletics and Gender important or even necessary? Don't women in postfeminist America have equal rights? Women work out, run, even wrestle and box. It's hip to be buff. Katie Sowers, who played in a women's football league, is now an assistant coach for a men's football team. Fans of women's sports cheer for the US women's national soccer team, follow Serena Williams, and bump fists whenever a woman holding up an Olympic gold medal gets her picture on a Wheaties box—unthinkable in the past, when Wheaties commercials exclusively targeted little boys with the ad jingle "He knows he's a man; he's ready for Wheaties."[1] Happily, today's young women can run, leap, slam-dunk, tackle, score, and sweat, whether in pursuit of basic fitness and self-confidence or as key players on Olympic and NCAA championship teams. Women and girls can find success in sports. But they sure won't find equal pay.

Sports history is the history of American opportunity: the opportunity to play, compete, win, and be a role model to the world. It's also the history of limitations placed on talent: "Whites Only," "No Girls Allowed," "Girls' Rules," "No dogs or Mexicans permitted in the park." Across US history, these messages shaped the fate of women athletes and all people of color, too many of whom lost the playing time and fame they deserved as they confronted barriers to their ambition and ability. The long story of women's fight just to get in the game is well worth revisiting, especially as we celebrate the fiftieth anniversary of Title IX law (1972)

WSTP 230. Athletics and Gender

Professor Bonnie Morris

This course is one of the only undergraduate seminars in the country to focus on the history of sex-role stereotyping in athletics. This course will investigate how out attitudes about male and female sports are reflected in our cultural beliefs; how men and women are trained to think about competition, winning, and performance; and if Title 9 has made any significant impact on equality of opportunity for female athletes. The course will also examine how the American media plays a role in constructing stereotypes about winners, losers, masculinity, and femininity. Through readings, films, guest speakers, class discussion, and analysis of current sports issues, we will explore the politics of athletics and gender--at our own university, in the larger society, and cross-culturally.

Mondays/Wednesdays 4:15-5:30 pm

Fig. I.1 Course poster, late 1990s.

and the fiftieth anniversary of Billie Jean King's historic victory over challenger Bobby Riggs (1973). Who were the first female athletes in America? When was the first women's college basketball game? Who were the real base-stealing heroines of the All-American Girls Professional Baseball League? How did Black women competitors win Olympic gold for an America that denied them a drink of water in a public park? And how did the era of feminist change help women demand the right to officiate at games, write sports news, and coach men's teams?

I was a reluctant athlete, preferring to read and write stories while my father and brother organized volleyball legacies. My brother, John Morris, played both soccer and volleyball at the University of Maryland, and my father, Roger Morris, personally built the sandpit volleyball courts near the Lincoln Memorial; he ran the DC Doubles tournament for at least fifteen years. My mother, Myra, taught dance and movement to schoolchildren in the Washington, DC, area. We were a high-energy family that rarely sat still, and from the time my brother and I could walk, my parents took us on hiking and camping trips four times a year.

I was an actress and dancer in high school; despite enjoying years of youth soccer, I didn't find my stride as an athlete. Instead, I was an early feminist, my antennae up for any perceived slight to girl power. My sport was social justice; I lettered in women's rights. I made sure to keep the *active* in *activist*, clumsy but constant, climbing mountains, camping, walking, ice-skating, and swimming. If team sports revealed my lack of reflex coordination, solo workouts let me write entire books in my head while moving—moving ever forward on pavement or ice, water or hill. By the time I was twenty-two, I realized that I was in fact more fit and daring than many women of my generation, that first generation benefiting from Title IX law. I dived through beach waves that other women dreaded, clawed my way up Sierra mountain trails on one granola bar, and rode camels into the Sinai Desert, unafraid. Later, I bought myself in-line skates for my thirtieth birthday; played on a women's soccer team called the Chico Weasels; and tested my muscles, endurance, and energy levels every summer working on crews at women's music festivals. But as I would discover, fitness is not the same thing as advocacy. The year I became a women's sports *advocate* is easy to pinpoint: 1994.

I had become a professor of women's history and was teaching in Upstate New York at St. Lawrence University, snowed in during the long winter months, and getting to know many student athletes. I attended all sports events, both men's and women's. In particular, I became a loyal ally to the women's basketball coach, but as I sat nearby admiring her complex plays, I pondered why I was the only member of the teaching faculty in the bleachers. And then at one game, the captain of the men's team—who was also my student—walked right through the gym, not even pausing to look at the women's game unfolding. Instead, he spotted me, grinned, and called out loudly, in earshot of the women's coach, "Nothing better to do on a Friday night?"

A few months after that, I was hired at George Washington University, where I would teach for the next twenty-three years. I discovered a great women's basketball team there as well. With so many of these fine players in my own classes, I was at every game, screaming, "Go, girl!"; boasting to anyone seated nearby, "That point guard's in my class"; and introducing myself to the players' parents. My pride swelled as GWU women won home game after home game, went to the Sweet Sixteen, went to the Elite Eight.

In my first year of teaching at GWU, there was a big homecoming event: two back-to-back basketball games, first the men's team and then the women's, one ticket for one great afternoon. When I walked into the Smith Center on that day in February 1995, I was surprised to pass through a metal detector. Bomb threat? Bad prank by the rival team? But no: "The president's here!" whispered a security guard. President Bill Clinton had brought his daughter, Chelsea, to a game, as GWU's Foggy Bottom campus sits mere blocks from the White House.

I watched President Clinton closely. After the men's game ended, he mingled with many supporters in the bleachers, shaking hands. But then he began heading toward the exit. Was he really leaving now that the men's game was over? Leaving even before the women's team had come out onto the court? What sort of example did that set? Other fans, too, were packing up snow boots and winter jackets, turning their backs on our women's team. I'd seen enough. So I pushed my way toward Mr. Clinton, stuck out my hand, and declared, "Hi, Mr. President. I'm a women's studies professor here at GWU. I'd like to thank you in advance for your ongoing support of Title IX and athletic opportunities for women and girls in America!"

"Why, thank you very much," he said. He had a warm handshake.

I pressed on. "And I'd like to ask that you stay to watch the women's game. Please don't leave now that the men have won. It would be important to our women's team, not to mention your own daughter, if you stayed to cheer the women. They're a terrific team."

"Well, I'd love to stay," said the president. "But I have an appointment at three o'clock."

I glanced at the clocks in our gym. "You can watch the first half of the women's game, sir," I insisted. "The first twenty minutes." And lo! He sat back down. He also became the first US president to telephone his congratulations to the winning women's team in the NCAA basketball championships that March. I had experienced sweet success in my first effort as a public advocate for women's sports. I never imagined it would involve giving a direct order to a US president, but this encounter gave me the confidence to propose a new class I called Athletics and Gender.

The timing was right for several reasons. We'd been experiencing a great deal of tension on George Washington University's campus over the possible recruitment of a young male basketball player who, it turned out, had a juvenile sexual-assault record. During the peak of campus debate about denying him an offer from GWU, the *Washington Post* contacted our women's studies program to ask what "campus feminists" thought about the controversy. I agreed to give an interview to staff writer Mark Asher. By telephone, I told the *Post* that my own students were definitely concerned about the intersection of male aggression and American sports culture, which paid millions to male athletic celebrities regardless of intimate violence in their private lives. How much of male sports culture involved disrespect of women? "You throw like a girl." "You're such a wuss." But, I added, my students and I were also fed up with the lack of fans at women's games, the lack of support for female athletic achievement. What if more women were visible as sports authorities? In what ways had feminism failed women's sports?

Overhearing this conversation, my program chair, Dr. Barbara Miller, offered her support. Here we were at the exact midpoint of the 1990s, and GWU proudly hosted the nation's longest-running graduate program in women's studies, yet there was no classroom forum or dedicated space in our curriculum for talking about women's sports. I proposed the Athletics and Gender course as a special topic for women's studies credit, a safe but scholarly forum for students to discuss their own identities and experiences in American sports culture. We'd bring an academic focus to athletic privilege and sexism, ideals of masculinity and femininity, opportunity and visibility, and the changing historic landscape of women's sports. I began teaching the class in January 1996, and on February 28, 1996, Barbara dashed off a crisp letter to university president Stephen Joel Trachtenberg, sealing the deal. Her letter helpfully reminded him that my class was already a success and that scholarship on athletics would fit well as a defined area of excellence for GWU's women's studies program. Supporting my own goals for our program, Barbara emphasized that women's sports history intersected with studies in public policy, the biomedical sciences, sports administration and management, and law.

I couldn't know then that I would end up teaching this special class every semester for the next twenty-five years at a half dozen top colleges; I am teaching it still. Having cracked open the door, I learned that almost everybody, in the United States and beyond, wanted to talk about these issues.

That was the beginning, at George Washington University in academic year 1995/96. Soon afterward, I was also hired to teach at Georgetown University, GWU's crosstown rival, and at American University, my own alma mater, and then on Semester at Sea, I traveled around the world with women's sports history. During the decades in Washington, DC, I attended hundreds of games as an honorary coach, occasionally at GWU-versus-Georgetown matches, where all starting players on both sides were my current students. I became GWU's Professor of the Year several times by vote of the student athletes and was appointed by the university president to the athletes' council. I became faculty adviser to women's rugby and flagged the line at our game against the Naval Academy in Annapolis. At Georgetown, my students included almost the entire football team and the Crown Prince of Jordan, and I lectured overseas at Georgetown's satellite campus in Doha, Qatar, on a panel with Paul Tagliabue, former NFL commissioner. Other opportunities followed: I was invited to be a women's sports consultant for Disney, for Harvard, for National History Day students; and one of my Georgetown class lectures appeared on C-SPAN (fig. I.2). In 2017, I was invited to bring my class into the curriculum of the University of California at Berkeley as a diversity requirement sponsored by American Cultures and the Department of History, and I became a finalist for the Excellence in Teaching award.

There followed invitations to teach the class at several private Catholic institutions—Santa Clara University, Saint Mary's College of California, and the list goes on. I worked with top student athletes from coast to coast. During broadcasts of the Winter Olympics, I watched my former student Elana Meyers Taylor medal in bobsled, commit to donating her athletic brain to science, and ascend to being president of the Women's Sports Foundation. At Berkeley, a modest male student confided to me, just before graduating, that he played pro baseball for the Dodgers—he hadn't wanted to receive any sort of special treatment. But he did give me an autographed bat.

In the early years at GWU, the course enrolled perhaps twenty-five to forty students each semester; at Berkeley, I enrolled two hundred. Many of the students, but not all, were Division I NCAA athletes, male and female, awarded college scholarships to play ball or row crew or run. Track, lacrosse, rugby, basketball, gymnastics, volleyball, swimming, football, cheerleading—everyone enrolled, and while several coaches and trainers begged to sit in, I maintained a strict students-only policy to foster uninhibited discussion. Other students were women's studies and history majors, business majors interested in sports marketing, health majors concerned about soaring national trends of obesity and eating disorders, and journalism majors hoping to analyze trends in media coverage of female athletes. With the exception of my wonderful returning adult students, all were born after 1972, heirs to the legacy of Title IX, the controversial law of the Education Amendments of 1972 that decreed that any educational institution receiving federal funds must offer equal opportunities to male and female students. But few students, regardless of their own backgrounds in competitive sports, were familiar with Title IX or with the complex social history of gender roles in American culture. Most didn't know how our traditional values, or cultural anxieties, had defined "male" and "female" athletics by law, custom, and fashion since Puritan times. As we analyzed the changing roles for women in society, the students' discomfort and outrage over legacies of discrimination were palpable. Discussions grew heated. I might have begun the semester by introducing myself as the professor, but during the class debates that developed over our fourteen weeks together, I soon felt more like the referee.

How did I plot the initial syllabus for a women's sports class? In the resources section at the end of the book, you'll find three sample syllabi:

one from the early years of the class at George Washington University, one from the 2019 class at UC Berkeley, and the global version from Semester at Sea. In chapter 6, I'll wrap up with a very candid look back at best practices: what worked, what did not work, what the student evaluations had to say over time, and which conditions at different campuses made success possible. The learning objectives I list in my syllabus today set out the same ideals I followed from the very start:

- Know the various codes and customs restricting female and minority access to sports participation in US history

- Demonstrate familiarity with athletes and educators who helped change attitudes, laws, and opportunities

- Identify the intersection of race, class, and gender in the construction of sports participation and facilities in the United States

- Analyze the evolving nature of the Olympics as a global geopolitical event with overlapping ideological narratives

- Identify biases and themes in media coverage of men's and women's athletics

- Compare restricted country-club sports and other membership-based facilities with public courts, YMCA and YMHA recreation, open versus segregated parks and pools, and street ball

- Understand and address the background of Title IX law and its ongoing applications

- Analyze aspects of social diversity (ethnicity, race, socio-economic status, gender, sexual orientation, age, ability, etc.) and how they affect American sports training

- Explain how social categories and structures of power may affect human athletic potential

- Articulate a critical account of double standards in health and fitness history

- Demonstrate your familiarity with the readings and other course content through exams and papers

This is, to be sure, a daunting list of objectives. On the other hand, apart from exercise science and kinesiology majors, most students came to this class through the humanities and social sciences, and I wanted, right up front, a menu of topics that offered something for everybody. It was clear to me that almost every issue pending in American politics was somehow linked to historical boundaries around gender and race. Sports offered a lens for looking at these hot-button issues over time and gave student athletes immediate roles in the classroom as authoritative narrators. But the syllabus also spoke to topics that on any given day offered students with other backgrounds the chance to shine: for English majors, we'd explore the literature of sports journalism and sports storybooks published for children; for art majors, we looked at sports in comics, anime, and ad graphics; for political scientists, we'd study Olympic standoffs and Title IX debates; for health and nursing majors, the body, fitness, and sports foods were constant topics. Even the one architecture major, who sat with his arms folded in a posture of distrust, grew alert and eager as we perused the design of racially segregated sports facilities and bathrooms, or discussed Nazi filmmaker Leni Riefenstahl's epic documentary *Olympia*, a propaganda masterpiece for the 1936 Berlin Olympics. There were films for film majors, ad campaigns for business majors, and discussions on pain and recovery for the trainers and kinesiologists. But knitting it all together was my expectation, stated up front, that everyone had to show up every day and make the effort to look at how sex roles and stereotypes shape what we think we know about the world of athletics.

Assuming that few, if any, students had been introduced to women's sports history through books assigned in high school, I had to construct a reading list that was informative, inclusive, approachable in tone, and affordable in paperback. To use my students' favorite adverb, I *blatantly* sought to interest athletes in the history major and to make women's studies or gender studies appealing to male and female students. These objectives required a balance of evidence, research, analysis, and open discussion that kept everyone feeling welcome but challenged. I intended to bring in sports documentaries and professional guest speakers as well. Fortunately, the first five years I taught the class overlapped with a surge in new publications and media attention devoted to women's sports.

That new media attention really began in 1994, with UNC–Chapel Hill winning the NCAA women's basketball championship with a three-point shot in the last second of the game. Then, in 1995, Connecticut emerged as a women's basketball powerhouse, followed by the astounding performance of the US women's basketball team at the 1996 Olympic Games in Atlanta. We began to see Laila Ali donning boxing gloves, teenage Cheryl Haworth powerlifting, and Britain's twenty-five-year-old Ellen MacArthur sailing around the world alone and setting the second-fastest time of any such sailor in world history. Suddenly the media was doubling and tripling its attention to elite female athletes. Moreover, a men's baseball strike left sportswriters stranded and annoyed, critical of well-paid male athletes holding out for more millions while female athletes held bake sales to buy volleyballs; sports journalists, both male and female, turned their pens to the phenomenon of women athletes playing for the love of the game. The United States saw the explosive emergence of women's professional basketball, followed by the gold-medal victory of the US women's ice hockey team in the 1998 Winter Olympics in Nagano—in the very first year women's ice hockey became an Olympic event. And then came the US women's soccer team victory in the 1999 Women's World Cup, symbolized by player Brandi Chastain's exuberant shirt removal. Her cousin Lindsay Chastain, a GWU student, later enrolled in my class.

During this five-year period, a new market niche—the loyal female spectators and fans ready to spend cash for season tickets and souvenirs—found their interest affirmed by television and print ads featuring new stars such as Rebecca Lobo, Lisa Leslie, Sheryl Swoopes, Chamique Holdsclaw, Mia Hamm, Julie Foudy, Venus and Serena Williams, Marion Jones, and scores of other women who quickly became household names and role models for young girls. Pat Summitt's reign as head coach of University of Tennessee women's basketball proved that attendance at women's games could break records; the ever-dominant UConn women's team had already shown that the women's game could sell out a stadium, yet at the same time, the University of Oklahoma athletic program tried dismantling its own women's basketball team to save money.[2] The ongoing popularity of Penny Marshall's 1992 film *A League of Their Own* introduced viewers younger than baby boomers to the World War II legacy of women athletes in America, and it created a new pop culture genre for movies that normalized women's sports; as Jenny Lyn Bader wrote in *Next: Young American Writers on the New Generation*, "I . . . never emotionally grasped it until I watched Penny Marshall's movie *A League of Their Own*. For the first time, I appreciated why so many women complain that sports bore them. I had enjoyed baseball before but never as intensely as I enjoyed the games in that film. The players were people like me."[3] But it took *Love & Basketball* to portray more contemporary issues for Black women athletes.

Physicians and health educators concerned with the burgeoning American waistline celebrated the new climate of competitive athletic participation for girls, as well as boys; around the country, a fresh fitness craze sent millions of adult women into gyms for kickboxing, cycling, and powerlifting workouts. Women brought home more gold than men at several consecutive Olympics. When Nike's new ads celebrating female athletes were unflatteringly juxtaposed with charges of oppressive sweatshop conditions for the many young girls assembling Nike athletic gear overseas, thousands of students and athletes, including soccer star Julie Foudy, joined campaigns to ensure that the increasing demands for designer sportswear and equipment were not fulfilled with child labor.

Because of these trends, I could choose from exciting literature on the history and contributions of women athletes. My key textbook, from day one onward, was Susan Cahn's informative study *Coming On Strong*. I also used Allen Guttmann's *A Whole New Ball Game* as an introduction to changes in American sports, along with athlete and advocate Mariah Burton Nelson's provocative *The Stronger Women Get, the More Men Love Football*. New writing on female athletes went well beyond academic studies. Popular titles appearing in bookstores included *In These Girls, Hope Is a Muscle*; *The Girls of Summer*; *Crashing the Net*; and *Full Court Press*. There were not one but two riveting overviews of the US women's gold-medal basketball team from the 1996 Olympics: *Venus to the Hoop*, an intimate look at the players, and *Shooting from the Outside*, the memoir by national team and Stanford coach Tara VanDerveer. Historical and contemporary photographs of sportswomen were displayed in the fall 2001 museum exhibit celebrating Jane Gottesman's volume *Game Face: What Does a Female Athlete Look Like?* Throughout the ongoing wave of publicity and homage, the Women's Sports Foundation mounted conference after conference, monitoring women's athletic progress on an ever-expanding website with a weekly newsletter. Very young girls flocked to soccer games at RFK Stadium in Washington, DC, wearing tiny T-shirts that declared "Girls can do anything," "Girls rule," and even

"Girls kick ass!" I was thus able to direct my students to relevant readings, exhibits in our capital city, new online resources, and a material culture that praised female sports achievement. Because there were suddenly so many books on women and sports where earlier in history there had been so few, I set aside two specific class meetings—one for reviewing works by women in sports journalism and the other for looking at children's sports books worldwide. Both topics yielded insights about gender stereotyping and equality, and I was able to bring in top sports journalist Christine Brennan as a class guest speaker on more than one happy occasion.

I also brought in guest speakers ranging from National Women's Law Center attorneys to members of the D.C. Divas women's football team, from D.C. referee Dorothy Hirsch—probably the first lacrosse official with lavender swirl designs buzzed into her haircut—to my own heroic eighth-grade gym teacher, Jackie Thompson, who was amazed to hear from me after all those years. I searched for relevant classroom films: *When Diamonds Were a Girl's Best Friend*, made by a communications professor named Janis Taylor, showed an actual reunion of aging players from the All-American Girls Professional Baseball League. HBO's *Dare to Compete: The Story of Women in Sports* shed more light on Black women's exclusion from the aforementioned baseball league—plus footage of runner Kathrine Switzer's expulsion from the 1967 Boston Marathon, because no were women allowed. *Pumping Iron II: The Women*, although campy and sexualized, revealed bias against female muscularity in the burgeoning culture of bodybuilding and gym workouts. We also used important documentaries on the racism perpetuated by American Indian sports mascots and the struggle for women, globally, to compete in or merely attend national games in countries ranging from India to Iran and Zanzibar.

I updated the books, films, and guest speakers every semester, but the final paper assignment remained the same: an overview of Title IX law. During the 1990s, many observers credited US sportswomen's phenomenal gains to Title IX, but critics, including speechwriter Jessica Gavora and the organization Concerned Women for America, denounced Title IX as a misguided affirmative-action quota system designed to emasculate existing men's college programs. A well-organized backlash, led by conservative women as often as conservative men, dominated airwaves, talk shows, and editorial columns. Would universities be able or willing to accommodate the post–Title IX generation of female scholarship athletes? Were female athletes merely a millennium fad? With high school girls demanding the right to wrestle, box, and even play football, should a line be drawn *somewhere*? Was that line really about protecting female physiognomy or about protecting male egos, turf, and coaching styles? And, most significant in a media-driven society, would television coverage include top-level women's events and sports highlights in evening news and on ESPN—beyond the mere tokenism of semiannual Olympic moments, Anna Kournikova's legs, Gabrielle Reece's swimwear, and shots of Pat Summitt or Gail Goestenkors screaming through NCAA March Madness? These were some of the questions my students explored in their Title IX term papers, where, I made clear, all political viewpoints and opinions were welcome and might result in an A-plus—so long as they were backed by scholarly evidence.

Grading was certainly a challenge. I never once met a student who fit the crude, uncomplimentary stereotype of being a "dumb jock." That slur seemed to be more of a preconceived bias held by other faculty, some of whom begrudged scheduling a makeup midterm for student athletes missing classes during competition season. Whatever assumptions I, too, had internalized—maybe the notion that college athletes were overprivileged beneficiaries of special treatment—quickly faded as I heard student athletes complain that other professors treated them with contempt for absences due to away games, injuries, and surgeries. Just being willing to listen and learn, I became known on every campus as a friend to athletes, which led to unexpected and wonderful alliances with university athletic directors, coaches, trainers, and NBC News. But I saw how hard these athletes worked, how they came to class clutching a bag of ice to a hyperextended knee or struggled to take a test with swollen fingers.

At no school was I ever subject to pressure, by any university authority figure, to pass or change grades for a struggling player—although I knew this shameful practice did occur at some Division I universities. Instead, I found most student athletes to be as competitive about doing well in class as they were about winning games. The course naturally attracted its share of athletes who expected to have a head start because of the subject matter, only to discover they needed practice in writing more academically about women's history or gender issues. Likewise, I enrolled some well-spoken women's studies majors whose

limited athletic backgrounds left them unfamiliar with the discrimination rip-offs their NCAA sisters were still experiencing in the post–Title
IX climate—everything from women's teams taking overnight bus trips
to track meets when the men's teams traveled by plane, to the utter lack
of advertising for some women's games. Quite a few campus feminist
activists, it seemed, had never turned their attention to sports as a space
of discrimination—had never attended women's games and did not possess the sports literacy to frame their arguments effectively. Sadly, some
of this was also true of other women's studies faculty. But there were
also star athletes majoring in women's studies, who dazzled us all with
insights that were both well researched *and* personally experienced; this
group included one student who played in the GWU band and became a
Title IX lawyer. In general, students who assumed they would earn an
easy A usually started off with a B-minus on the first paper and then
tried harder. What concerned me over time was a pattern where many,
many White students neglected to cite the experiences and contributions of Black women in American sports history, even when asked to
do so on the midterm.

A different challenge came from international students. Most were
quick to tell me how excited they were to participate, there being no such
thing as a class like this back home in Kuwait, South Korea, Turkey, or
Belarus. A student from Bahrain asked for my help in starting a women's
sports history archive in her home country, and another welcomed me
to her small basketball club at Georgetown University's campus in Doha,
Qatar, when I traveled overseas to give a guest talk in that oil-rich and
very sex-segregated emirate. These students were learning on the fly
about American social history, customs, and language, in addition to
the class lessons on gender and US sports teams. Did English-language
sports humor translate well for them? Could they, like me, chuckle when
a Pac-12 sports announcer unwittingly punned, "The Ducks are going
to foul"? Eager to show his proficiency in American slang, a student
from Bhutan informed me that he found our class "out-of-the-box cool,"
while Vesna, GWU's Serbian basketball player, shared that in communist Yugoslavia, where she had spent her girlhood, older women had
always played soccer on their factory teams after work: "In my country, grannies were chillin'!" A student from Myanmar sought counsel
on the important difference between the term *woman of color* and the
now discouraged *colored woman*. As the international students labored

to master English-language sports references, I became very aware of how frequently our American politicians and journalists borrow from football and boxing rules to make a point, often sidelining women, who are less likely to have participated in these activities. Throughout US election year 2020, my international students struggled to interpret the intended political message when Senate Democratic leader Chuck Schumer complained, "We're still on the twenty-yard line?"; MSNBC host Rachel Maddow described a lobby group as "punching above their weight"; Attorney General William Barr declared, "Everyone can be a Monday morning quarterback"; and former Missouri senator Claire Mc-Caskill declared, "Georgia is a total jump ball." You'll find many more examples of political sports talk in later chapters.

"Open discussion" could be a minefield. In the beginning, some male students in my class did not hesitate to express their contempt for Title IX or for the level of play in women's competitions. "Women's sports suck" was the mildest of remarks certain young gentlemen felt perfectly comfortable saying to the Division I female athletes seated next to them in class, often women whose teams were enjoying season records superior to those of their male counterparts. At the most extreme end of the misogyny spectrum were a few male students who expressed their prerogative by informing me, on the first day of class, that the only reason they had enrolled was "to make sure the male viewpoint is upheld." In few other fields of study do students hand over tuition money just to defend male dominance or introduce themselves on day one by impugning the professor's ability to be objective. Over the years, those attitudes changed and improved as society grew to place a higher value on women's sports. But for decades, peer pressure from male classmates was just one more form of daily harassment that female athletes endured unless I stepped in. For the first fifteen years of the course, I assigned an ungraded class journal so that more reserved students intimidated by the lively talk-back atmosphere could share additional insights privately. This elicited such an outpouring of detailed information on sexual harassment that I had to discontinue the assignment—more, on all of this, in chapter 6.

As elite athletes, and as women choosing to enroll in a women's studies course, female students also dealt with constant speculation about their sexuality. Those who were in fact gay rarely mentioned it in class. A few students worked overtime to prove their femininity and heterosexuality, prefacing every comment they made in class with "Well, my boyfriend says . . ." Because I, the professor, am famously out and proud myself, students knew they could speak to me in private about any homophobic hostility they experienced on campus. My office became the site of many personal discussions about campus policies—for instance, the discomfort some gay athletes felt being scheduled in conference against Liberty University, a school prohibiting LGBT students and faculty altogether. Would the athletic program make Black players, in the 1990s, engage with a segregated, Whites-only rival? Wouldn't that be a unique burden and aggravate tensions on the field of play? Eventually, we brought this conversation back into the classroom, and I shared the memory of my Quaker high school competing against a Whites-only religious academy—how our racially diverse basketball team felt walking into their gym, the underhanded injuries they sustained. We hosted their softball team on our own field, a game that left me, the third basewoman, with a permanently scarred shin.

Over the years, my students and I negotiated the learning curves of racism and homophobia; the problem of Native American sports mascots exemplified right there in DC, with the 'Skins' logo on display all over town; the rights of trans athletes; traumatic brain injury in young players; and alcohol and tobacco companies' sponsorship of sports tournaments and arenas. We looked at cheating scandals, sports foods and diet culture, the cost of a sneaker, and the salary of a CEO versus the starvation wages of children who sew our soccer balls. We ventured into the topic of abusive coaches, overly ambitious parents, and systematic doping of teen Olympians in East Germany. On some days, we all went home exhausted, drained, and emotionally triggered by what had been shared in class. But for twenty-odd years, every semester, I had a long wait list of students begging to join the conversation. In the week before classes began, my email would fill with cajoling letters asking me to add just one more body.

> Dear Professor Morris: My name is Michael, and I am a senior. I know that this class is very popular and equally difficult to get into, but it includes content matter that is of unparalleled interest to me. I come from a very athletically minded family that includes two sisters who surpassed me in athletic prowess. This is my plea, and I will be anxiously awaiting your response.

Dr. Bon: I just got my registration results, and I didn't get into your Athletics and Gender class. I NEED to be in that class. It's more important to me than life itself. So I was wondering what the deal is with add-drop, and if there is any way to get into the class, I'll be your best friend.

I set firm academic standards in the classroom and was rarely disappointed. The high grade point average maintained by most female athletes appears in NCAA studies reported by the *Chronicle of Higher Education*; women graduate on time more consistently and with fewer disciplinary problems overall than male collegiate athletes. However, there are few financial rewards for such merit: I've yet to see a female player graduate right into a six-figure income, though this can happen for male athletes recruited directly into professional leagues. The reduced opportunity to earn a living doing what you're best at, even while in the peak of condition and promise, pushes female athletes to succeed even more in a practical academic major. It's hard for me to counsel women about this sobering reality because as an overworked, untenured adjunct assistant professor, I know the mixed blessing of playing your heart out for scale. Perhaps this is what binds me to the athletic women—the awareness that we're *all* doing what we do for the love of the game, unable to depend on financial gain as our incentive. Their love of playing; my love of teaching; the stereotypes we all endure as strong women, as athletes, or as gay women—all of us pathbreakers on the field or in the classroom—become a curious equalizer. We don't intimidate one another.

Riding in vans with my athletes, going to cheer at their games, I learned things I'd never hear about in the classroom. At one GWU women's rugby match, which ended in a major victory against Washington College on Saturday of parents' weekend, the referee charged that GWU players were taking too long with substitutions. The reason: our poorly funded club team did not own enough team uniforms to go around, and each exhausted or injured rugger coming out of the game had to tear off her bloody jersey and hand it over to the incoming replacement. At another match, a player's father stood beside me as my student Dre coached tackling maneuvers. "Hit your opponent here, this way, and she won't be going anywhere," Dre advised, and the visiting dad turned to me and confided, "That's good advice for handling my wife." His casual remark spoke volumes. Girls now turn to sports to learn strength and self-defense skills necessary for dealing with adult males who might "handle" them. But many male coaches are not eager to see strong, athletic girls besting boys in any situation, on or off the playing field. Dre's own final paper for my class in the spring of 2001 contained this poignant anecdote about growing up as a girl baseball star in Texas and Florida: "When trying out for the men's baseball team in high school, I was informed by the southern male coach that 'Women belong in the kitchen baking cookies, not out on the field playin' ball.' Although I enjoy cooking very much, I proceeded to walk out onto the field, asked the pitcher to burn me a good one, and I hit a home run. I went home and baked cookies for the whole team the next day. They tasted almost as sweet as that home run."

During the years that I taught in Washington, DC, it was a city of women athletes—the WNBA Mystics; the Washington Freedom soccer team; collegiate basketball, lacrosse, and volleyball victories; and the D.C. Divas football matches. In all those years, athletic women were seldom rewarded with money or media coverage. After dutifully covering women's historic victories in the Summer or Winter Olympics and NCAA basketball, the *Washington Post* would return to its standard disparity: entire sports sections featuring no mention of women. For example, on one Saturday, I was shuttling between a women's crew regatta on the Potomac and my rugby players on the National Mall in the Cherry Blossom tournament. Personal bests and broken legs, wins and losses, sweat and heartbreak, and victory celebrations were happening all over town, but you wouldn't know; you wouldn't hear—unless you cared personally about the women's events. My own calendar became a seasonal athletic daybook as I raced from game to game to cheer my students onward. What was happening all around me was a feminist revolution from the biceps down, and it was one I didn't want to miss, if only for moments such as this: once, a rugby reporter at the Cherry Blossom tournament informed me, "Ah, come on. There are no women in rugby"—and then gaped, saying, "*Whoa*," when the GWU and Georgetown women's club teams took the field. I knew every player by name.

A great deal has changed since I first started teaching sports history in 1996—the US Women's World Cup soccer victories; the September 11, 2001, attacks that transformed all security practices and airline travel;

the explosion of internet culture and social media; activist scrutiny of Nike and other brand-name sportswear manufacturers; doping scandals; the expansion of Title IX into a tool for addressing sexual assault and harassment on campuses; better accountability for abusive coaches, as well as team doctors, like Larry Nassar; modified sportswear and inclusion of Muslim women athletes who wear the hijab; and the Black Lives Matter movement and the practice of taking a knee at a game. As I write these words in late 2020, the COVID-19 pandemic has effectively paused sports altogether. There will likely be even more significant changes, both to college sports and global play, by the time these words are published; I address these uncertainties in the book's conclusion.

In the following pages, I will walk readers through a typical semester of my Athletics and Gender class, reflecting on the social changes that shaped and informed class discussions over twenty-five years. It's important to note at the outset that this is *not* a complete or formal history of women's sports. It is a memoir of teaching and a template for teaching, drawing from remembered and successful best practices to pass on. It is not a list of scores but a twenty-five-year discussion between me and more than 1,500 bright students on how we might get women's scores into ordinary dialogue and media. You'll hear a great many of my stories, exactly as my students did in every class; every one of them learned how I confronted President Clinton at that GWU basketball game and how proficiency with a soccer ball got me out of security detention in Borneo (see chap. 5). For all students, coaches, and fans of women's sports, I hope that the questions raised, resources offered, and peek into our approaches to thinking about change can lead others to informed conversations and advocacy. And as we celebrate the fiftieth anniversary of Title IX law and the fiftieth anniversary of Billie Jean King's historic tennis victory over challenger Bobby Riggs, I hope these tales from the classroom will serve as talking points for multiple communities.

The first four chapters correspond to what's covered over a college semester as my student athletes and I explore the social history of American sports. In chapter 1, I introduce the class to the religious, gender, race, and class divisions unique to American heritage, all of which lent boundaries to who might play which sports where and when in American life. We familiarize ourselves with the boundaries of slavery and segregation, as well as the approaches of schools, state interests, and wartime in setting up physical education ideals. Chapter 2 investigates headlines and sports marketing as we apply modern media literacy to the coverage of athletes in the news. What are the sources we turn to for multicultural stories of female athletes? Why aren't more women's events broadcast on television, reviewed in daily newspapers, or promoted on campus? How are women hidden in online search engines about athletics? In chapter 3, we turn to the ever-changing definitions of masculine and feminine roles, especially how sports have been used to test who is a real man or a real woman and how the shame of "playing like a girl" incites misogyny from a very early age for young boys. This conversation of course spills over into the social ills of homophobia and transphobia, the fickleness of sponsors, and the ways coaches have used gender tropes to motivate or humiliate players. Addressing a defeated boys' team as "Hello, ladies" is the mildest example. We also look at the ways that media coverage for women's sports has too often relied on the athlete as beauty queen or the marketing of sex appeal, the equation of fitness with diet culture and high-end gym memberships, and how these practices marginalize women whose bodies don't fit high fashion.

Chapter 4 covers Title IX law from its earliest incarnation to very current challenges from the US Department of Education itself. The final paper on Title IX law, our most significant class assignment, consistently resulted in some spectacular critiques, suggestions for change, and personal narratives, and I share some of my students' ideas here.

Chapter 5 draws on my experiences teaching Athletics and Gender for Semester at Sea in 2004 and 2019, as well as lecturing in several different countries and addressing global efforts to bring girls from traditional Islamic societies into athletic participation. In contrast to the Olympics, which brings competitors from every land into one uniform venue, Semester at Sea scatters eight hundred college students and faculty into a dozen cultures over a hundred days, allowing exposure to contrasting social standards of gender roles, national pride, strength, and political ideology. And chapter 6 concludes with lingering questions of backlash, pay inequity, the problem of funding women's athletics, and the cultural expectation that women should always play for less—or simply for the sake of fitness and attractiveness. This chapter features a thorough self-reflection on what worked and what did not work in the arc of the class over almost twenty-five years. What changed? Did the students change? Did I change?

That would have been the end of the book, except for the completely unexpected thunderbolts of 2020: the cancellation of in-person classes *and* scheduled athletic events during the global pandemic, interrupting so many collegiate athletes' championship brackets and professional opportunities. My students' unique writings from that one spring semester addressed the frustrating setbacks for women's sports following so much public progress the year before. Even more dramatically, the Black Lives Matter protests of the summer of 2020 put athletes in the spotlight as NBA and WNBA players walked out, while President Trump, speaking at the Republic National Convention, demanded the return of seasonal college football. These tensions brought fresh attention to both long-standing critiques of risking Black athletes' health for purposes of White entertainment and the charge that sports in too many ways has resembled a plantation system. These issues are exactly what my students would ordinarily be analyzing in class, if only campus had not closed, so I added a postseason chapter with input from my pandemic-semester students at Saint Mary's College.

Throughout the book, I draw from my students' class conversations and written reflections, which offer a truly diverse and intersectional range of opinions on opportunity, fair application of law, and the future of gender issues in competitive sports. The viewpoints included here come from students at George Washington University; Georgetown University; Georgetown's overseas campus in Doha, Qatar; American University; the University of California at Berkeley; Santa Clara University's adult education Osher Lifelong Learning Institute; Saint Mary's College of California; and the students from dozens of US and international colleges who enrolled in Semester at Sea. The students I worked with identify as male, female, LGBTQ, nonbinary, Black, White, Asian, South Asian, Arab, Latinx, African, eastern European, Pacific Islander, mixed race, Indigenous, Catholic, Jewish, Protestant, Hindu, Buddhist, Muslim, Wiccan, conservative, progressive, affluent, working class. They include returning adults, single mothers, first-year students, transfer students, international students, student athletes, ROTC students. They are learning challenged, veterans, homeless, refugees, Olympic medalists, and a few occasional guests or guest speakers visiting for the day. The athletic department steered prospective student athletes touring the campus to my classroom. With advance notice, I also welcomed onetime visits from students' parents, partners, and children.

I include the prompts we used for class discussions and writings, as well as some of the media images and sources that, across time, provoked good debates and discussions. It's my hope that this intimate look into a long-enduring, successful college class will inspire any and all readers who care about women's sports: students and teachers, NCAA athletes, women's sports fans and veteran players, coaches and trainers, parents, Olympians, sports journalists and historians, school administrators, feminist advocates, women's health strategists, educators, Title IX lawyers, and ESPN anchors. Every one of us can move the needle of knowledge forward, sharing women's sports history as American history when given the opportunity to speak. And here I'd like to acknowledge some of the women and men whose research, support, and advocacy made teaching this course possible: my women's studies program directors at both Georgetown and George Washington University, Professors Diane Bell, Barbara Miller, Dan Moshenberg, Bonnie Oh, You-Me Park, Sue Thomas, and Suzanna Walters; athletic administrators Pat Thomas and Mary Jo Warner; author and athlete Mariah Burton Nelson; referee and sports commissioner Dorothy Hirsch; exercise science professor and former GWU volleyball coach Pat Sullivan; Gay Young at my alma mater American University; and my heroic, insightful junior high PE teacher, Jackie Thompson. From Semester at Sea and the Institute for Shipboard Education, I thank Ray Owen, Greg Luft, and Marti Fessenden. In California, thanks are due to Mark Brilliant, Anne Meyers, Victoria Robinson, Doug Parada, Denise Oldham, Peter Zinoman, and Derek Van Rheenen at UC Berkeley; to Claire Williams, Chi-An Emhoff, and Skye Ward at Saint Mary's College; and to the Osher Lifelong Learning Institute at Santa Clara University. For introducing me to Nadine Seltzer's tomboy cartoon character Sweetie Pie, I thank Joan Walker; for insights into coaching a champion high school girls' volleyball team, I thank my brother, John Morris, who taught me the phrase "Earn your turn"; and for inspiring me to write about the lessons that students teach *us* in any classroom, I thank Jeanne Henry.

The historian Gerda Lerner, whose works I studied in graduate school and whose granddaughter I taught at George Washington University, theorized that throughout women's history, every feminist organizer felt she was acting for the first time, not knowing whether others before

Fig. I.2 Author lecturing on C-SPAN, March 5, 2014. *Photo courtesy of C-SPAN History Channel Archives; used with permission.*

her had made similar attempts. After I had taught Athletics and Gender for many years, I discovered that similar courses on women and sports were offered through women's and gender studies programs at Stanford University and Duke University. I learned about the award-winning sportswriting and teaching being done by Susan Cayleff at San Diego State University and the research supported by the University of Minnesota's Tucker Center for Research on Girls and Women in Sport. And during 2019–20, I consulted with South Dakota social studies teacher and coach Trent Dlugosh as he developed the first women's sports history class for high school students in Sioux Falls. Seizing opportunity where there's obvious interest, Trent wrote to me proudly:

> If you don't know, South Dakota is home to two of the best women's basketball programs in the entire nation. . . . Last year when the women and men played a doubleheader at the University of South Dakota, the arena was packed to the rafters for the women's game and it was an all timer that went into triple overtime. Sioux Falls is also home to the most attended women's basketball conference in the nation. We annually sell out the arena here in town for the Summit League. It's really cool to be a part of that environment and see so many people really care about women's sports.

Yes—and imagine the ongoing local impact of introducing women's sports history to high school students. May it soon become a nationwide, twenty-first-century trend.

I'm humbled to acknowledge these esteemed curriculum colleagues, knowing I am not now and never was alone in establishing women's sports history as a credible and credited field. Let us recall the words of Hillel, my ancestor and Gerda Lerner's too: "It is not up to you to complete the task. But neither are you free to desist from it."

Fig. 1.1 Fort Shaw girls' basketball team, 1905.
Photograph by Louis Heyn. Courtesy of Montana Historical Society; used with permission.

THE STRENGTH OF OUR FOREMOTHERS

Engaging Students with the Past

On the first day of class, I look over my new students—hardworking scholarship athletes, mostly. Plenty of women's studies majors too. Caring, committed people. They've never studied women's sports heritage for credit before, and they are equal parts doubtful and hopeful as they take their seats. Some arrive direct from practice, already icing a strained ankle or knee.

Can an accelerated, one-semester remedial history of women's sports satisfy interested students, offer an academically rigorous environment, and avoid predictable charges of "political correctness" all at the same time? It's the challenge I accepted long ago.

They're wondering how I'll begin. One approach might be a force-fed presentation on famous women athletes, reviewing glorious moments at the Olympics, Wimbledon, Iditarod. Such a course would rely on media images plus rote memorization of athletic achievers: "All right, class, who is Kathrine Switzer? Who is Cathy Freeman? Who is Susan Butcher? Who is Nawal El Moutawakel? Who is Faye Dancer? Thirty points each. Pencils down!" Of course, this is how most of us, women and men, were taught history, all throughout school: memorizing facts and taking tests—on the life achievements of famous *men*. Their triumphs may or may not have seemed connected to our own lives; what mattered was mastering their names in order to do well on the SATs.

Certainly, I want those heroines' names known. But today's students have a better-than-average chance of working for government, news bureaus, nonprofits, and lobby groups, as well as in youth sports. Someone's going to put a microphone in front of them for the evening news one day, and they need to be ready to offer an informed conversation about women's sports, a sound bite that's meaningful and lasting—*more* than a score. I prefer a learning strategy where students begin by examining the larger social and cultural histories that first established a hostile environment for athletic women. When, where, and why were women first prohibited from taking part in sports? Which medical, moral, and state authorities eventually acted in concert to discourage the interests and achievements of "tomboy" girls? What's the uniquely American history for talented females in any field? After all, we are a nation that thrives on competition and winning, as well as ideals of fairness, justice, and equality. So how have women and girls fit into those national ideals as citizens and as would-be athletes? How have men and boys?

But that comes later. Before instructing them to crack open the textbooks, I ask students to think back to their first experiences with childhood games. "Let's each make a list of our favorite ones, the playtime after school or even before we started school—stoopball, double dutch, red rover, capture the flag, freeze tag, four square." Are these early and beloved activities with peers also their first memories of competitive play, of mastering an athletic skill? Students comply eagerly. Pencils scratch; keyboards tap. Nostalgic sighs fill the air. "Ghost in the graveyard." "Oh yeah!" "What about wall ball?" "Sure, that counts." Then we share aloud, and these are the most common:

Capture the flag, cops and robbers, dodgeball, double dutch, duck-duck-goose, four square.

Freeze tag, Frisbee, ghost in the graveyard, handstands, hide-and-seek, hopscotch, house.

Hula-Hoop, jacks, jump rope, kickball, kick the can, king of the hill, leapfrog, marco polo.

Miss Mary Mack; "Mother, may I?"; musical chairs; red light–green light; red rover.

Ring-around-the-rosy, "Simon says," slides, swings, tag, tetherball, tree climbing.

Students' individual lists become the first documents in their per-sonal narratives, their own sports histories, the lifetime of experience that athletes draw on. And the lists make *everyone* in class an athlete by universalizing early memories of physical play. We break down our lists into common categories of children's games: Crime and punishment characterize games like red light–green light and "Simon says," where kids wield adult power. For girls, domesticity and caregiving are central to playing house or playing with dolls; girls also learn shame through chants like "I see London! I see France! I see Janie's underpants!"; and games often involve handclapping with rhyme and music. We talk about all the close-to-the-body hand games reserved for girls, along with games that keep them close to home, seated in the yard or on the stoop, where they can mind a baby and stay within calling distance. I ask, "When did you begin to play sports? If PE is required of every American schoolchild, male or female, when does play, or gym class, first begin to take on segregated overtones of boys' sports versus girls'? Who coached you? Who were your role models, sports heroes, or heroines? Did you like your body and its power, or did you begin to loathe your build in adolescence? Who encouraged you to keep playing; who discouraged you or pushed too hard?"

The lists reveal my students' own regional and ethnic differences. The students thus become maps of history themselves. And they can recognize how early culture and politics creep into child's play: we take apart capture the flag, "smear the queer" (yes, ouch), cowboys and In-dians, and the plague-derived ring-around-the-rosy. With the under-standing that we will gradually fit these narratives into the framework of a larger social history, most students find the readings relevant, the discussion more important, their own years of sports practice living texts of sex-role socialization and tradition. And so we'll begin the read-ing assignments with the notion that there is a "national" athletic body with a social heritage we belong to as Americans—a body with very different standards and rewards for male and female, Black and White, working class and country-club rich, gay and straight, urban and rural, bookworm and jock.

When do we first begin to learn that certain sports are for boys and others are for girls? One student says, "Sixth grade." His female class-mate shakes her head and says, "No, earlier—like five or six." "I got smacked for taking the football instead of the doll in nursery school," another says. "It's the toys your parents give you," some students argue, while others disagree: "I played with my five brothers right up to when I was fourteen." "We all played touch football after school. It didn't matter who you were . . ."

The media—and racism—creep into the youngest of American lives. When do we develop notions of who is "naturally" good at what? With the caveat that we're going to take apart certain obvious stereotypes— so students should mention whatever comes to mind—I invite answers to touchier questions: "Which sports are Black athletes 'supposed to' play and do well?"

"Basketball," everyone sighs. "Track," adds a young woman. But no one mentions Simone Biles, Dominique Dawes, or other award-winning Black gymnasts.

Quickly, I ask what Whites are good at. Laughter from students of color: "Golf." "Polo." "Downhill skiing." They name sport after sport associated with affluence, restricted country-club memberships, and exclusivity—sports that until recently kept out Black athletes. This is a gateway to many weeks of discussion on socioeconomic class and race in sports.

"What about Latinos?" asks one student, and others shout out, "Boxing," "Baseball," and "Soccer." "And Jews?" I ask, and there's derisive laughter—hmm, let's interrupt that. I pass around a 1923 photo of my handsome grandfather holding a basketball for Boys State, explaining that Bed-Stuy in Brooklyn was once a Jewish neighborhood full of tough guys and pro ballplayers. I share some Jewish names: Senda Berenson, Sandy Koufax, Mark Spitz, and Kerri Strug. We'll get back to antisemitism soon. And when I follow that with "Can you name a Muslim athlete?" everyone's stumped, except for the guy in the back row who calls out, "Yeah. Ali. Muhammad Ali!" But no one names Kareem Abdul-Jabbar.

Finally, I ask about their perceptions of popular Asian or Asian American athletes. Here old stereotypes come out in force: "Kung fu." "Ping-Pong." "Chess." "Sumo!" The long-dominant Winter Olympics ice-skaters of Asian heritage, from Kristi Yamaguchi to Michelle Kwan to Apolo Ohno, are forgotten. We talk about the dangerous stereotyping, in the United States, of Asian women as exotic beauties. No one knows about the huge role that Rep. Patsy Mink (D-HI), the first Asian American woman elected to Congress, played in securing the passage of Title IX. No one knows of Kitty Tsui, bodybuilding medalist at the Gay Games.

"Can anyone name the sports that Pacific Islanders introduced to American culture?" It takes a while, even in my California classroom, for someone to mention surfing. When I ask in my East Coast classrooms which state has the largest percentage of athletes with Asian heritage, and the largest US participation in sports like sumo, surfing, and dragon-boat racing, everyone says California. But the correct answer is Hawaii.

These are the biases up front. Few students bring up Native American athletes except those who are themselves Native American or from Alaska. "Where do we get these biases?" I ask, and they answer, "TV, movies, comic books, and video games." Sometimes it's "my dad" or "my uncle" or even "my Scout leader" or "my coach."

In the coming weeks, I explain, we'll look at resources and films about Native athletes; Black athletes under Jim Crow segregation; women banned from sports; gay athletes expelled from teams; Jewish athletes banned by Hitler; Muslim, Jewish, African, and Asian Olympians; women in baseball; and men in field hockey. Students whose parents were Olympians, whose grandfathers played Negro League baseball, or whose aunts were Roller Derby queens or bodybuilders eagerly offer to bring in film footage from home. I explain that similar to this first day, open discussion will mean open discussion—we can examine our historically inherited stereotypes, prejudices, and preferences, but not to the point of hurting one another. In the 1990s, syllabi didn't include policies on triggering or microaggressions; those guidelines evolved in the twenty-first century by department and major. I also make clear that there's a difference between the permitted, informal language of open discussion and the scholarly, academic writing I expect in papers. Too many students over the years have written essays telling me how women "really got the shaft" in US history as they negotiated "crap" rules, "crap" uniforms, and "crap" pay—assessments I readily support but prefer to see submitted for college credit in more Nobel Prize–winning terminology.

On our first day together, we also look thoughtfully at how the colorful language of sports is woven into American slang and street talk. We make lists of popular sports expressions that appear everywhere from TV comedy dialogue to ad campaigns to presidential speeches: *struck out*, *level playing field*, *bull's-eye*, *red flag*, *three sheets to the wind*, *slam dunk*, *left field*, *raise the bar*, *sudden death*, *score*. I share that critic Mariah Burton Nelson has an entire book chapter on the sexual usage of *scoring* in communities of young athletes. Did you get to *first base*? Are you a

Monday-morning quarterback? Do you tend to *miss the mark* or *cry foul*? Are you a *team player*? This easy use of sports talk in, say, a business plan is one reason experts argue that athletic participation will help young women's political and boardroom skills—benefits men have conventionally accrued through sports. Evening news hosts and guests convey important political information in sports terms: four times in one night on MSNBC, reporter Bob Woodward declared, "He's got the ball and kept a hammerlock on the investigation," followed in the very next hour by host Brian Williams declaring, "That was a layup shot and then a fumble on the one-yard line!" in reference to political action.[1] The metaphors spill over into top Washington, DC, think tanks. For example, the prestigious Woodrow Wilson Center grants fellowships for international research along the theme "Great Powers Game On: Competition and Cooperation."

Thinking athletically—in terms of rivalry, strategy as game, and dominant power as physical—has historically been taught to young men and praised as a masculine attribute. Yet in the United States, sports literacy has been used to test certain measures of intelligence for both boys and girls on the SAT. During the decades just before and after Title IX, standardized tests featured sports analogies for both math and verbal assessment. Adolescent girls' unfamiliarity with sports terms led to charges of gender bias—as well as race and class bias, since some questions required knowledge of elite or country-club sports. Such wording placed young women of color, who were most likely to have been excluded from football or golf and sailing, at a particular disadvantage.

But if we measure athletic intelligence in students preparing to leave high school today, we find more sophisticated sports know-how among American girls. This is due in part to greater participation in athletics, and it's also because of our burgeoning, ubiquitous sports media, which introduces new celebrities and extreme sports to young viewers almost hourly. Not only are we each walking narrative texts of our early play years; we all gain exposure to the slang language of professional sports, whether or not we participate. Exposure, however, is not the same thing as knowledge.

What should students know about key events in US women's sports history? How can a class like this engage students of color, and which aspects do? Is it possible to improve on a victims-and-trailblazers approach to women's history? In every community, women in sports sought recognition and a fair platform for competing with and against other athletes. My approach is to familiarize students with the highlights that represent cultural shifts: achievements, controversies, and breakthroughs leading to more enlightened public views on equal participation. I tell my new class that by the end of the semester, we'll cover all the hallmarks from women's sports history that I've listed on a handy timeline of 101 turning points. With the ease of the internet, today anyone interested in women's sports can access and learn more about such key moments and perhaps also watch restored film clips of the athletes in competition. (Similar historical timelines are presented in a range of the books and articles we use in class; you will find these listed in the bibliography, with additional recommended readings and typical class discussion questions in the Critical Thinking Resources.) What I assume most of my college students do *not* know is how both men's and women's sports opportunities have mirrored the social structures of American economics and law, or race relations and culture. For the long first month, we concentrate heavily on the changes in culture that developed American ideas about work versus play. Students who walk into Athletics and Gender eager to jump right into a modern-day conversation about Colin Kaepernick or Megan Rapinoe have to recalibrate, for we begin with the White Puritans' arrival in Native America.

In the first week, I flip cultural assumptions by showing that once upon a time, men, too, were shamed and even punished for enjoying sports, which were linked in the Puritan mind to hedonistic body worship and devilry. That American manhood should gradually come to encompass physical glory and revenue-producing playtime, that Christian church services should end in time for the real ritual of Sunday football viewing, was definitely not part of the Founding Fathers' plan. Masculinity, and boundaries placed around male athleticism, evolved in response to changing cultural values, so shouldn't we expect transformation in femininity and female strength? Not necessarily; a popular colonial American toast was "May our sons exceed their fathers and our daughters be equal to their mothers." As male opportunities expanded in the public sphere, the proper female role of domesticity remained static.

I explain that we'll start with historian Allen Guttmann's excellent book *A Whole New Ball Game*, an overview of men's sports in America, and read it paired with Susan Cahn's *Coming On Strong*, an overview of women's entry into sports competition in the twentieth century. There's no masculinity without femininity as its foil, and vice versa. Eventually we'll disrupt the binary as well.

The history of sports in the United States is rooted in complex manifestations of Christianity. In the beginning, religion defined male and female as separate beings, their bodies formed and marked for different tasks. To question that order was blasphemy, and still is, for devout evangelicals worldwide. The body shame of Judeo-Christian doctrines gradually moved in to change the existing male body worship seen in Mediterranean civilization. Long before the early church fathers landed in Greece and Rome, the first Olympics were male only—and performed naked, glorifying the male body.[2]

Homoerotic admiration between men, captured in rippling-muscled statues, was definitely part of an earlier culture that valued masculinity and considered women at best mere vessels for reproduction and, at worst, deformed males. We do know that Greek women had their own sacred festivals and athletic events—Sappho speaks of this, writing in the sixth century BC, "I taught the talented / And furthermore, I did well in instructing Hero, who was a girl track star from Gyara." It's a pleasure to see that Hero was originally a girl's name. But except for the warrior state of Sparta, where fit motherhood was required to birth soldier sons, women's exercise in the ancient Mediterranean consisted mostly of household and slave labor. Male narcissism and excess came to a halt with the Christian revolution, whose leaders disdained the corporeal, earthly body as a mere vehicle for transmitting sin from one generation to the next. New Christians learned to valorize the spiritual over the temporal and to cover up bodies, abstaining from temptation. For millennia, in Judaism, Christianity, and Islam, women were specifically charged with dressing modestly or remaining in the private sphere so they would not corrupt men. This quickly extended to bans on women preaching, teaching, singing, and acting. To be an athlete—a public performance of the body, after all, and in front of *men*!—became unthinkable, comparable to harlotry.

Allen Guttmann's *A Whole New Ball Game* deftly introduces readers to the ways these European attitudes shaped early American rules about outdoor sport and recreation. Native Americans' sacred games and long-established spiritual practices honoring physicality, with a special place for those of "two-spirited" gender in some tribal nations, disturbed

White Puritan settlers, who were hostile toward "pagan" merriment and the human body's expressiveness. From as early as 1650, Puritan laws went to the extreme of banning certain physical *motions* on Sunday: anyone caught running or jumping received ten lashes and a fine. My college students in the late 1990s were shocked by the Taliban's ban on sports in Afghanistan, as entire soccer arenas outside Kabul turned into sites of flogging and capital punishment, yet a close reading of early colonial American law hints at similar zealotry.

But those were the Northern colonies. Meanwhile, Guttmann shows how the increasingly affluent Southern colonists imitated English landed gentry by indulging in a love of horse racing, gambling, and the eventual use of slave jockeys competing for hefty prize purses. This split between religious abstainers and plantation-owning "sportsmen" set the stage for a young America hyperaware of the boundaries between permitted activities for White and Black, men and women. After the American Revolution, men from all regions of the country were gradually pressed to identify with "muscular Christianity," the ideal of keeping the body fit and ready for God and country. The repetitive drills of early fitness culture were thinly distinct from the military exercises required of a new US army. Because women were not expected to serve in the military, they were seldom introduced to basic calisthenics, except through their brothers and sons.

Male students digest the first week of class with discomfort. This is a history of sports very different from what they expected. The original Olympics were kind of *homoerotic*? The Puritan parliament *burned* James I's Declaration of Sports and made it illegal to work out on Sundays? Most of these students grew up associating Sunday, in the United States, with football. We used to put the rebellious joggers and dancers in stocks and stone them, sort of like . . . the Taliban? And America's first big Southern sport, the reason for the mascot of teams like the University of South Carolina, was not football but *cockfighting*?

The gap of what we don't learn about women's history is large, different, and, again, painful. We follow up on our week of early American manhood by looking at what *womanhood* has meant in terms of strength and delicacy, work and play.

Most public authorities across history referenced God or the holy scriptures of religious belief to justify male control over women, with male clerics interpreting, banning, or permitting female roles. The female body was already considered especially sinful, different, impure, and problematic for public life by the time Christianity reached southern Europe, on its way to influencing American law and culture. Religious and medical leaders alike cautioned against the female body as a site of agency, independence, or health, making a public athletic identity close to impossible. Sports would masculinize women—and for a woman to take on a man's role violated the separate spheres intended by God, who created Adam and Eve. This religious argument against women's sports later intersected with warnings from medical authorities, as scientific methods began to edge out spiritual interpretations. Yet right up to the late nineteenth century, Western physicians supported Aristotle's theory of the wandering womb and believed a menstruating woman had limited energy in her delicate body—energy that could be sapped or just badly misdirected by sports or study. Hysteria, purportedly caused by an imbalance in the womb, would damage reproductive health, and too much exercise thus spelled infertility. Furthermore, sports might spoil a young girl's good looks, which along with her presumed fertility and virginity were assets for a good marriage arrangement. Religious, medical, and marriage concerns combined to form a trifecta of prohibitions against serious sports for women, as well as firmly establishing men and women as "opposite" sexes.

This was the prescribed wisdom for elite White women in the nineteenth century: strenuous exercise hurt the womb. Strenuous effort was not, however, banned for enslaved women, the working poor, or mothers of ten children. The most important question on the midterm, I revealed to the class right at the start of week 2, would ask whether concerns about protecting women's health applied to *all* women in America's race- and class-stratified past. Yet no matter how many times I gave this hint in week 2, more than half the class every semester neglected to mention slavery or the abuse of working slave mothers on the midterm, a chilling reminder of how deeply students had internalized a White view of history. The great contradiction of the nineteenth century was declaring women's bodies too weak for sports, while simultaneously exploiting the labor and reproductive potential of female slaves. This continued long after slavery had ended as a legal institution, through articles such as the infamous "The Leading Cause of Diseases Peculiar to Women" from *Massachusetts Medical Journal* (1897). There, physicians named conditions hurtful to women's health that were unavoidable for most enslaved

mothers: "insufficient sleep, overwork, faulty dress, improper schooling, late marriage, carelessness after parturition, imprudence during
menstruation . . ."

Starting in the early nineteenth century, however, fixed "truths"
about gender and race were openly challenged by first-wave feminists,
female and male abolitionists, and religious reformers appalled by slavery's perversion of parent-child ties. White women continued to be kept
out of sports and colleges because of their supposed delicacy, but that
patriarchal protectiveness hardly extended to Black women or serving-
class Whites. Few White Christian women beyond Sarah and Angelina
Grimké dared to mention, additionally, the sexual abuse that was a con-
tinual part of slave women's lives. Sojourner Truth's famous "Ain't I a
Woman?" speech (1851), summarizing the harsh physical labor and maternal heartbreak demanded of female slaves, shamed other Americans
into understanding that ideals about "delicate womanhood" and sacred
motherhood did not privilege women of color:

> That man over there says that woman needs to be lifted over ditches,
> and into carriages, and to have the best place every where. Nobody ever
> helped me into carriages, or over mud puddles, or gives me any best
> place—and ain't I a woman? Look at me! Look at my arm! I have plowed,
> and planted, and gathered into barns, and no man could head me—and
> ain't I a woman? I could work as much and eat as much as a man (when
> I could get it), and bear the lash as well—and ain't I a woman? I have
> borne thirteen children, and seen them most all sold off into slavery, and
> when I cried out with a mother's grief, none but Jesus heard me—and
> ain't I a woman?[3]

The idealized White woman's modesty and the association of White
femininity with delicacy and illness set up a dual standard with roots
in ancient history: Elite women should not exert themselves; their servants would do the manual labor in the home. But those servants, too,
were women.

After the Civil War, newly freed Black men and male immigrants competed with Whites for the prize money and public acclaim available
through some late nineteenth-century sports. Events such as boxing offered a venue of masculine triumph. Through physical prowess and open
competition, working-class men could prove their might as individuals,
even when denied their right to vote as citizens. Black-against-White
contests grew limited after the 1896 *Plessy v. Ferguson* decision upheld

separation in public accommodations. But for women, there were far fewer sporting outlets, especially for the working-class girl with athletic gifts and aspirations. Instead, elite women's colleges and country clubs associated with the wealth and leisure of the Gilded Age made certain sports acceptable for aristocratic ladies: tennis, croquet, archery, and bathing-beauty swimming—often at racially restricted lakes or beaches. In *Coming On Strong*, historian Susan Cahn notes that these endeavors were also more socially acceptable because they required elaborate outfits, pasting an assurance of femininity onto competitors in costume. Healthful beauty, not aggression or the personal or political desire to triumph over competitors, remained the watchword for active women—with the interesting exception of field hockey, an occasionally bruising contact sport legitimized as girlish because of its association with British boarding schools for daughters of the elite.[4]

Throughout these troubling decades from slavery to Reconstruction to Jim Crow segregation, from religious repression to debates over evolution and Darwin, women faced an additional barrier. Barred from the ministry, law school, and medical school, kept off juries, they could not gain the degrees and public authority necessary to change sexist teaching and to reimagine woman's place in society. The feminist struggle for educational and professional opportunities was fueled by hope that if they could graduate, or be elected, or practice law and medicine, women would decide what women were allowed to do. In the twentieth century, however, given more empowered opportunities, quite a few women chose to reinforce traditional ideals, placing limits on what other women and girls could do in the name of "moderation."

It's a lot to take in during the first week of classes. My students groan as they read Cahn's account of the warnings against female strain one hundred years ago. Medical authorities feared that bicycle riding and other unladylike sports would render nice women infertile; worse, the bicycle seat might injure virginity. Putting on bloomers came dangerously close to a woman wearing the pants in the household, prohibited in the Bible. Whatever a woman did athletically had to be done differently than a man, whether that meant riding a horse sidesaddle or being pushed out of baseball and into softball. Sports might be part of all-women's colleges, but very few women overall went to college in the nineteenth century, and of their numbers, quite a few athletes found college "play days" to be less than the full-on intercollegiate contests they longed for.

Campaigns against higher education for women had clear racial and class overtones: women who graduated from the elite Seven Sisters colleges were indeed less likely to reproduce, but this had more to do with the lure of professional service careers, such as teaching and nursing, which required women to remain unmarried. Still, the popular connection between higher education and spinsterhood led to notions that learning, like sport, "desexed" women; even President Theodore Roosevelt, a strong advocate of sports and military manliness, believed that America's oldest White families were conspiring to commit "race suicide" by sending their next generation of daughters to college. White women were urged to save their energy for motherhood. Thus, as nineteenth-century America honed White masculinity through warfare and capitalism, baseball and basketball, it also restricted women's competition in public spheres of sports and politics.

At the same time, public reformers pointed to ways that women were already exhausted from manual labor and injury in the wildly unregulated world of industrial capitalism. In textile mills and factories, women and children worked all hours in life-threatening conditions, captured in Sarah N. Cleghorn's poem "The Golf Links": "The golf links lie so near the mill that almost every day / The laboring children can look out and see the men at play." The sacred role of mother had been legally violated every time a female slave suffered the sale of her children for someone else's profit, and in 1885, the age of consent for a girl child to be pushed into sexual union with an adult male was as young as ten years old in thirty-six states and seven years old in Delaware.[5] It was legal for any man to beat his wife and kids. Clearly, socially sanctioned ideals of protecting women and children from harm had enormous gaps.

Most women had to be tough to survive—as mothers, child brides, farmwives, sharecroppers, factory girls, mill hands, and, in the case of many Asian immigrants, railroad workers. But where silent stoicism and physical endurance were highly sought-after qualities in farmwives, most women's real or potential strength was kept separate from *athletic* identity. Endurance and heroism were to be saved for childbirth, admittedly a very dangerous game in a country with a high maternal death rate at the onset of the twentieth century.

Before long, my students raise their hands to protest. "But didn't giving birth prove to men that women were incredibly strong and able to handle pain and effort? All those women were giving birth in fields and back rooms with no painkillers. Why didn't men know women were tough?"

This is a hot discussion. Why does a woman's ability to strain for forty-eight hours, producing healthy twins, not prove her untapped athletic potential? There are many possible responses. Giving birth, the most feminine sex-role act celebrated, is also a private and family-directed act, and such are the traditional values defining modest womanhood. The most physically difficult things that women do are what they do for others, not for athletic glory. Boasting about the strain and endurance of childbirth at a women-only gathering is not the same thing as posting Olympic track records for public discussion; many taboos of modesty and secrecy surround pregnancy and childbirth because of the obvious associations with sexuality. In some religious communities, it is possible to violate standards of modesty even during childbirth, if a woman allows her head to become accidentally uncovered. That women endure high levels of pain in childbirth is not even seen as honorable: Genesis 3:16 declares such pain as Eve's punishment for disobeying God, and centuries of religious authorities reinforced this concept of woman's sinfulness, the monthly "curse" proof of moral impurity. In the Middle Ages, midwives who eased the pain of labor were burned at the stake; today, destitute women giving birth in charity wards are not always well medicated—they are still scorned as society's moral strays. No one denies the muscular effort involved in carrying a child and giving birth. It is women's and girls' public muscular strain, as well as their athletic performance unrelated to childbirth, that has historically been condemned as immodest, selfish, and attention seeking, the trinity of bad-girl behaviors. Thus, sports risks undertaken in childbearing years have been portrayed as ill advised or even antifamily.

After studying the glaring contrasts in physical expenditure between affluent, elite women and the working underclass of women who served them, my students examine physical stress levels once common for women in the rural middle—the homemakers of the past who ran a household or family farm with no labor-saving devices or hired hands. Their daily workload rivaled the bricklaying or hay baling assigned to the strongest men, but rural and small-town wives rarely had their femininity impugned, as their athletic chores involved proper domestic duties. One student, Justine, shared her thoughts on this: "Disadvantaged women have never posed a threat to masculinity, despite the immense physical demands they were expected to meet as slaves or factory workers." What were these immense physical demands? We make a list of the standard weight-bearing chores required of past homemakers and farmwives, most of which would eclipse the upper-body strength-training regimen at any modern gym today.

Globally, a woman's day once began with collecting firewood, hauling it across fields, and chopping it as well. Then fetching water and building a fire for breakfast—all before sunrise. (This remains the daily domestic work for girls in many lands even now.) Breakfast might be eggs just collected, milk squeezed from the cow and carried in a heavy bucket, butter churned and churned again, and cheese pressed in forty-pound tubs. There followed daily chores: scrubbing floors, wringing laundry, ironing, lifting children, tending animals, hauling more water, gardening, canning, hoeing, haying, harvesting, more milking, and dressing freshly slaughtered game. From this midwestern demographic of bulging female arm muscles came the first female softball players and, ultimately, the All-American Girls Professional Baseball League of World War II.

Why has it been easy to forget the athletic strengths of farm women? Eric Schlosser's best seller *Fast Food Nation* points out that in America, once-prevalent family farms have given way to corporate agribusiness. And public reformers' concerns about child labor have given way to public contempt for undocumented migrant workers, who harvest so much of our produce. Our collective national memory is slowly erasing images of those American women, Black and White, who grew up farming or going out to factory work at age five. My grandmother Mia could split an apple in two with her bare hands, a casual act of kitchen athletic power that delighted me as a child; my grandmother Nonnie immigrated from Poland to a Brooklyn neighborhood of Jewish factory girls who yearned to wear—and embody—the very flapper clothing styles they manufactured. Both of my grandmothers struggled to define their womanhood and find their place in middle-class America against their backgrounds of hard work, difficult families, and the breadwinning burdens that were expected from daughters, as well as sons.[6] Sports were inaccessible to them. What they had in common was a basic longing for love and respect. Eating disorders, free playtime, and college sports for elite women at the Seven Sisters were completely alien to their youths. At a certain point, marriage, they magically turned into "ladies," White privilege and hardworking husbands permitting them to leave Idaho and Brooklyn for the good life of Los Angeles, where their grandchildren, male and female, would one day swim and surf in skimpy athletic gear designed to celebrate the American spirit of leisure, play, and sex appeal.

In the first few weeks of class, the purpose of immersing students in so much social history is twofold. First, it is to make clear that the course involves hard study, with assigned readings providing important intersectional context. Students expecting just sports movies with free popcorn brought in by the professor tend to drop the class by week 2. Second, it's necessary to explode the myth that women have always been weak or were always in the home and not factories or fields, and it's also a myth that good men always protected the potential mothers of the nation from harm and strain. Working-class women, Black women, imprisoned women, migrant workers, and rural homemakers have traditionally contributed the greatest physical labor for the lowest wage return. And their combined numbers make up a hefty percentage of American womanhood. In addition, each group has been dismissed as somehow naturally promiscuous—consider the endless cultural stereotypes of the loose factory girl, the lascivious Black woman, the caged female prisoner who seduces the "new fish," the willing farmer's daughter, the repressed housewife awaiting a liaison with the hired hand. Somehow, we have made critical value distinctions between the effort involved in toting a fifty-pound milk pail or a fifty-pound child and the effort involved in bench-pressing fifty pounds in a public gym. All of this is crucial for understanding our social resistance to female athletes—for they are women competing, through physical merit unrelated to childcare, for prize money, attention, and immodest glory comparable to what elite male athletes enjoy.

By the fourth class meeting, prepped with background, we're ready to meet the heroines. Who were the first female athletes embraced by Americans? What allowed them to break through restrictive cautions and conditions? Susan Cahn's textbook, along with supplemental volumes like Jean Hastings Ardell's *Breaking into Baseball*, Jennifer Ring's *Stolen Bases*, and Madeleine Blais's *In These Girls, Hope Is a Muscle*, teach us about the first women's baseball teams, the college teams and "play days" of early women's colleges, tennis and swimming stars, and sandlot sluggers and daring drivers. We look at the first intercollegiate women's basketball game, Stanford versus the University of California at Berkeley on April 4, 1896—no men allowed and a whopping final score of 2–1: "As the Armory game tipped off, many of the 700 women spectators felt themselves witnesses to similar societal change. All three big San Francisco newspapers sent women writers and artists to cover the historic contest, for men were banned for modesty's sake. Denied admission, men climbed the roof and peered in the windows. Women inside fended them off with sticks."[7]

We look at the different athletic programs for women at historically Black colleges and universities and at the construction of public parks during the growth of cities in the 1890s—parks that allowed for roller-skating, rowing, walking, and cycling (in bloomers yet). Hot class debate: How much of women's "hysteria," illness, weakness, or presumed reproductive delicacy was caused by tight-fitting corsets that crushed the internal organs, limiting healthy lung and kidney function? When does beauty make women sick, a vicious circle authorities used to prove female inferiority? When did women and girls begin going to educated gynecologists for real remedies? After the first two weeks of class, if they've done the reading, every student is well versed in initial timelines of race, class, and gender. That's when we start to look at the Western obsession with classifying race, ranking physical difference, and exhibiting bodies to audiences for profit (see fig. 1.1, the Fort Shaw Indian School girls' basketball champions of 1905). At the end of the nineteenth century, the United States had become an empire, with more Americans living in crowded cities than on farms and a rampant maternal death rate that led medical authorities to recommend light exercise for women to stay fit for motherhood. *Plessy v. Ferguson* decreed the separate-but-equal ruling that determined segregation in sports for decades to come, and the modern Olympics began. Most women weren't allowed in the Olympics until the 1920s, but there was a special Women's Olympics convening in 1922 and well into the 1930s. We didn't know the names of the fastest women in the world until well into the twentieth century, an absence that handily perpetuated the notion that women couldn't run fast or set records. Moreover, segregation limited the interaction between White athletes and athletes of color. From the popular schoolgirl fiction aimed at a new generation of female students one hundred years ago, we can glimpse how ordinary girls already loved sports like basketball. Consider this scene from *Grace Harlowe's Third Year at Overton College*, a 1914 novel by Jessie Graham Flower for Altemus's College Girl Series:

> With the shrill notes of the whistle began one of the most stubborn conflicts ever waged between two Overton teams.... In the last half the doughty sophomores rose to the occasion and tied the score with their first play. Then Elfreda, with unerring aim, made a long overhand throw to the basket that brought forth deafening applause from the spectators. The sophomores managed to gain two more points, but the juniors again managed not only to gain two points, but to pile up their score until a particularly brilliant play to basket on the part of Elfreda closed the last half with the glorious reckoning of seventeen to twelve in favor of the juniors.
> ... For the present, at least, she was the most important girl in college.... "You deserve it!" exclaimed Gertrude Wells. "You were the pride of the team. I never want to see a better game. That last play of yours was a record breaker."[8]

This author's writing offers the reader more game details than many newspapers would give to women's basketball in the twenty-first century.

Historian Susan Cahn suggests that country-club sports like tennis and swimming, which had leisure-class and feminine-fashion associations, allowed White heroines like tennis star Helen Wills and swimmer Gertrude Ederle to capitalize on the flapper era's love affair with youthful outdoorswomen. "They helped fashion a new ideal of womanhood by modeling an athletic, energetic femininity with an undertone of explicit, joyful sexuality."[9] But first, as so often happens, it took a world war to liberate sex roles. Off came the corsets as American farm girls and the Land Army of women completed grain harvests in 1918; women went to work, volunteered as Red Cross nurses, and, in France, drove ambulances during the Great War. Men, however, failed army physicals so often that after the war, PE classes were introduced in America's public schools, giving us that familiar authority figure: the gym teacher.

With bobbed hair and shorter skirts, and the ability to vote in all states if White, flappers of the 1920s leaped into sports culture with greater acceptance, symbolizing healthy young womanhood and American superiority. Too quickly, that vitality was seized on by the lurking eugenics movement. Racism reached extraordinary levels in the 1920s, a decade that saw burgeoning Ku Klux Klan membership and lynchings.

Few tennis courts or park pools were open to Black athletes, male or female. While White swimmers brought home Olympic gold and White tennis beauty queens made headlines, African American "race girls" brought pride to their own communities at segregated track and basketball meets. This pattern of White celebrity athletes versus local grassroots heroines heralded only by their own minority communities remained in place for decades, further obscuring how many women and girls were in fact committed to sports. White women were themselves limited in school sports by the guidelines of the women's division, which enforced modified "girls' rules" intended to protect womanhood.

Young women in the twentieth century workforce risked a reputation as "rough" girls by playing softball on factory teams or running track in industrial leagues, producing champions such as Babe Didrikson. But after the attack on Pearl Harbor and the US entry into World War II, gender codes changed to permit and reward muscular competence in war factories' Rosie the Riveter workers and Women's Army Corps recruits, and wartime America embraced an unlikely symbol of victory: the All-American Girls Professional Baseball League. Though all-White, and requiring strict obedience to set standards of femininity in dress, curfews, and hairstyles, the league is today praised as groundbreaking for its day (see fig. 1.2). Penny Marshall's 1992 blockbuster film *A League of Their Own* and Janis Taylor's documentary *When Diamonds Were a Girl's Best Friend* make plain the league's selling point, conceived by Chicago Cubs owner Philip K. Wrigley—that his "girls" would play like men but look like ladies. The novelty of contrast, and the presentation of strong-armed women as a wartime emergency resource not unlike the military's Women's Army Corps and Women Accepted for Volunteer Emergency Service, made escapist athletic entertainment profitable. Since the league continued well into 1954, an eleven-year run, it's not accurate to suggest that women's pro baseball ended as soon as the men returned from war, when women were urged out of factories and ballparks and back to the home. But that social shift certainly influenced the league's postwar wane, along with other factors, such as boys-only Little League and the advent of television. Female sluggers were steered to softball, with industrial leagues such as the Connecticut Brakettes very popular with local fans from 1947 on, yet once again, those players dealt with social stigma of being mannish tough girls or lesbians, since during the postwar baby boom adult women were supposed to be back in the home and pregnant.[10] It would take decades for the very successful, active story of postwar women's softball to win mention in history books, as my Georgetown student Haley Lowrance shared in class: "Today's lecture reminded me that my grandmother, a farm girl from Glendale, Arizona, played softball for the Chicks in the late forties / early fifties. My mom was perusing books at Costco when she recognized her own mother in a picture!" Originally sponsored by the Glendale Hatchery, these players were in fact called "chicks" for business reasons; when Webster's Creamery took over sponsorship, the Chicks became simply Webster's.

The Cold War dramatization of American femininity versus Soviet women athletes' masculine appearances was a key part of the 1952 and 1956 Olympics. However, as women's sports historian Ashley Brown has noted, during the same Cold War era, the US State Department eagerly sent Black women athletes like tennis champion Althea Gibson on global goodwill tours. Sports became a means for the United States to impress on important allies the *look* of an idealized democracy, in which African American women, too, symbolized achievement.[11]

A side note here: most college students today were born after the Berlin Wall came down and require a quick review of Cold War politics. Otherwise, papers and exams reveal American students conflating World War I and World War II, confusing the Korean War with the Vietnam War, and mistaking East Germany for Nazi Germany, and most are unaware that the Russian Revolution occurred during World War I, when Russia was a US ally. Once this background is up on the whiteboard in class, it's clearer to all students how the demonization of Soviet Bloc athletes shaped American sports pride and gender codes for more than forty years. In 1952, at the Helsinki Olympic Games, a Soviet gymnast won *seven* medals, the most ever won in a single Olympics by a woman. This Jewish gymnast netted glory for the Soviet state during an era of official antisemitism. But no American student I've taught has heard of Maria Gorokhovskaya. And few students understand why the United States boycotted the 1980 Olympic Games, or what it had to do with Afghanistan, or that the United States supported the Taliban and Osama bin Laden's pushback against Moscow at that time.

After the advent of film and television, more women's sports events began to be documented; today we can view and analyze some remarkable earlier contests. The HBO special *Dare to Compete* covers a fantastic range of female athletes' constrictions in the 1950s and 1960s: efforts to feminize superstar Babe Didrikson; the exultant triumph of the Tennessee State Tigerbelles track team at the 1960 Olympics, when the team's Black female medalists could not get counter service in much of their nation's capital; the daring participation of two forbidden women in the male-only Boston Marathon; and the ongoing women's rules of half-court, three-dribble basketball. When some of my students struggled to believe the ways women had been held back, I brought in my mother as a class guest and passed around my parents' high school yearbooks from Fairfax and Los Angeles High of the mid-1950s. While my parents' soon-to-be-celebrity classmates Dustin Hoffman and Jack Kemp were lettering in track and football, the girls of West LA had two choices: join the Neptunettes (and be like glam swimmer Esther Williams) or the Bowlerinas (and meet boys). Most important, the 1950s established the dominance of television, which broadcast free ballgames, sports-themed commercials, and images of a race- and gender-stratified America no patriot of the McCarthy era was supposed to question. Television made possible a national rejoicing in US sports heroes once only glimpsed in movie shorts or at actual games. But its prime-time fare of westerns, spy series, and family sitcoms reiterated the dichotomy of strong, protective, occasionally outlaw men versus domestic, perfectly coiffed White wives and daughters.

The civil rights movement and second-wave feminism would change society forever, making equal opportunity a hallmark of activism and legal challenges. There could be no measure of progress, however, without awareness of the past. Although in the 1960s and 1970s women began to gain greater roles in sports, most had no map to the foremothers who had competed before them. It's not just that we don't learn about Maria Gorokhovskaya or about America's own Vicki Manalo. Women's sports history simply isn't included in school—or, as it turns out, in the media.

Fig. 1.2 Souvenir sweatshirt promoting the All-American Girls Professional Baseball League and the film *A League of Their Own*, signed by original players.
A gift to the author from Connie Wolver. Photo by the author.

Female athletes need to raise their own bar—not the one handed to them by men or the media. The female athlete is changing the game, and media coverage of women's sports needs to follow suit. Men don't need to be threatened by strong female athletes and offset their power by sexually exploiting them in the media—in the majority of today's media coverage, the female athlete is either nonexistent or naked.

—LIZA YANNUZZI PASCALE, GEORGETOWN CREW

HOW FEMALE ATHLETES DISAPPEAR
Headlines, Publicity, and Media Activism

What's the score? How do we know what we know about women's sports, past and present? Unable to attend every game of every sport ourselves, we depend on the media to give us game outcomes; to make game viewing possible at certain times online or on television; and to provide backstory and coverage at large global-scale events, like the World Cup and the Olympics. There is no women's sports history without informed, detailed description. Yet women's history in general has been shaped by rules concerning women's bodies: how those bodies are controlled, the effect of those bodies on male viewers, and whether women should be out in public at all. As one scholar put it, "We judge female athletes on everything but their athleticism."[1]

In the past, when there was no professional sports journalism, no photography, no radio, and no electronic or even print media, someone, somehow, served as a credible witness to every event we know about. Stories, sketches, oral narratives written down by a literate family member, songs, poems, and legends tell us about a unique talent or contest. And over the years, nearly every report and retelling was filtered through bias. How were women athletes described? Were their achievements celebrated, questioned, or mocked? The Greek statesman Pericles, for instance, declared that the greatest compliment to a woman was when no man spoke of her, meaning that she had no "reputation" and was never the subject of gossip. Pericles's long-lasting guideline for

Fig. 2.1 Sports journalist Christine Brennan, 2018.
Photo courtesy of Christine Brennan.

modesty frowned on fame; simply by achieving, in any arena, a woman invited scrutiny—of her looks, virtue, virginity, sexuality, and family honor. To this day, an appearance in the Olympics can be a death sentence for some women, if public exposure on the world stage violates the community standards of their traditional cultures.

To analyze sports media in class and consider where and how women have been included or excluded, I start with some historical reminders: You may never have heard of an event, but that does not mean it didn't happen. Because of the pressure to remain separate and modest, women often held their own sports festivals or competitions apart from men, or in secret, with the proceedings never inscribed by historians. In modern times, communities outside the American sports mainstream hosting their own championships included the Gay Games, the Women's Islamic Games, the All Native Basketball Tournament in Canada, and many more.

How we define media reporting depends on the decade. Again, I put a brief history timeline on the board—this time, a lesson on the progression of media and technological innovation. When did we first have sports columns in newspapers in the United States? What about radio broadcasts or photographs of competitions? When did sports films first show up on a big screen? When did talking pictures become the norm? When did television enter the home? How about cable TV, the promise of seeing movie after movie in your own house? And the VCR—permitting a sports fan to rent, or own, and play *any and all* sports movies all weekend long; for a kid's sports-themed birthday party; or as a team energizer before the big game? When did all-sports channels like ESPN make their debut? I discover that many of my students think television screens were in American homes as early as the 1920s. They can't imagine a twentieth century without small screens.

In fact, we learn that once upon a time, before the era of Hollywood film and television, quite a few American spectators gathered to watch tall or muscled bodies put on public display not in a gym but at carnivals and zoos.

During the late nineteenth century, industrialization and urbanization crowded more and more unrelated people together in towns, cities, and workplaces. Waves of immigration from eastern and southern Europe; racial segregation supported by law and custom; and the US military takeover of distant lands, including Cuba, Puerto Rico, Hawaii, and the Philippines, fostered an explosion of interest in ranking human diversity and difference. New scientific classification by anthropologists, sociologists, zoologists, archaeologists, and psychologists resulted in a taxonomy of body types, races, and sexual categories as well, with official terminology like *Caucasoid*, *Negroid*, and *Mongoloid*; *mulatto*, *quadroon*, and *octoroon*; and *deviant*, *abnormal*, and *invert*. Darwin's controversial research on the survival of the fittest sparked additional interest in population statistics—which people were the tallest, fastest, most fertile, and longest living? Scientific explorers ranked and rated the peoples they encountered in service to ideals of Western, White dominance, with American and colonial British leaders subscribing to the "white man's burden" doctrine of control over darker-skinned races. The scientific interest in classifying non-White bodies and seizing their skeletons for display in museums has become a shameful controversy, taking us from anthropology to apology, and is now addressed in books like Samuel Redman's *Bone Rooms: From Scientific Racism to Human Prehistory in Museums.*[2]

One hundred years ago, many ordinary Americans, Black, White, and immigrant alike, remained illiterate and were unlikely to read science journals, but the American public did begin to visit museums. A 1915 exhibit in San Diego titled the Science of Man was just one early twentieth-century American installation promoting views of dark-skinned races as primitive. A good hundred years before that (1810–15), overseas, we find the sad life story of Sara Baartman, known as the Hottentot Venus. Taken from South Africa and displayed onstage to high society in England, she fascinated voyeuristic White audiences and scientists obsessed with her large buttocks. Being well endowed was an ordinary characteristic of her Khoikhoi tribe, but for a fee, onlookers could even touch Baartman's body. In an era of intense body modesty, White men projected hyperfertility and sexuality onto the Black African women who colonial explorers had "discovered." This framework of discovering, and publicly uncovering, African women's bodies informed social practices for well over a century; after dying in poverty, Baartman was dissected by an anatomy professor at the Museum of Natural History in Paris, her bones and genitalia put on display. Finally, after years of organized protest, her remains were returned to South Africa for burial in 2002.

Popular culture continued to commercialize displays of human difference through large-scale events, including the St. Louis World's Fair. A young African man named Ota Benga was exhibited at the 1904 World's

Fair in St. Louis, along with Igorot from the Philippines; Ainu from Japan; and America's best female basketball team, from the Fort Shaw Indian School. The young athletes performed exhibition games against White teams, handily defeating them—and then donned cumbersome dresses to sit in an exhibit stall on raised platforms, sewing and ironing, demonstrating their femininity and domestic skills to White visitors. Placing young Native American women on exhibit confirmed for fairgoers that White values were superior and could be taught. In 1906, Ota Benga was put on display in the Bronx Zoo, encouraged to play with an orangutan for the amusement of visitors. Eventually, the man in the zoo took his own life, shooting himself through the heart.[3] Although this history was unfamiliar to my students, they quickly made the connections, as my UC Berkeley student Rachel Sumadi noted, "The public display of the body brings back the horrifying history of slavery. . . . Sports and the body cannot be separated."

As early as 1907, a University of Chicago sociologist named William Thomas suggested that women "resemble the child and the lower races, i.e., the less developed forms . . . a very striking evidence of the ineptitude of woman for the expenditure of physiological energy through motor action."[4] His comment comparing "women" to "the lower races" both stigmatized and disappeared women in those races, a phenomenon repeated throughout the twentieth century whenever writers disappeared Black women by using the phrase "women and minorities." Thomas's words also emasculated the smaller-bodied men of non-Western tribal groups by suggesting they were physiologically feminine or childlike. These attitudes reflected US foreign policy seeded as a result of the Spanish-American War. When the Philippines came under American control, the new governor-general and eventual twenty-seventh US president William Howard Taft famously suggested that "our little brown brothers" would require "fifty or one hundred years" of White control "to develop anything resembling Anglo-Saxon political principles and skills."[5]

In the United States, athletic women and men became part of the new order, helping make America number one in a global hierarchy by maintaining strict codes of race and sex. These codes included displaying Black talent in service to White interests, organizing other groups to perform for White audiences, emphasizing that "primitive" aspects were natural in non-White races and naturally led to strong athletic performance, valorizing physical size as a prized attribute of Western ruling power, and limiting Black achievement to sports and entertainment venues. Thirty years later, racial classification systems and scientific attitudes embedded in US policies became models for Nazi Germany's taxonomy of Aryans and non-Aryans, with the official expulsion of Jews from the top sports clubs and national teams just before the 1936 Olympics in Berlin. Hitler sought to make the Olympic Games into a showcase of the master race, with any German Jewish athletic talent excluded. Local county fairs, carnivals, and circuses continued to showcase living human bodies right through the twentieth century, migrating on-screen into exploitation films, starting with Tod Browning's 1932 circus film, *Freaks*. Even more problematic, the long tradition of displaying and treating people of color as subhuman shaped our media in ways that can be seen every day, from comparing Black athletes to animals like gorillas, gazelles, antelope, or monkeys, to characterizing Black women's muscularity as threatening or unfeminine. Few public figures endured a cruder, more-racist examination of their muscular arms than First Lady Michelle Obama: In 2012, diplomat Richard Grenell, later the acting director of National Intelligence for President Trump, mocked Michelle Obama for "sweating into the carpet" of the White House. In 2016, a West Virginia mayor was forced to resign after she commented, "Just made my day, Pam!" on her friend's Facebook post, which had described the First Lady as "a Ape in heels."[6]

We study this appalling background to bear in mind that even now, much of sports viewing is about ranking and staring at extraordinary bodies the average person would otherwise never see. Sports is where much of recorded history describes who is fastest, tallest, strongest, and biggest. Sports can also reward unusual bodies with positive attention and significant income, turning the human oddity into a glorified global hero. Today most viewers accept that unique types of bodies suit unique sports: small men as jockeys, men over seven feet tall sought after by basketball programs, swimmer Michael Phelps's atypically big hands slicing through pool water to win Olympic gold. Oversize feet? A special shoe may yet be *named* for you. Biceps that bust a dress shirt? Well, being *bigger* than average is expected of male football players. And other men may envy athletes whose powerful physiques, symbolizing hyper-masculine endowment, hint at possibly impressive penis size. But the bigger-is-better yardstick does not apply to women, who are supposed to be smaller than men; less muscular, if muscular at all; soft skinned;

and, above all, private about their bodies. Both in the Western heritage of Cinderella and in traditional Chinese foot-binding, women were praised for small feet. My students were quick to point out that we reward men for size and women for sizing down—and not without complications: tellingly, in one Georgetown class, every male student "knew a guy" who had abused the supplement creatine in hopes of bulking up rapidly, whereas every female student "knew a girl" whose obsessive dieting had turned into an eating disorder. Through the many side glances, I understood that some of these self-harming practices were ongoing or recent among the group right in front of me. And it wasn't hard to find the messages encouraging such unhealthy behaviors, as one student, Sarah Trice, reported to us: "In the magazine *Tennis*, I found an article entitled 'Most Improved Body.' Jennifer Capriati received the award for having lost thirty pounds while Andre Agassi received the award for having 'bulked up'!"

Not only is this difference romanticized and embedded as normal or correct—making it harder for tall, big, bulked-up women to win admiration—but nice girls are supposed to suppress the actual normal functions all *humans* are born with: Don't sweat. Don't spit. Don't belch. Don't bleed.[7] Don't swear either. In sports culture, what's permitted for men is not well received by the media or some fans if a woman does it.[8] In some classic sports editorials, female effort and ability have also been framed as turnoffs for men. Arthur Daley, sports columnist for the *New York Times*, declared in 1953, "There's just nothing feminine or enchanting about a girl with beads of perspiration on her alabaster brow, the result of grotesque contortions in events totally unsuited to female architecture. . . . Don't get me wrong, please. Women are wonderful. But when those delightful creatures begin to toss the discus or put the shot—well, it does something to a guy. And it ain't love, Buster."[9]

When we study both women and men in today's sports headlines, we see when, where, and how past biases shaped American culture. These biases lurk in the inkwell of the sports journalist, whether or not that writer personally intends to perpetuate stereotypes. To understand the cultural ambivalence toward *female athletes* in America, one only has to look at the images in our media. A picture or editorial cartoon declares to us the position of women's sports in American society. How are women posed, photographed, or caricatured, presenting a nonverbal message readers may take in with one glance?

In our second month together as a group, we get busy honing critical media literacy, meeting the sportswriters and editorial cartoonists of America's past. In addition to the essays cited previously, we scan suggestive headlines such as "Eve in Trouble as Usual" (1928); "Sports Is Unfair to Women" (1972); "Female Athletes Guard Figures, Complexions" (1974); "Uta's Victory a Female Thing" (1996); "Chastain Is Topless, Er, Tops in World Cup Win" (1999); "Romanian Mother, 38, Takes Gold" (2008); "No Balls? No Balls: In D.C. Public School Sports, Most Girls Stay on the Sidelines" (2010); "Pregnant Malaysian Shooter Aiming for Historic Gold" (2012); "One Brave, Tough, Tough Girl" (2012); "Womanhood Is Dying at the Olympics" (2012); and "A Coach First, a Female Coach Second" (2018). As these titles indicate, while sports pages are often devoid of women's accomplishments, what we *do* hear about women and girls in sports directs our attention to femininity, figure, or motherhood and marital status. Fans of women's sports hoping for broader media coverage are often frustrated by the few images that do circulate. When we look beyond the nonathletic women modeling swimsuits on the cover of *Sports Illustrated*, we're still directed to identify female athleticism with Brandi Chastain in her sports bra at the moment of World Cup victory, style articles featuring the tennis dresses of Venus and Serena Williams, or the hair-pulling YouTube video of UNM soccer player Elizabeth Lambert. Such images continue to reduce female athletic power and competitiveness to sexiness, fashion, and "catfighting."

Profiles of female athletes also heavily emphasize rivalries, reinforcing tropes of tension and distrust between women and taking glee in conflicts that make headlines: Martina Navratilova versus Chris Evert, Mary Decker versus Zola Budd, Tonya Harding versus Nancy Kerrigan. Of course, well-branded rivalries attract fans and drive sports marketing whether athletes are male or female. At UC Berkeley, my students' T-shirts declare "Voldemort Went to Stanford," and Stanford Athletics' department phone number is 1-800-BEAT-CAL. For American women, rivalry branding often has an implicit good girl / bad girl binary, drawing on sexist ideals of female behavior in order to promote women's individual sports, like tennis and skating. Or, in team victories, news headlines focus on the attractive individual rather than the group effort, a marketing trend female educators in the women's division had foreseen and warned about in the 1920s. Women in sports may be exoticized; depicted as freaks of nature; compared to animals; or flirted with *and* infantilized as little girls simultaneously, as when Winter Olympic Games reporter Dennis Murphy said of women's snowboardcross medalist Lindsey Jacobellis, "What's a cute Goldilocks like this doing in a cutthroat event like that?"[10]

From cartoon strips to magazine covers, we also find ongoing tension between *female* and *athlete*. And the mainstream media, including newspapers with family-inclusive material such as comics, have an enormous impact on how children see women athletes. The children's publication spin-off *Sports Illustrated for Kids* purposely featured very few girls on its covers, catering to boy subscribers. When managing editor John Papanek was challenged about this, he replied, "It is reasonable to think that a cover that features only females will be repugnant to those people who are most likely to buy the magazine."[11] One DC-area parent wrote in to the *Washington Post* explaining that her nine-year-old daughter had stopped reading the *KidsPost* insert because its sports columnist had not mentioned women's sports in more than two months.

On other occasions, the *Washington Post* failed to include any coverage of women's sports in its daily sports section, yet it included cartoonists' nods to Title IX and Mia Hamm on the comics page. This marginalization of the women's sports world, forcing newspaper readers to hunt for the tiniest reference to female athletes, is certainly frustrating to those who seek fair, in-depth, daily coverage of women's events, but those smallest comics-page images have much to teach us. Many of us grew up with Peppermint Patty playing against Charlie Brown in the *Peanuts* strip; cartoonist Charles Schulz later became a devoted Title IX advocate. Female cartoonist Nadine Seltzer, whose 1955 comic strip *Sweetie Pie* featured a feisty football-playing tomboy, both confirmed and questioned traditional sex roles by having Sweetie Pie's father boast to a neighbor, "We hoped for a boy. . . . We got the next thing to it." Positive images of girls playing sports, usually soccer, now appear regularly in conventional, family-centered cartoons like *Family Circus* and the Latinx-themed *Baldo*. But sexist messages and images also appear. In 2008, the year of the Women's Baseball World Cup, *Argyle Sweater* cartoonist Scott Hilburn debuted with a panel depicting "The Throw-Like-A-Girl Baseball League Tryouts," showing weak-wristed boys with pained expressions and rear ends pushed out. In April 2013, a Sunday funnies edition of Rick Kirkman and Jerry Scott's *Baby Blues* showed father and son relishing a ball game while mother and daughter sweat resentfully, comparing baseball to a migraine or a math test. "Why are they even here?" asks young son Hammie, and his father answers, "Probably to pay us back for how we acted at the *Nutcracker*."

In the first class assignment, handed out by week 3, I invite students to analyze the depiction of women athletes in local, national, or world coverage of sports. Immediately, the class discovers what is *not* there: reliable, daily reports on women in competition. Even now, representations of women in sports news are rare compared to the endless coverage of male athletes; women make up about 40 percent of all sports competitors but only appear in 4 percent of sports reporting, according to the Women's Sports Foundation. Women officials and referees lack representation as well, though these role models are so important for both boys and girls to see (fig. 2.2). Students quickly line up for my office hours, bewildered, explaining, "I couldn't find anything." They're outraged to discover that entire editions of influential newspapers, including those from their own hometowns, rolled off the presses with no mention of female athletes. To give an example, the *Washington Post* Sunday paper on September 4, 2016—right in the middle of Labor Day weekend—had an eleven-page sports section. Those eleven pages included exactly *one* paragraph about women's sports: a note on the Washington Mystics, deep at the bottom of page 10. There were also three women listed in the Digest section for having won races, plus one throwaway mention that pro basketball player Tina Charles had just scored the four thousandth point of her career, making WNBA history. One needed a magnifying glass to find any of these marginalia. Ironically, the lead story of the sports section was about Paralympic swimmer Brad Snyder, an article challenging readers to expand their concept of just who is an athlete.

Happily, some national and regional newspapers are consistently representative of women's sports. A few worth singling out are *USA Today* and the *Santa Cruz Sentinel*; the latter's July 15, 2018, Sunday paper featured news and images of local women athletes on the entire first page of its sports section and on two-thirds of the second and third pages that day. And newspapers from the *New York Times* to the *Wall Street Journal* are aware they're on watch for how they depict women athletes. Shannon Scovel, a swimmer and journalism major at American University, found both defensiveness and an arc of improvement in her study "Complaining, Campaigning, and Everything in Between: Media Coverage of Pay Equity in Women's Tennis in 1973 and 2007," a paper she presented at the Association for Education in Journalism and Mass Communication conference.

My students are always delighted to find peers in collegiate sports, sports journalism, or women's studies who succeeded in publishing critiques like the one I assigned, and I make it very clear that I am available to help them fine-tune a paper for possible publication if they produce quality original work. "Original" becomes the sticking point; in recent years, it's been easier for students to find professionally written news features *about* sexism in sports. Top national writers have looked critically at Serena Williams's penalty for "verbal abuse" at the women's US Open in 2018, as well as at the French Tennis Federation's chastisement of her for the catsuit she wore at the French Open in 2018. However, I ask students to become critical writers themselves instead of just summarizing what established writers Sally Jenkins and Deirdre Clemente have to say about bias. This catch stumps quite a few first-year students. Isn't it enough for them to find cool articles *about* sexism? "No," I explain. "This assignment asks you to find a sports article and then show me where, or why, *you* believe the author of that piece embedded subtle or obvious gender bias. Sally Jenkins doesn't get to do your homework for you. You're the acting authority here." But the course and syllabus are designed so that by week 3 in our semester, the students have all the historical tools necessary to write a three-page critique themselves.

Once the first class papers come in each semester, I begin by evaluating writing skills, identifying who might need help and who might be on their way to a Pulitzer one day. (These are sometimes the same person.) I make sure to start any attached notes with a compliment, telling a student, "Your paper really awakened me to an issue I did not know about—good for you! Now, about spelling . . ." Students who struggle with writing usually know that they need academic support. But professors can also reward for what's there, to paraphrase a guideline used in AP US History exam scoring. Every paper I've received over the years has offered at least one smart insight about bias in sports media, impressing me over and over.

"So what did you find in your searches?" I ask the class after returning the first graded assignment a week later. There's an explosion of opinions. Everyone's eager to share. Here are just a few of the best responses from over the years:

The way sportswear is marketed to women is based on a complex history of exclusion turning into inclusion with judgment.

Because the neutral has taken on the face of a White male, everyone else therefore becomes a minority, including women—in the sports world especially.

We want men as the heroic champions and women as their supporting cast.

The sports media advertises men's *sports* versus advertising women's *bodies*.

We cannot forget that the generation that controls most of the money in this country grew up before women could play on an organized sports team.

It's a tough battle for women athletes in a society where the terms *women* and *athletes* are personified as opposites.

With news heavily tilting sports coverage toward men, women are left feeling like the last kid chosen in gym class.

To be both female and strong today, as female athletes are, violates traditional codes of feminine identity, and therefore advertisers compensate by oversexualizing or glamorizing the women.

The woman is not permitted to stand alone on her merits. The media feels a need to place feminine adjectives in front of the female athlete.

[An additional note to me was scribbled across a bar napkin and attached to the paper.] The ESPN Zone where I work does not have one damn women's sport playing on any of their TVs!!

I took a look at the *Sports Illustrated* website today and was very disappointed by the lack of attention to women's sports. There was virtually no coverage of other professional teams [other than the WNBA], but there was a big link to the swimsuit issue. I finally typed in the word "women" to see if I could find additional articles on women's sports, but what I got was a blank screen that said "Women is not a valid keyword." I then typed in "men" and was sent directly to an NBA site. I thought, "Even the search engine is sexist."

I found these two newspaper sections from 1997 about Wil Cordero and how he was so quickly allowed back into baseball after beating his wife. I happened to be in Boston when he was playing the first game back from his suspension. What was most of the crowd's reaction when his name was announced in his first at bat? Primarily cheers and applause. I sat there stunned and speechless as fathers with their sons cheered for this man and in essence supported his actions.

Several students addressed the mixed messaging of *Sports Illustrated*'s swimsuit issue, where more commercial attention went to a posed swimsuit model than to her athletic sister, sweating, just off camera, on an actual basketball court. The unspoken question, my students complained, seemed to be "Would you rather look like an athlete or a fashion model?" And many women resemble neither. As Rosie O'Donnell noted in her foreword to Kelly Whiteside's *WNBA: A Celebration*, "Sport mirrored a society where women are always taught to compete against each other. Who's better? Who's better looking? Who's got the best figure?"[12]

When I taught the class in a spring semester, during March Madness NCAA basketball, students' papers also described the ways that women's "difference" informed the selection of commercial sponsors, sometimes embarrassing male announcers and viewers. Here's one example: "I don't mind so many commercial breaks if it means they show us the women's games on TV—at least they acknowledge that women's sports fans also buy cars and eat pizza. I know that a couple years ago male announcers were red in the face saying the name of the feminine hygiene sponsor. My teammates and I cracked up when we heard the commentator say, 'We'll be right back with the Monistat halftime report.' But so what? Our coach says the men's games used to be sponsored by commercials for a product that treated 'jock itch'!"

In the process of sharing what they had learned, several students weighed in on how assumptions about sports know-how are gendered and how such stereotypes insulted their intelligence in differing ways. From a male student: "I asked the woman next to me if I could read the newspaper she had put away. And she replied, 'Oh, of course—here is the sports section.' As if I'm not concerned about what occurs in the world! I actually wanted to read the world news section, which I study every day, faithfully. I replied, 'Despite your stereotypes about young men, some of us really do care about things beyond sports.' This is the gender discrimination *I* experience."

From a female student: "I had another run-in with a male who thought I was sports illiterate because I'm a girl. I wore a light purple sweater to work today, and when I got into the elevator, the guy who was already in there said, 'I'll bet you don't even know you're wearing a Baltimore color. Did you even know they were in the Super Bowl this year?' I looked at him and told him that I happen to be a huge Ravens fan, had attended many of their games last season, was looking forward to seeing them beat the Giants."

From another female student, who went from playing soccer at GWU to playing on the Canadian women's national team:

> My journalism professor flat-out told me I couldn't possibly know enough about football to do commentary on a game for my assignment. I pleaded with him, but he didn't seem to care. My anger grew, and then my frustration turned to determination. I asked one of my best guy friends to let me sit in on his football practices, and I brushed up on all the lingo and plays. For an entire week after my own soccer practice, I drew out plays, jotted down words; I knew our team inside and out. I waited until I was nice and ready, and then I made my move: I told my teacher I did not appreciate sex discrimination, and if I wasn't given a fair opportunity I would bring this to a higher authority. I told him I wanted to sit in our classroom studio, with him, and do the play-by-play of last week's football game for my final assignment. To his surprise, my teacher received enormous feedback from the rest of the class about having a female announcer, all good reviews.

From Georgetown lacrosse player Jennifer Welsh: "My cousin has been promoted to work for the *Philadelphia Daily News* as a sports enterprise writer. She has always been the only full-time female reporter on every sports staff she has ever worked for, which shows just how male dominated the field is. When she answers the phone and says, 'Sports, this is Dana,' the person on the other end often responds, 'Can I speak to someone in sports?' They assume she is the secretary."

And Shannon Scovel, the AU student who had already presented a conference paper? She noted wryly that as a college senior covering the 2017 NCAA men's wrestling tournament in St. Louis,

> a woman came up to me in the hotel and said something along the lines of "You must not be here for the wrestling tournament." I was so taken aback and bothered that she just assumed I wasn't there for the perceived men's sporting event that I have continued to cover the sport. I became even more motivated to bring other women into the space. Still, people tell me things like "Wow, you really know a lot about the sport" when they read my work. I'm sure it's meant as a compliment, but to me it sounds like they're surprised that I am knowledgeable about sports.

Beyond their critiques of gender, students were also wary of the prolific coverage of Black male athletes, concerned that this trend both disappeared Black women and reinforced a stereotype. Athletes were often the only men of color featured in daily news, their celebrity branded and sold, crowding out views of role models or success stories from other fields of achievement. We had been studying the exploitation of the Black male athlete, his very body directed, disciplined, commodified, and traded by White management, in specific texts, from Harry Edwards's *The Revolt of the Black Athlete*, to John Hoberman's *Darwin's Athletes*, to William Rhoden's *$40 Million Slaves*. I reminded the class that sports events can and do confront American racism. Few who were alive at the time can forget the iconic photo of medalists John Carlos and Tommie Smith raising fists from the podium of the 1968 Olympic Games in Mexico City. Yet in our anguished, ongoing national forum on race, perspectives from Black *women* in sports still go missing—overlooked, ignored, buried, muted, or just less visible, aside from ubiquitous profiles of Serena Williams. How might we better incorporate the heritage and authority of Black women in sports? In a battle for representation, equality, and the inscription of Black leadership, half the story is no story.

One particular year, in the middle of navigating my students' questions about bias and invisibility, I took the class to a local event where we watched Black women's sports history vanish right from the auditorium of a historically Black university.

In 1997, as female athletes prepared to celebrate the twenty-fifth anniversary of Title IX, African Americans were also celebrating the fifty-year anniversary of Jackie Robinson's integration of Major League Baseball. Numerous exhibits around Washington, DC, paid homage to Robinson's daring legacy and to the decades of Black male athletes who crossed the color line into pro sports. To examine the hard question of racism in American sports, with feedback from the larger DC community, ABC's *Nightline* program filmed a "town meeting" on racism in sports at the Howard University campus. College athletes from all local schools were invited to be in the audience, and I brought students from my women's sports class at George Washington University, along with members of our women's basketball team.

That auditorium was packed with male and female athletes, Olympic veterans, sports fans, students, coaches, trainers, journalists, and concerned Black parents of young competitors. But onstage, there was not one woman among the otherwise splendid coaches and athletes who spoke about fifty years of racism in sports. Not one woman had been included in that panel of experts, and during the excruciating hour moderated by host Ted Koppel, my students looked to me with questions brimming in their eyes, waiting for just one mention of the numberless Black *women* who overcame double discrimination to set world records. Women, too, brought home gold medals, trophies taller than their children; ran eight hundred meters only to be refused a cup of water from a cooler; or won tennis tournaments while unable to take a bathroom break at the White country club. Where were their names? We began rumbling. Alice Coachman, Toni Stone, Wilma Rudolph, Peanut Johnson, Althea Gibson, Willye White . . .

When at last the panel invited questions from the audience, up rose the cocaptain of GWU's women's basketball team, Tajama Abraham. TJ politely asked Ted Koppel why Black women were not represented on this important occasion. Were they not part of this story? Had women not experienced racism as Black athletes? Or had Black women never participated in sports?

The audience roared approval, awaiting Ted Koppel's response. Caught off guard, he was defensive, saying only, "We can't cover everything in an hour. And let's face it—sports is a man's world." Hisses and shock radiated from the disappointed audience. I watched my student athletes' faces burn as a White man told a Black woman, who had just led her team to the NCAA Elite Eight twenty-five years after Title IX became law, that *her* effort, sweat, experience, and victory simply weren't part of history. We were supposed to accept that her exclusion was not because she was Black, which would be wrong. It was simply that she was female, and in the man's world of sports, the media didn't have time to address female achievement or experience.

That night, Black women were disappeared from the record, and we watched it happen in sports journalism. I've never forgotten the mood on the bus ride back to campus. *This is how it happens. This is why we never know the score.*

Ten years later, in 2007, the tables turned—for a brief moment. An on-air slur from radio shock jock Don Imus, who referred to the players of Rutgers University's women's basketball team as "nappy-headed hos" after they won the NCAA championship, forced a fresh national conversation on race. This time, the focus was specific to the double burden borne by Black women athletes, who, we saw, could be the best in the world yet instantly reduced to White scrutiny of their hair and sexuality. My classroom simmered with critical analysis of this legacy: One could win as an athlete yet fail as a woman on the national stage—by whose standards? But within days, we watched the national conversation switch from the pained perspectives of Black women and eloquent interviews with Rutgers coach C. Vivian Stringer to the hurt feelings of Don Imus. Should he be fired, after all? Wasn't he sorry, as well as a frequent donor to charity? I listened as White women defended him. In one unique response—the book *Burying Don Imus: Anatomy of a Scapegoat*— Black professor Michael Awkward argued that Imus had only said aloud what too many White racists thought and that he should be understood in that greater context. Sympathy also grew for the public space of talk radio, popular with powerful conservative listeners. Wasn't this really about freedom of speech?

Less and less was heard from Black women athletes. By 2017, another ten years later, my students at UC Berkeley told me they had never heard of the Don Imus controversy, coach C. Vivian Stringer, or that glorious championship Rutgers team.

My students were alert to the many instances, in sports reporting on women, when journalists referred to adult winners as "girls." "Girls Rule!" was the banner headline on *Newsweek*'s July 19, 1999, cover, announcing the Women's World Cup victory across the photograph of Brandi Chastain tearing off her jersey. It was surely an exuberant moment that showed all girls, worldwide, what was possible, but in contrast, both *Time* and *People* featured the whole team on their covers that week, and only *Time* stressed the women's athletic ability with the headline "What a Kick!"

In the past, *girl* could either be meant as a compliment, in terms of having "girlish good looks," or serve as a warning to stay in the assigned place—below men, who are less often referred to as *boys*. Historically, *girl* has also been a patronizing and unwelcome form of address for adult African American women. One standard that has not changed in our culture is the taunt "You play like a girl." Top women competitors simmer at the implication. In her memoir *Raise the Roof*, coauthored with sportswriter Sally Jenkins, famed women's basketball coach Pat

Summitt tore into the word *girl*, suggesting it represented a person who didn't know how to keep score, rather than the championship players she built at Tennessee.[13]

Unfavorable comparisons to women are normal in men's sports conversations. The example that follows appeared on page 1 of the Metro section of the *Washington Post* only eight days after the newspaper took an editorial stance in support of Title IX:

> The college kids on the sidelines can't believe their eyes.
> "Without a doubt, the worst basketball player I have ever seen," Geremy Coy says, shaking his head.
> "He might be able to play in the WNBA," Andrew MacKinlay adds.[14]

During that same winter (2003), both the Jack in the Box fast-food chain and Mercedes-Benz ran television commercials devaluing girls in sports. In the former, a jester-like Jack explains to a ball-playing boy that girls are "different" because they take dance. In the Mercedes ad, very young boys in football uniforms taunt their rival team by saying, "Excuse me, ladies." When former PGA champion Mark Brooks shot a seventy-two to Annika Sörenstam's one-over-par seventy-one, he declared, "To tell the truth, I played like a girl today."

Ah, but what if the "girl" in question is beating the man? That, too, results in a type of news headline, as other class papers addressed. The hype around golfer Annika Sörenstam's entry in the all-male PGA tournament led an entire country to look at the gender-war issue. News headlines on May 23, 2003, the day Sörenstam scored one over par, discussed not her golf swing but the sex-role tensions on the links: "Why All the Fuss When a Woman Beats a Man?" was the title on *USA Today*'s page 1, while inside, another headline noted "Sorenstam Hangs with Guys" and an editorial cartoon jested "Terror Level—PINK." The conservative *Washington Times* ran a front-page headline, "Playing with the Boys," but conceded on C1 that "Sorenstam Holds Her Own." The *Washington Post* was neutral: "Sorenstam, History Take Course," on page 1, and "On the Cutting Edge," on D1. The content in each newspaper's coverage delved into the drama. *USA Today*'s Erik Brady asserted, "This much seems certain: She won't finish last. And there's the rub. Then men who finish behind her could be ridiculed. *Sports Illustrated* columnist Rick Reilly suggested on NBC's *Today* show that 'feminine hygiene products' might be left in their lockers." Brady added, "What is it about male sports culture that equates ability with masculinity—and losing to women with emas-culation?"[15] Considerable buzz surrounded golfer Vijay Singh's ungra-cious public remarks, particularly his wish that Sörenstam would fail to make the cut at the Colonial.

The previous night, Ted Koppel hosted yet another *Nightline* special called "Not One of the Boys," conceding, "Most of all, this is about the fragile male ego." Koppel returned frequently to the theme of male em-barrassment in being defeated by a woman, and he turned the discussion to economics: today women often earn more money than men, or have more education, or both. Do these trends add to the sense of male inad-equacy? If women succeed in sports, where will men prove their might? Lingering in the air was the unspoken suggestion that high-achieving women and girls must hold back, even voluntarily retard female prog-ress, in order to protect male sensibilities. Soccer star Julie Foudy, a guest on the program, said, "The amazing thing to me is that we're even having this discussion—it's sad." My own mother, visiting class that week, shared that her algebra teacher once wrote in her yearbook, "To a girl who's smart enough not to let the boys know it."

Sportswomen like Sörenstam can certainly be made to feel that their talent and ability are unwelcome. During the 2002/3 academic year, my class papers also addressed the very public debate about the very pri-vate Augusta National Golf Club, which hosted the prestigious Masters golf tournament while continuing to prohibit women from being club members. Students noted that Tiger Woods participated in the Masters. His own recent rise to stardom had hastily integrated certain all-White golf clubs; according to the *Washington Post*, the PGA Tour had prom-ised to boycott racially discriminatory clubs only after the 1990 PGA Championship at Shoal Creek Club in Alabama, and Augusta admitted its first Black male member that same year. "The Masters founder, Clifford Roberts, once declared: 'As long as I'm alive, golfers will be white, and caddies will be black.'"[16] One of my Georgetown students volunteered that both her father and grandfather were loyal members of Shoal Creek; our class discussion hit close to home for her.

The students debated whether Tiger Woods should have refused to step on the links at Augusta or any other discriminating institution. What was the mixed message sent to Black women golfers? Why was racism no longer socially acceptable while sexism thrived? Passionate diatribes from all sides appeared in newspapers across the country, pitting defenders of the male-only tradition against feminist activist Martha Burk of the National Council of Women's Organizations. The debate drew published comments from athletes, managers, sportswriters, and corporations, giving my students plenty to write about in their first papers. Never had so many people weighed in on whether discrimination in *golf* should count as a burning feminist issue. Eleanor Reissa, writing for *Women's Sports Experience*, said, "To me, golf was a rich white man's game, until Tiger Woods popularized it. All sports in the United States were white men's games. Until Jackie Robinson cracked open baseball. And Arthur Ashe smashed open tennis. . . . No matter what terms they may use to couch it, the men of Augusta National choose to stand alongside repressive minds instead of standing for openness and accessibility."[17] But Sally Jenkins, in the *Washington Post*, suggested to women athletes, "Rather than bemoan the cruel fact that you just can't make some folks invite you into their club, maybe the thing to do is simply get on with putting together the shattered pieces of your life."[18]

And then there were the comic-strip reductions of the issue. One of the most challenging editorial cartoons my students analyzed, by Mike Smith of the *Las Vegas Sun*, showed a poor single mother telling a feminist, "I need equal pay . . . I need equal treatment in the workplace . . . I need affordable day care." The "feminist" responds by pointing toward Augusta and saying, "If you'll excuse me, I see a fancy golf club that needs to admit women." Here the cartoonist refused to make the connection between the many concerns confronting female athletes—equal pay, day care, respect—and portrayed the integration of golf clubs as a petty issue dividing have and have-not women. A different cartoon, in the January 2003 issue of *Ms.*, depicted separate drinking fountains for men and women at Augusta, linking the general question of women's limited sports facilities to powerful images from the Jim Crow South. And the December 6, 2002, opinion page of the *Augusta Chronicle* showed a buzz-haired Martha Burk ramming open a locked door with a tree trunk, only to have a mixed-race male group tell her, "For the last time, Miz Burk, this is not an exclusive males-only club . . . it's the men's restroom!" This touched on fears that are perennial in America: shared bathrooms.

It's easy to find worrisome gender and race bias in sports reporting, but are we prepared to do anything about it? Although students were eager to spend hours of class time complaining about the sexism they saw in sports coverage, few seemed ready to take action. Silence greeted me when I gently inquired, "Who's written a letter to the editor?" When I discovered that most in the class were unsure *how* to do this simple civic act, I dropped everything and changed our topic to media activism.

Never has it been easier to compose an email to a prominent newspaper, not just on a laptop but now on a cell phone the size of a cookie. Feeling ancient, I heard myself explaining to students that back in my college days, one had to type a business letter on onionskin paper with a carbon beneath it in order to make a copy, then find a business-sized envelope and a stamp, and go to the post office. That didn't stop eight-year-old Abigail Pogrebin, daughter of feminist writer Letty Cottin Pogrebin, from writing to General Mills in 1973 about the marketing of Wheaties as a boy cereal for boy athletes. The response she received at the time came from a female manager: "In presenting the Wheaties story to the public we have endeavored to capitalize on the brand's long heritage as a male-oriented product. As you know, many products, such as Virginia Slims, Grape-Nuts, and Marlboro have spoken primarily to one sex. . . . Our research for the product is that as a boy matures, his taste matures, and he is ready to eat an unsweetened, adult-tasting product."[19] My students were amused to examine how cereal and cigarettes were gendered, and they were impressed that an eight-year-old had taken on corporate America "way back then," during the banner year when Billie Jean King defeated Bobby Riggs.

Today my students can send a protest tweet round the world to millions while still in their pajamas. But when I first began teaching the class in 1996, few students had cell phones or were social media activists. Writing a letter to the editor on appropriate stationery was the right step for the tri-captains of GWU's women's basketball team, who paid an unscheduled visit to my office in April 1997.

As their collective height filled the doorway, I gulped, wondering what was up. These women had just returned from playing in the NCAA Elite Eight. They represented the absolute best of campus athletic ability and pride. And, of course, we'd just experienced that galling town hall at Howard University where Ted Koppel had told Tajama Abraham that sports were "a man's world." Now, as TJ crammed into my suddenly way-too-small office with its low ceiling, I told her about my own then recent experience with sports sexism. I'd returned east from a spring-break trip connecting through the Denver airport just as the Elite Eight game was being broadcast on television. Intent on catching even a few minutes of my own students' competition, I lunged off my plane and into the airport sports bar, which boasted five televisions, all broadcasting lower-bracket men's games. When I begged the bartender to accommodate me, he reluctantly put the women's Elite Eight match on one small TV screen embedded in the restaurant's floor-to-ceiling support column. As I strained to see this screen, a male traveler with a large hiking backpack walked into the bar, removed his heavy frame, and leaned it up against the post, completely covering the event I was watching.

We all shook our heads. But what was on their minds? Lisa, Colleen, and TJ thrust a *Washington Post* letter to the editor into my hands. The author had written in to complain about the "excessive space devoted to women's basketball." He blamed Title IX for the amount of coverage on the GWU women's NCAA ranking, "far out of proportion to what the quality of competition would command and the place women's basketball occupies among sports fans in general." Comparing women's basketball to the minor leagues, he declared, "There is no team sport in which men and women compete where the physical skills of women come anywhere close to matching those of men, and there never will be."

I looked at the pain in the eyes of my elite student athletes. I had to set aside my own distress as I realized that the letter to the newspaper came from a local man I knew—I had in fact attended junior high with his son. "What do you need from me?" I asked.

"We want to write our own letter to the *Post*," they asserted. "So . . . how do we start?"

In a few days, their response appeared.

Over time, more students wrote letters, on a variety of issues. My Georgetown student Madeline Wiseman published a thoughtful piece in the campus paper, the *Hoya*, describing her experience at a Georgetown men's basketball game. In a pregame activity for the audience, teams of selected students competed for prize money to see who could be first to make a basket. But male students were awarded larger sums, as Maddy reported.

> Besting her opponent, my friend won $25. Not five minutes later, two male students participated in a similar race that resulted in making a basket. The male winner was awarded $100. . . . A prize discrepancy between competitions whose only difference was gender reflects badly on Verizon Center and, by association, on Georgetown.
>
> On average, women earn $0.77 for every $1 that a man makes. . . . The gender wage gap significantly disadvantages women over the course of

their lifetimes. As fellow seniors and I join the workforce next year, it will become a very real part of our lives.[20]

Another Georgetown student shared that she had already been active in high school, publishing a thorough critique in her high school newspaper on sports inequality at their campus and in the state of Connecticut. Her high school happened to be the highly regarded private academy Choate. Taylor quoted one Choate classmate who had said, "Multiple male athletes have repeatedly been found guilty of honor code violations but were allowed to stay because of their value in athletics." A different student had told Taylor, "Male athletes can get away with almost anything if they are a hockey or lacrosse player. It shocks me what boys can get away with."[21] Just a few years before, two star football players from Kenton High School in Ohio had pleaded no contest to a vehicular "prank" that disabled two other teenagers in a car crash. At their hearing, the judge sentenced them to community service plus sixty days of juvenile detention—to be served once football season had ended. When Taylor emailed a copy of her article to me, she commented that "it caused quite a stir at school, which was strange for me because I'm pretty quiet and don't usually start conflicts."

Yes, there are risks to engaging in a public forum, and they include public backlash from those who disagree—which in our contentious era can include very personal, even sexual attacks on women in the comments sections of online articles and, on social media, what's known as trolling and doxing. This also affects men who write editorials in support of women's sports: in a 2016 *New York Times* op-ed titled "The NCAA's Women Problem," Andrew Zimbalist examined preferential treatment for men's sports—and received posted comments such as these:

> More Liberal nonsense. Women want equality when it is totally undeserved and without merit. The truth is no one cares about women's sports. How many people go out on Friday night to see women play any sport? Answer—NONE.

> With the exception of volleyball and mud wrestling, most women's sports wouldn't exist at all without government intervention. Government-mandated women's sports in the U.S. colleges are about as exciting as school political plays in North Korea.

> Women's sports are less watchable, and consequently less important. . . . Title 9 has destroyed a number of men's sports at many universities. . . .

All so that women can play ice and field hockey, and delude themselves into believing that anyone cares.

No one wants to watch women play.

Have females become afflicted with "male envy"? Why not wear pants on their wedding day?[22]

In class, I share my own experience. I wrote a brief letter to the *Washington Post* in 2010, expressing dismay that their TV Week sports overview listed only men's games. None of the women's NCAA games being broadcast on ESPN, ESPN2, or CSN were listed in TV Week, though women from many local university teams were playing in those games. The newspaper printed my letter, and within hours, I had quite a few responses in my email box. Some praised my initiative. But a retired military officer wrote this to me: "I watch men's games because the athletes can run faster, jump higher, be stronger, and have better basketball skills than women. Why would you watch a women's game if you had no personal connection to a particular team? You mention you teach a course on 'Athletics and Gender' and the GW website says you are a 'professor of gender studies.' Is that one of those majors that prepares students for life in the work world? Will your course prepare students to help get the economy going again? Will it give students a skill?"

It astonished me that a retired colonel would take the time to look up my website and professional title and then, having never met with me personally, compose a letter impugning my years of work in academia—all because I had asked the *Washington Post* to list women's NCAA championship games in the TV Week schedule. However, as we discussed in class, this incident is a reminder of how passionately and personally some men resent the intrusion of women's sports. Three extra lines in TV Week, or in a flyer promoting fall games at a university, is all it takes to achieve equality in print. In any discussion on the costs of adding women's sports teams or equalizing salaries, it's easy to argue that the *least* expensive act is advertising games. Yet even here we find resistance. As my frustrated student athletes pointed out in class, the arguments are often circular: women's games don't bring in revenue because no one attends them, but often that's because they aren't advertised. How can we "prove" that fans aren't as interested in women's events if they don't know about them?

At every campus where I taught, I found the athletic department or alumni association promoting homecoming or parents' weekend events by offering special deals on tickets for the men's games. Women's games scheduled over those weekends were not similarly listed as options for guests. Although statistically each university enrolled more female undergraduates than male, the likelihood that some tuition-paying parents were arriving to visit athletic *daughters* in competition went overlooked. Gradually, this changed, after my students and I brought pressure to list some women's games along with the usual football homecoming attraction. Thoughtful letter writing and follow-up communication do produce results. After several seasons of contacting the *Washington Post* about women's sports coverage, my students and others in the greater Washington region had a response from the *Post* ombudsman Patrick Pexton: an editorial titled "Is Women's Sports Coverage Lacking?"

> Matt Vita, the *Post's* sports editor, is aware that coverage is unbalanced and says forthrightly that no matter the sport, coverage will rarely be equal gender-wise. He does have a strategy, though, for paying attention to female athletes. One is his staff. Although still male-dominated, two of the five sports columnists are women, two of the four daytime editors are women, many women are covering men's sports and vice versa. . . .
>
> In the past month, only three women made it to the front page of the Sports section in feature photos. . . . I think the *Post* can do better in its treatment of women's sports, if only to feature more women on the front page of the Sports section and to cover more extensively the problems, and successes, of female athletes and teams as they strive to gain and keep a corner of the vast sports entertainment market.[23]

Though speaking out steadily for equal representation can be time consuming and exhausting and bring crude challenges from critics, we know that throughout history other female trailblazers endured far worse hostility. In some classes, I show the film *Shirley Chisholm: Unbought and Unbossed*, a documentary about the first African American woman to run for president in 1972. Not only was Chisholm a dynamic speaker; she used considerable skill in responding to her critics. Typically, she repeated a rude question or comment back to the challenger, thus inviting him to hear his own offensive words while giving herself time to prepare a devastating retort, instead of first responding defensively. In class, we occasionally did role-play exercises to practice handling difficult or even insulting questions, and this also proved helpful in preparing nervous seniors for their first job interviews. I usually shared a few of my own experiences—for instance, the time a university dean began my job interview with the charge "Look, are we even going to need women's history five years from now?" (FYI: I did get that position.)

Over the years, I frequently hear from former students of mine who put their media-activism practices to good use:

> I'm studying abroad this semester, but I used information from your class in a letter to the editor I wrote today. My conservative hometown paper printed a George Will opinion piece agreeing with Larry Summers's comments that women's biological differences prevent them from excelling. I used information from the films we watched to talk about the history of bigotry-inspired "science." Just thought you'd like to know!

> I just wanted to send you a quick link to a column I wrote that was published today, about the funding of women's sports. I wanted to share it with you because I couldn't have written it without being a student in your Athletics and Gender class—some of the points I make were based heavily on our class discussions. So, thanks so much for the inspiration! (I would have loved to interview you for it!)

As my students gain confidence as media activists, we start to examine the role of women in sports journalism. The majority of sports journalists and syndicated cartoonists are male; men are more likely to be the image makers inscribing beliefs about female athletes via camera lens and pen. African American feminist Flo Kennedy, interviewed at the 1972 Democratic National Convention by filmmaker Sandra Hochman, once declared that men were so invested in sports coverage they would never concede time for women's media. In the fall of 1995, that seemed particularly true: Hillary Clinton's important "Women's Rights Are Human Rights" speech at the UN's Fourth World Conference on Women, broadcast from Beijing, China, was cut from US television news so that American viewers could see a birthday tribute to retired ballplayer Cal Ripken. However, since the 1970s, women have succeeded in producing a new genre of sports media in print, with publications like Billie Jean King's *womenSports* magazine, *Women's Sports and Fitness*, *Amy Love's Real Sports*, *ESPNw*, and more. The internet has made possible an infinite number of women's sports interest groups—although, as Australian scholar Jessica Megarry pointed out in her 2019 study *The Limitations of Social Media Feminism: No Space of Our Own*, women's online publications and support groups today are overseen and controlled by the men who own and administer Facebook and Google.

As part of our media unit in class, we read the works of dynamic sportswriters Christine Brennan (see fig. 2.1), Sally Jenkins, and Joan Ryan; study interviews and broadcasts with radio hosts like *World Football Daily*'s Sophie Nicolaou, who founded the *British Soccer Diva* blog; and look at sportswriting by women of color, including Ashley Brown, Nina Revoyr, and Lisa Bowleg. The class learns not to expect that women in sports journalism will automatically write about women or "women's issues"; many fought hard, as knowledgeable fans of football and baseball, for the basic right to write about football and baseball. But there is a long backstory in women's battle to cover men's athletic events, to use their press passes and credentials to interview men, over the objections of male athletes who grant male but not female sports reporters access to postgame locker-room interviews.[24] And women in journalism whose focus is not necessarily sports but rather human-interest writing and literary nonfiction have produced some of the most piercing, up-close books on women's sports by embedding themselves with an elite team during a winning season—authors such as Madeleine Blais, Sara Corbett, and Marcy Turco.

Paired with memoirs by successful athletes and coaches, journalists' perspectives supply alternatives to the limited information by and about women in sports. I bring in a stack of books from my personal collection and fan out the titles on a table, inviting students to borrow any they wish. These include children's books with girls as prominent athletes, old beauty-and-fitness advice books from one hundred years ago, photo-essays of older women in sports, autobiographies of LGBTQ athletes, and texts on athletic body image and eating disorders. Every semester, I loan out three or four books that are never returned to me, and that's OK. Those missing copies matter fiercely to someone encountering women's sportswriting for the first time—someone grateful to find herself in those pages. I can always order more. And I remember how it felt to be eighteen, in college, and hungry to see books about lives like mine.

Fig. 2.2 International lacrosse official Dorothy Hirsch.
Photo courtesy of Dorothy Hirsch.

Did you know? Joan of Arc was born on January 6, 1412 in the village of Domremy, in the Meuse River valley of France. She was a military leader, fighting against the British, on the behalf of Charles VII of France.

Fig. 3.1 Joan of Arc coloring-page image.
Image courtesy of Crayola LLC; used with permission.

TOMBOY IDENTITIES, MUSCULAR IDEALS

Discussing Gender Roles and Homophobia in Sports

During the first half of the course, Athletics and Gender students find that American social history is riddled with contradictions about the body and its functions, performances, and meanings. We learn that authoritative recommendations about the right sports for men or for women changed continually, bending to fit American priorities. For every "truth" about male and female sex roles, history shows us cultural contradictions and reversals in public and private adherence to such roles, usually when race or class designations take precedence over gender to define social position. Evolving fitness standards, labor laws, wartime, Hollywood film culture, and even the shape of children's toys contribute to public ideals of who should be muscular and who should be curvy. In evaluating what human bodies can do, sports fans, coaches, and athletes all bring along and apply learned ideals of masculinity, femininity, and attractiveness.

Tomboy culture has a signature, a recognition so undeniable that its symbolism can be handed to very young children or marketed to adult sports fans. Baseball player Toni Stone, one of the few women to play in the Negro Leagues in the 1950s, autographed souvenir baseballs with the signature "Tomboy." Today, Crayola's coloring pages of great women from history include the masculine-dressing Joan of Arc (see fig. 3.1.). But when more and more girls and women gain opportunity to compete and excel, in the military, business, or politics, as well as sports, we find fear of equality masking as concern. *Where will this masculinizing trend lead?* Put differently, if women continue to improve, lead, and excel, who will be defined as the weaker sex? Different social scientists across the nineteenth, twentieth, and twenty-first centuries also raised the question of women becoming their future husbands' economic rivals. In the public sphere, men have traditionally been urged to compete against one another, with women competing for the attention of the top-ranked men. While American society has changed, different communities still place limits around female power in order to keep certain spheres or traditions male—and to ward off female authority over men. For many faith-based organizations, schools, and individual believers in the United States, maintaining separate spheres for male and female is also a central tenet of religious doctrine. Many evangelical Christians oppose placing women in authority over men, citing the biblical passage "Wives, be subject to your husbands." One Kansas boys' school forfeited a game rather than have their student athletes accept calls from the female referee sent to officiate that day.[1]

"Where will this lead?" is not only a religious question. The fear of young women behaving like young men speaks to idealized sex-role differences too. Girls' rules were plotted to protect growing bodies but also to limit the tactical aggressiveness permitted and even cultivated on boys' teams. One classic example is lacrosse, originally a Native American game of skill and now a Division I sport with entirely different rules and gear for men's and women's teams. In quite a few contact sports that are designated male, "winning" qualities permitted for boys and men may be ugly, aggressive, and violent, associating manliness with brutal conquest. In male sports, these are seen as exciting, crowd-pleasing aspects of the game, and over the years, many of my male students defended the excitement of men's games as their drawing card and, by extension, the reason women's events will never sell as many tickets. Writing in 1967, Stephen Ward suggested, "The real enigma is the reconciliation of the soft, physiologically, socially and culturally determined maternal inclinations with the harsh phallic requisites of competitive sports at a superior level."[2] Some parents and educators quick to agree that girls *can* learn to play at the same level expected from boys nonetheless question whether they want athletic daughters to enact behaviors tolerated in athletic sons. That concern contains an implicit indictment of masculinity, but it also drives a wedge between male and female athletes in important ways, supporting male violence as natural and condemning female aggression as deviant. Consider the pushback from our media when female victors celebrate too boisterously, as we saw with the US women's soccer team's goals and victories at the 2019 Women's World Cup and, in 2010, with the Canadian women's ice hockey team's champagne and beer following their win at the Vancouver Olympics.[3] Critics who suggest that sports inappropriately masculinize women ask, "If everyone becomes rough and tough, boisterous and rowdy, who will we turn to for models of tenderness?" As one of my Berkeley students noted, "These rules and laws protect 'femininity,' not women."

This system punishes men, too, in forcing them into models of aggressive competition from birth onward. We have come to associate athleticism with kicking ass, glorifying violence. Consider this rivalry over sons still in utero, between then Washington Redskins owner Dan Snyder and his personnel director, Vinny Cerrato: "Cerrato learned his wife was pregnant with their first child, a boy. Snyder and his wife, Tanya, who have two young daughters, were coincidentally expecting their first boy. So, from the obstetrician's office, Cerrato announced his big news by calling Snyder and leaving a message on his cell phone: 'My boy's gonna *kick* your boy's ass.'"[4]

We devoted a full class period to this quote the day it appeared in print. Students pointed out that the pregnant wives carrying the sons to term were entirely absent from the conversation, though the women, too, might have had hopes, feelings, or aspirations for their sons. Rarely do we hear of any mother heralding the news of her pregnancy by phoning a best friend from the ob-gyn's table to declare, "My girl's gonna kick your girl's ass!" But in sports news, aggression sells. It's a reminder that as girls and women gain equality with the men who set the standards and define the norms as male, we can expect to be handed mixed messages about competition from the minute we're born. The assumption of assigned sex roles and superior male performance also haunts the designation of women's team names, as I often pondered during GWU women's games against the Lady Rams. "But, Daddy," said a wise eight-year-old girl seated behind me, "a lady can't be a ram." Today there are many Lady Rams basketball teams throughout the United States, in Upper Sandusky, Ohio; Chicago, Illinois; and Rochester, New York, just to name a few.

Is it a normal expression of masculinity to like sports? And a violation of femininity to do so? How do such values drive the limits placed on female athletes today? This is the heart of the semester, and to extend the metaphor, these class discussions are not for the faint of heart.

Much of our Western cultural anxiety is sheer homophobia: Girls who excel at rough sports and boys who hate rough sports (or play them poorly) are assumed to be at least a bit queer, making clear our association of high-end athleticism with male virility. If women become *too* good at sports, they risk becoming male impersonators, or "garcon manque," as would-be soccer girls are called in France.[5] And women are never allowed to neglect their duty to attract. Remaining attractive even midgame is the collective burden on female athletes, although the hierarchy of whom to be attractive for is constantly redefined, as it can include critics with self-serving priorities—corporate sponsors, boyfriends, fans, male TV viewers, university officials, and coaches. Having to satisfy performance criteria as an athlete and a "babe" simultaneously is a familiar challenge for my students.

"You can be athletic right up to the point where you become unattractive to men," a female student argued one October day. "If you don't care about being attractive to men, maybe you'll push yourself to go that much further in musculature and strength. But the not-caring factor makes everyone think you're a lesbian, a bad role model. It costs you endorsements—look at Martina Navratilova!"

How do we first begin learning these messages? And how are they directed at boys, as well as girls? In class, students are quick to share childhood experiences of negotiating adults' expectations and advice about sex roles and sports from a very early age. For the young men in class, family and childhood memories included a father pitting his sons against one another and berating them as "pussy" or "sissy" midgame, an older male friend declaring he would "smother his son in his sleep" if he didn't turn out to be good at sports, and other stark expectations of masculinity through athletics. For the young women in class, early memories included being warned how to sit on a bike to protect genitalia (no warning given their brothers), being called "butch" or even "faggot" for excelling at sports in elementary school, and excelling only to realize they had no athletic future because few pro leagues existed for women. Here are more specific student examples:

> I hate that when I'm in a bad mood, guys say, "Are you PMSing?" When did PMS become a verb? Even now, men still say things like a woman can't be president because she menstruates and that could jeopardize

the national security of the United States. Why are antiquated medical beliefs that women are physically weak utilized to separate little girls and little boys?

Although I was born in Seoul, South Korea, I never had a chance to grow up there. In the two years I lived in Suriname, my parents had me take swimming lessons, and I got very good at the sport, fearless of the water. The following summer, my parents and I took a trip back to Korea. When I jumped into the deep end of a pool, the lifeguard blew his whistle and had me taken out of the water. He went over to tell my parents about the danger of leaving a girl in the deep end. He refused to believe that a nine-year-old girl had any swimming skills. After arguing with my parents, he made me take a swimming test in front of him. I did my freestyle laps without a rest. Finally, the lifeguard apologized to my parents for doubting my ability.

All my relatives are huge Patriots fans and season ticket holders. My aunt recently found out that she's pregnant with twins, so my mom and I bought them little Patriots outfits. Now that we know the twins are a boy and a girl, my uncle commented to my aunt, "You're not going to dress her in a Patriots outfit, are you?" Thankfully, she responded by saying, "Of course! I wear Patriots shirts, don't I?" But then my mom chimed in: "Just put a bow in her hair, and she'll be fine." It really bothered me that wearing a Patriots shirt was too "boyish" for a baby girl and that the problem could be solved by tying a bow in her hair, thereby reaffirming her sex.

Trying to score a goal, I accidentally kicked the ball into the face of one of my opponents. The girl started to cry, her mother and team members rushed over to her, everyone stared at me as if I had just committed a crime, and I overheard the girl's mother call me "an aggressive little brat who plays like a boy." From then on, I was always afraid to try too hard, in that I would be looked upon as dangerous, ugly, and mannish.

In fourth grade, I was in prime shape athletically, I was in Catholic school, and I was the type of girl who wore shorts underneath her skirt so I could really play during snack time. One day, a third-grade boy wanted to race me. Everyone put in a dollar toward who they thought would win. Most thought the third grader would win because he was a boy. We ran a sprint, 150 meters, and I won. That boy would no longer talk to me, and no one would give me my money.

Crew practice didn't go well today. Our women's team is much better than the men's team in the rankings, and we are taunted by them while racing. The guys yell out things to us like "pussy" or "Let's pass these sluts." When we got angry at them, their retort was "What's wrong? She must be on the rag." So when they are angry, it's manly, but when we are, it's seen as a weakness. Hello? When will men realize that they all got here on Earth by passing through a woman's vagina?

Why are being feminine and being strong contradictory goals? Kate T. Parker refutes this notion in *Strong Is the New Pretty*, and Colette Dowling explores it in *The Frailty Myth*—two different texts I've used in class. Dowling's thesis is succinct: "By keeping themselves physically undeveloped, girls and women have fulfilled the myth of the weaker sex."[6] She adds that "emphasized femininity begins in the cradle"[7] and laments that "only recently . . . have sports scientists attempted to investigate possible environmental causes for the performance differences."[8] Studies available through the Women's Sports Foundation suggest that girls are comfortable with an athletic identity, even outperforming boys, until the social shifts of puberty begin in middle school. Then sports participation lags, although those girls who remain athletically active show significantly lower risks of drug use, teen pregnancy, osteoporosis, and depression.

A significant change in American society is that the onset of puberty and menarche, a girl's first period, starts at an earlier and earlier age— possibly because of growth hormones added to the meat we consume, or because of our higher caloric and fat intakes and the general overeating in America, all of which can accelerate the body's preparation for fertility. With more girls beginning their menstrual cycle at age nine or ten—that is, before middle school—self-consciousness about the body, parental fears about early pregnancy, and postponement of formal sex education until later school years all interrupt what used to be the long "tomboy" time from ages nine to thirteen. For transgender athletes, girlhood isn't necessarily defined by a menstrual cycle; moreover, any athlete's menstrual cycle can be slowed or paused by hard training—and by extreme dieting, in the case of young gymnasts.[9] Throughout different regions of the world, an earlier menarche and thus earlier marriage were the cultural norm for girls. But a unique shared burden for many competitive female athletes over time has been having to monitor and attend to period symptoms throughout the peak performance time of a sports career and in front of peering audiences and media cameras during events where contestants traditionally wear white.[10]

When I was invited to participate in an *NBC Nightly News* segment in November 2002, the subject was otherwise healthy and athletic girls who abandon regular exercise during adolescence, when attracting boys and staying put together throughout the school day take on new urgency. I showed the resultant TV clip to my Georgetown class, and one student spoke up about her own experience:

> I really liked PE when I was younger, but once I hit high school, I became that typical girl who doesn't like gym. I would make up fictitious injuries so I wouldn't have to participate. What was it about gym class that repulsed me and so many of my girlfriends? We did not want to sweat, mess up our hair and/or our makeup. Looking good became a priority that superseded the need to be active participants in PE class. It was acceptable for girls to do this, and no one ridiculed us. But I noticed that the guys who did not demonstrate athletic prowess were ridiculed and criticized by the other boys.

Other students revealed that some girls still hear a negative and inaccurate warning when they hit puberty: that sports injuries will instantly, permanently cost them their femininity. Georgetown student Michelle Masone learned this while playing youth lacrosse in the late 1990s, when she was told that as a goalie, she would not be able to have children if she were hit. She noticed that her male counterpart in the cage was not similarly advised that he might be risking his future fatherhood.

Author Colette Dowling also comments on this double standard: "No one talks about the 'major biological disadvantages' of the smaller, weaker boys and men who are injured in football every day. . . . Seventy-eight percent of retired football players suffer from permanent disabilities. The average life expectancy of a pro football player is fifty-six years!"[11] Dowling introduces women's pervasive fear of rape and battery, noting that even conservative surgeon general C. Everett Koop once called domestic assault the number one health risk for American women.[12] In many instances, a woman's bruises are more likely to come from intimate violence than from team sports, yet self-defense training for women, popularized in the 1970s, became an unkind caricature of feminism itself. These issues are further explored in Jennifer Lawler's book *Punch! Why Women Participate in Violent Sports*. Does a strong woman somehow signal that she doesn't *need* a man's protection, therefore alienating or intimidating men?

In my own tenth-grade physical education class, during the spring of 1977, these ideals of attraction and strength were spelled out in very conflicting messages: If you're fat, men won't want you. But you'd better learn self-defense, girls, because men out there are waiting to harass you sexually. At Walt Whitman High School, we fifteen-year-old girls endured a PE unit that no boys had to take: first, the humiliating fitness workout where we marched robotically to an album blaring, "Go, you chicken fat, go!" and then rape-prevention class—with our two gym teachers pretending to attack each other so we could learn to fight off random sexual predators. Preparing for a glum future of trying to attract and repel men simultaneously composed our one hour of gym each day. Although I definitely supported my gym teachers' agenda of fitness and self-defense for girls, I knew my male classmates were spending their own PE hour in actual play, competition, and sport, working hard to impress us with their growing strength. This lesson in difference took place five years after Title IX became law. At this same school, my brother trained as a soccer goalie and led his team to win the regional championship.

In sports, where is "difference" most emphatic? Endless class conversations revolve around the pressure on female athletes to *look good*. With beauty standards constantly changing, it's easy to fail society's tests. I share a story in class: While teaching at Northeastern University just outside Boston in 1991/92, I enjoyed lunch-hour workouts on the big ice hockey arena where faculty could indulge in a noon skate. I skated energetic laps, plotting out class lectures in my head, dressed in my brother's old University of Maryland sweatshirt, a pair of shorts, and big warm knee socks. A former ice dancer who worked out at the same time, re-creating graceful routines in her original skate costume, came up to me one day to reprimand me for my appearance. Pointing to my boyish clothes, she said, "The whole point of ice-skating is to look pretty."

Pretty gained importance, even urgency, long ago as a factor in getting the media to notice and record female athletic achievement. From the 1950s to the 1970s, as television cameras beamed sports events right into the family living room, coaches and competitors pushed a telegenic femininity that would satisfy sponsors and reporters, especially in events like track, where both White and African American women had to prove they were "ladies" beneath the sweat. Ed Temple, who coached the Tennessee State Tigerbelles to multiple national championships and Olympic medals, famously said, "I want foxes, not oxes." In 1974, the *Durham Morning Herald* highlighted a female athlete by reassuring readers that "she is a fierce competitor on the track, but 'when I get to the winner's circle,' she says, 'I reach for my false eyelashes.'" That so much of public femininity is based on pretense, like the use of false products to construct commercial womanhood, is an irony the newspaper did not care to explore further.

For much of the American twentieth century, an accepted masculine/feminine split in sports was the popular image of high school football players posing with (and dating) perky cheerleaders. By the twenty-first century, that binary had been destabilized by the participation of male gymnasts and lifters in competitive cheerleading and, in some cases, the advancement of young women to placekicker positions on high school and college football teams. I watched the D.C. Divas women's football team take on and defeat Erie in front of a multiracial crowd of fans, while small boys and girls led traditional cheers from the track below.[13] Cheerleading is now also being recast as a high-profile sport, paired with football, in terms of calculating girls' Title IX dollars and opportunities. Few of my students were aware that cheer had once been a male-only activity, particularly in the early twentieth century, when few women were admitted to college.

Powder-puff events, in which female students temporarily don football uniforms while male students act as cheerleaders, still draw audiences, often for fundraising events, precisely because they flip game-day roles Americans have come to expect. One Georgetown student, Megan Krug, organized a faculty panel discussion on the symbolism of powder-puff football. In her editorial for the *Hoya*, Georgetown's campus newspaper, Megan questioned the value of women playing hard-tackle football professionally, asking, "In catching up with men: What are we catching?"[14] The same question was posed after a different powder-puff contest. The nation watched in horror as a homemade video of Glenbrook North High School's powder-puff game aired on the evening news May 7, 2003. Senior girls hazed junior players with sadistic physical abuse and humiliation, sending several girls to the hospital with broken bones and head wounds, all caught on tape with a rapturous male onlooker exclaiming, "This is the most beautiful thing I've ever seen!" Several students were suspended from school the following week, but the incident sparked an entire year of media inquiry into female aggression.

Most Americans have embraced the ideal of equal opportunity—that competence alone, and not preconceived racial or gender roles, should dictate the opportunity to compete. Yet we still come up against extraordinary cultural tension over female athletes who are "as good as men." Add points for athleticism, but deduct points for femininity, and somehow the elite female competitor loses on the balance sheet, becoming a freak, a threat, or, at the very least, an interloper. Although every few years new female athletes break into those sports events once forbidden to them—the Boston Marathon, Olympic ice hockey, Olympic pole-vaulting, boxing, and wrestling—female successes in once male-only fields bring on new pressures to play like a man but still look like a girl. If male strength and muscle power still serve as norms of athletic superiority or heroism, how far can a woman develop her natural build before being accused of betraying the feminine aesthetic? And how harshly do our media and sports judges rate buff women when they win the gold but leave off the lip gloss?

To get this discussion rolling, just before the midterm exam, I treat my class to the film *Pumping Iron II: The Women*, George Butler's documentary of the 1983 Caesars Palace World Cup female bodybuilding competition. The film allows us to look at an arena of muscular competition that is not a contact sport, not ranked by aggression or tackling, yet is still marked by gendered boundaries of appearance. My students prepare for the film by reading Gloria Steinem's excellent essay "The Strongest Woman in the World" in her 1994 book, *Moving Beyond Words*, and their jaws drop when they are introduced to Australian powerlifter Bev Francis on-screen.[15] Bev's extreme muscle-bound physique so disturbed the 1983 Caesars Cup judges that while she was clearly the most built woman in that competition, Bev was openly scorned by both male and female judges, as well as by a few sister competitors. The judges' on-camera dialogue reveals a very early, predetermined consensus that big Bev must not win, even though one or two male judges support Bev's extraordinary training regimen and achievement. In the film, we hear the following exchanges:

> Judge A: I object to being told that there's a certain point beyond which women can't go in this sport. It's as though the US ski federation told women skiers they could only go so fast!

Judge B: We want what's best for our sport and what's best for our girls! We don't want to turn people off—we want to turn them on. We're here to protect the majority; we are following what the majority want.

Judge C: If they go to extremes and start looking like men? The winners of this contest will set the standards of femininity!

(Lone female) Judge D: [If Bev wins], it would be a total disaster. The sport would totally go in reverse. Bev does not represent what women want to look like.

The other female bodybuilding contestants also debate Bev's appearance, with one insisting that a more "feminine" look should prevail as a standard, while another disagrees, explaining, "We're talking about a developed shape. We're not talking about God's given shape. We're talking about a shape that's been created in a gym through hard work." In another scene, Bev Francis herself acknowledges the ambivalence swirling around her body: "I want to really shock people, show them that a woman can develop muscle and still look like a woman."

"Ew!" "Gross!" and "Oh my *god*!" are my students' initial responses to Bev's first appearance on-screen. Lexa's eyes pop. Erin's mouth hangs. Jessica's hand claps over her lips. But as they adjust to Bev's unique figure, my students also begin to admire specific aspects of her musculature. Soon, I hear envious and impressed whispers about her arms and abs and the amount of weight she can press in workouts. "She's jacked!" mutters one football player. This new generation of scholarship athletes is far more at home in the weight room than any previous era of young women. While they do not identify with Bev as Bev Francis, whose total-body look as a final product of extraordinary training sits uneasily on their eyes, they keenly identify with the discrimination Bev experiences in a rigged competition ostensibly about bodybuilding and power. Though she is the most built competitor, Bev places last in the competition, winning just $400 of the $50,000 prize purse—no surprise to my students, who observe the judges snarling, "Bev does not look like a woman." In the film, Bev's loyal fans in the contest audience can be heard shrieking, "It's a beauty contest!" when Bev places last. Of Rachel McLish, the most feminine of the contestants and aesthetically a consistent favorite of the judges, Bev's fans sneer, "You can't flex bone, Rachel!" Though the events portrayed in *Pumping Iron II* are now thirty-five years into the past—my students rock with laughter when a more liberal judge scolds, "We are in the *eighties*, gentlemen!"—many attitudes have not changed. In the film, most judges imply that they will favor, as a winner, whichever woman suits the agenda of marketing women's bodybuilding—a winner other women will hope to become, not avoid becoming. That there must be a beauty quotient, a femininity quotient, involved in selling women's athletic workouts is simply assumed. The mainstreaming of gym memberships and strength training for women did change American fitness ideals in the 1980s. But fitness workouts in college gyms continued to be a particular kind of subculture, a performative space where students gave side-eye to their own peers. During one class at GWU, a female student described what she thought were accepted norms on campus: "When you go to the gym, you'll see girls doing sit-ups and elliptical and guys doing chest presses. I mean, when's the last time you saw a *girl* do chest presses, right?" Rugby player Erin replied to her classmate, "Today. And that *girl* was me."

By this point in the semester, my students are sufficiently immersed in larger US history to see Bev's connections to past debates about the ideal female body. They're ready to talk back. The midterm exam includes an optional essay question on the bodybuilding film, and most students select it: "Many authorities believe there is, or should be, a natural limit on female strength. We see this in the film *Pumping Iron II* and in Olympic sex testing of female athletes. Are such standards of femininity realistic? Why does someone like Bev create discomfort and backlash? Is this debate about biology or culture?" Here are some of the most thoughtful responses over twenty-five years:

> It seems awfully ironic that our society tells us muscular women are "sick" and "unnatural," "freaks" even, and yet silicon-stuffed women are "hot," "sexy," . . . *ideal*.

> Bev is *as woman* as any other woman I have seen. Every woman is different, ranging from flat chested and no hips to very large breasts and large hips, to no muscles, to a lot of muscles—and many in between. I showed my boyfriend a picture of Bev, and he said, "Eww, she looks like a man." I responded, "Well, you're a man, and you don't look like that." It is not man, nor woman, but Bev.

> Bodybuilders were all on the side of Bev. This points out that the judges' ideals for femininity were not able to keep up with the progression of the competition. Bev encountered resistance in the judges but was

successful with the crowd. As long as the competitors are not taking banned substances, limits on strength for women are unrealistic.

Patriarchy is built on the subjugation of women. When science allows women to reach their full potential, men feel threatened. Who will have the kids if women are the same as I am? How will I distinguish myself from a woman who has co-opted my main defining characteristic? What is left for the boys when women take our strength?

In the film, even the camera angles objectified the bodies of the female bodybuilders, encouraging the idea that women should work out to please men. I also noticed there were no female trainers, which means that the male trainers were sculpting the female bodybuilders into the shape that they identify as "normal" for a woman.

Bev opened the eyes of women. She changed athletics from a beauty pageant to a true competition and test of strength and power. From then on, more and more women bodybuilders began looking more muscular. I feel that Bev was heroic for refusing to conform.

And Rose Wetzel, one of Georgetown's many thoughtful track athletes, offered an intersectional analysis, touching on gender, race, and class: "Muscles used to be a symbol of poverty, but now they're a symbol of affluence. Likewise, having a tan used to be a symbol of poverty because it meant you had to work outside in the fields, but now it's a symbol of affluence because it means you travel to exotic places. Society's standards of beauty change often and are very subjective."

Muscles now have an economic status based on gym membership. "You look great: Where do you work out?" is a modern greeting we often overhear. Part of what made our class discussion crackle with energy was the controversy over women *developing* their bodies to potential never before seen—never before permitted, athletically. In class, we also talked about accepting possible harm to the body in pursuit of extreme training or in events with obvious risks, such as rock climbing and football. When does society allow males to be injured, framing their risk-taking as masculine and heroic, while discouraging women from joining similar physical challenges? One year, we went around the room, each student proudly showing off scars or dents from memorable championship games. "Her cleats were in my neck, but we won." "She clawed me, below the waterline, where the ref couldn't see, but we won." "They stopped the game and restarted the clock because I was bleeding." We talked about why it's heroic in ice hockey for a star player to be missing his front teeth but disturbing when a woman has a tooth knocked out. And this led to our heightened awareness of how bruises on women suggest partner violence, not the Heisman Trophy. After several years of this very popular class discussion on athletic battle scars, I deliberately discontinued it. Though for most students it was engaging and memorable, I had grown sensitive to the students in class who did bear skin scars and missing teeth from accidents, violent relationships, or earlier family abuse.

After the midterm on historical background, we move on to new topics that are more contemporary. I introduce a unit on homophobia, which now includes more on transgender athletes as well. First, of course, I fill in some of the history my students have never heard of. I explain that in the 1950s, '60s, and '70s it wasn't uncommon for lesbian bars to have softball teams or to sponsor tournaments, creating community in a time of intense homophobia. Closeted LGBT athletes competing in the mainstream spotlight had no legal protection against expulsion, loss of an athletic scholarship, or denial of sponsorship. When isolated and excluded gay athletes organized their own Gay Olympics in the era of AIDS, the International Olympic Committee demanded a name change to Gay Games, although the committee allows dozens of other events, such as the Puppy Olympics, to adapt the brand. And the 1990s were marked by officially tolerated homophobia at universities like Penn State, where women's basketball coach Rene Portland openly declared she would not allow lesbians to play on her team. Profiled in Dee Mosbacher's documentary film *Training Rules*, Portland joined other coaches in the practice of negative recruiting, warning prospective players during home visits that the other schools they were considering were "gay," whereas her program at PSU tolerated none of that. Eventually the subject of a lawsuit, Portland long wielded power over a generation of frightened athletes desperate to retain their scholarships and playing time.

Today, not only is there more legal, political, and cultural support for out LGBT athletes, as WNBA All-Star player Layshia Clarendon found working with women's basketball coach Joanne Boyle at UC Berkeley, but there's historical interest in knowing about those silenced players of the past. In the summer of 2020, many viewers watched the Netflix documentary *A Secret Love*, about a member of the All-American Girls

Professional Baseball League who kept her female partner a secret for nearly seventy years.

What's changed? We discuss why the lesbian label is still routinely pasted onto all female athletes and whether being a lesbian athlete is still a stigma.[16] Women who achieve conventionally "male" levels of muscle or whose chosen sports demand "male" styles of competitive aggression are taunted with accusations of lesbianism—a genre of name-calling seldom intended as a compliment. "We are *constantly* assumed to be gay," the softball players complain. "Oh, sure, we're gay baited all the time," the soccer and rugby players say. These top-level athletes, many playing for their schools on college scholarships, experience unkind harassment from coaches, boyfriends, and even salespeople. Here are some comments from class discussions:

> At one of my girlfriend's games, more than once the coach tried to stop some of the girls' cheering on the bench by saying, "Stop that queer bullshit." My girlfriend exchanged looks with another lesbian teammate and then left the bench. The coach attempted to apologize and to explain away her "poor choice of words" as akin to making "blonde" jokes. This, as my girlfriend told me later, did not cut it. She very bravely spoke to the whole team explaining why she was upset and why her coach's use of language was unacceptable, officially outing herself for the first time.

> The most common comment made about female rugby players is that they are all lesbians. When we went shopping at the rugby supply store, we were asked by some guys who work there if we were straight. When we said we were, one guy yelled to his coworker, "Hey, I told you there had to be at least one straight one!" To which his coworker replied, "Yeah, but they're a college team. All the club ones are queer."

> At our women's basketball game this year against Notre Dame, their mascot came over to the section where Georgetown fans were located and handed us a sheet of paper. The paper had Georgetown's roster with crude notes about them. Almost every comment was about our players being gay, like one of our players had mono and gave it to another one because they were dating. The list just went on and on.

> As a captain of the soccer team here, I have had to deal with lesbian stereotypes and homophobia in sports. In the past I got extremely defensive when people would call me a lesbian—because just by virtue of being a female, and playing a sport in which you don't wear skirts, I was of course homosexual? Even when it was my guy friends joking around,

you can only hear the phrase "dykes on spikes" so often before it starts to get old. Sometimes I just get sick of constantly having to prove my heterosexuality. It's embarrassing to admit, I guess, but I do really care what people think about me. Recently I have changed the way I react to these comments, though. The fact that the name-calling pissed me off hasn't changed—now I am pissed off because I am realizing what my teammates who *are* lesbians have to go through.

This sampling is typical, in that only one student identified as lesbian—and even then chose to speak from the context of her girlfriend's experiences with sports homophobia. Gay and lesbian athletes often remain silent. In a typical teaching semester, one or two athletes come out in class discussions, and maybe two more students reveal their orientation to me through their written work or email correspondence. Most students are aware that their instructor for this class is an out lesbian, but this doesn't prevent a few from using stereotypes when the class discussion shifts. At one point, we were debating the use of Native American monikers and mascots for sports teams. When a male student advocated dropping designator names like Chiefs and Braves, his female classmate across the aisle remonstrated, "But then what are men's teams supposed to be called? Some sort of *pansy* name?" "Yo! Miss! The *professor's gay*," whispered one of my loyal, bighearted football players, and the student who had disparaged "pansies" came up to me after class and apologized. This incident is worth citing because it flips other familiar stereotypes—that of the homophobic quarterback and his supposedly more feminist classmate. Many of the football players who enrolled in my class were sons of single mothers, keenly sensitive to working women's concerns, well informed and active on other social-justice issues.

To break the ice in these frequently tense discussions, I joke that if being a lesbian truly gave women an unfair or unnatural athletic advantage, as some believe, then I'd be a medal-wearing Olympic speed skater. Instead, I was the student who scored fewer baskets than anyone else during the required eighth-grade PE test. This elicits much-needed laughter, but the students grow thoughtful: Hmmm, so not all lesbians are gifted sportswomen. Then why the stereotype? Does excelling at high jump automatically put a girl on the path to gay marriage? Does every woman with an ACL surgery scar from playing college ball also have a girlfriend on her arm? There's plenty of humor as we unpack the contradictory assumptions for men and women. Revolving rapidly in a tight circle is part of a traditionally masculine sport event: preparation for throwing the discus. But somehow it's "gay" when a male body turns in tight rapid circles on ice skates. What's the difference? What makes the skater's *body* gay in that Olympic minute? And everyone shouts out, "Spangles!"

Yes, humor helps. I have a treasure trove of song recordings to play in class on the days we address sports, LGBT athletes, and homophobia. Typically, I'll start with the Broadway hit "One Hundred Easy Ways to Lose a Man"; then Meg Christian's classic "Ode to a Gym Teacher" and her follow-up song, "Gym II"; then "Outfield Blues" by gay male duo Romanovsky and Phillips; and finally the rap "Croquet" by Bitch and Animal. Students who had no idea there was music by, for, and about the queer jock legacy line up after class to ask, "What are these recordings?" "Where can I find these recordings?" and, more recently, "How do I download them?"[17]

Over the years, my student athletes at Georgetown University, Santa Clara University, and Saint Mary's College of California have confronted official church opposition to LGBT rights in different ways at their Catholic campuses. However, as faculty, I found that these schools also offered support services and commitments to diversity that far outpaced many other colleges with or without a religious affiliation. I also heard many students in class address ways that their own Catholic identity permitted acceptance of women's sports—after all, Immaculata University, the Mighty Macs, won the first-ever national women's college basketball championship in 1972. A large number of Georgetown students come from highly competitive single-sex parochial schools, where team sports for girls are both expected and an aspect of daily, visible female leadership. One student boasted, "At my high school, Ladywood, run by Franciscan nuns, everything went to the women! Sports were huge; if you didn't play, you were in the minority. We were also damn good. Our athletic director built a huge gym, two softball fields, a soccer field, and began a turf field for field hockey and tennis courts." Traditional single-sex education does produce top-level female players, many of whom, especially in Catholic families of eight to ten kids, are groomed to win athletic scholarships from Catholic universities. We all overheard certain dads of top-ranked Georgetown players make homophobic remarks

now and then on game day, but there was a refreshing ease among the
GU women athletes. They told me that during their adolescent years, being good at sports had simply been an expected part of family tradition.

How did the well-educated, athletic girl become accepted as normal
in America? Nineteenth-century sexologists assumed that a dislike of
girlish hobbies like needlework and a preference for boys' games marked
a girl as a possible "invert." Spinsters dispensing education at all-female
academies abruptly lost their sheen of respectability when medical models of lesbianism warned parents to think twice about sending a daughter to a single-sex school run by unmarried women. In her review of girls'
boarding school literature, *A World of Girls*, scholar Rosemary Auchmuty
examines the theme of school sport in popular and wholesome juvenile fiction produced in Great Britain during the first sixty years of the
twentieth century: "In attempting to persuade reluctant parents that
games would be good for their daughters, reformers also drew on the
moral advantages beloved of Victorian educators of boys. Team games,
they argued, encouraged discipline, loyalty, and determination: qualities
as relevant to girls as to boys."[18] Auchmuty draws a chilling portrait of
the shift, between the First and Second World Wars, from greater support of female exercise to critical pressures on unmarried educators.
While teaching was the main profession open to middle-class women,
both in England and the United States, laws requiring teachers to be
single or to resign upon marriage persisted in both countries well into
the 1940s. Respectable women desperate to retain their livelihoods, as
well as those genuinely committed to the vocation of educating girls in
sports and scholarship, confronted conflicting messages attacking their
moral character:

> The influence of the spinster teacher—sexual failure, neurotic, even
> deviant—could scarcely be healthy. Girls needed models of truly
> fulfilled married women to ensure their own normal development and
> socialisation. Women teachers could not win. As guardians of children's
> morality, they could hardly choose to live in sin with men; yet if they
> married, they lost their jobs. . . . And after the successful prosecution for
> obscenity of Radclyffe Hall's novel of lesbian love, *The Well of Loneliness*,
> in 1928, spinsters were subjected to ever more aggressive attacks . . .
> media publicity ensured that everyone now knew what lesbianism was
> and, moreover, defined it as dangerous and obscene.[19]

Historian Lillian Faderman, whose research examines lesbian lives
and female friendships of the nineteenth and twentieth centuries, makes

the point that the tomboys and spinsters of yesteryear often envied male privileges and freedoms, while chafing at the legal and social restrictions marriage imposed on women. These desires for greater individualism, personal expression, public leadership, and freedom of movement may be understood as separate from sexual orientation and gender identity, especially as what marked a heterosexual woman as a tomboy one hundred years ago was very different from today's LGBTQ cultures. Riding a bicycle, for example, or daring to put on trousers or bloomers instead of a corset might have been shockingly boyish behavior in the late nineteenth century. Women in today's America enjoy and take for granted once forbidden, male-only privileges, such as smoking, hiking, drinking beer, driving a motorcycle, and sitting alone in public cafés. My parents' friend Naomi Sobo broke the existing rules for female students at Santa Monica City College in 1954 by smoking a pipe in the student games lounge, a privilege then reserved for men only: "So I got a cute little pipe, very feminine. It was black and red and had rhinestones. The Dean of Women was not at all pleased, but I won my case for equality."

The post–World War II boom in materialism and televised toy ads helped normalize bikes and blue jeans for all American boys and girls. Yet not long ago, pants in public and a solo bike ride were scandalous behavior for adult women. Men's gender roles, too, have changed in every era—from the powdered wigs of George Washington and Thomas Jefferson; to the crew-cut machismo of 1960s marines juxtaposed with hippies' long hair and colored paisley shirts; to the ascendance of drag performer RuPaul as a media icon; to President Barack Obama's telephoning NBA player Jason Collins to call him "a role model," offering support when Collins came out as a gay man in April 2013.

For this section of the course, I assign many different readings: Pat Griffin's excellent *Strong Women, Deep Closets*, which examines bias against lesbian athletes, and numerous essays by Mariah Burton Nelson—who has also served as a guest speaker in class. We pair films such as *Training Rules* with the documentary *It Takes a Team* from the Project to Eliminate Homophobia in Sport. For young-adult fiction centered on fierce athletic competition between two young lesbians of color, one outstanding book I assign is Nina Revoyr's *The Necessary Hunger*; my students also like Linnea Due's *High and Outside*. Along with these sources, we study provocative readings on femininity testing at the Olympics. Beginning in 1967 and ending only recently, all female athletes were forced to endure either nude parades or buccal swabbings to prove their gender to a team of doctors. Women with chromosomal differences that did not affect athletic performance were nonetheless eliminated from competition and sent home in disgrace.[20] Students interested in transgender athletes' rights, as well as the experiences of people born or classified as intersex, raise a number of questions: Where does an intersex athlete play? Do women with XXY attributes have an unfair edge? Who decides? Consider the global media assaults on South African runner Caster Semenya, a woman accused of looking too masculine. Why are men not tested for possible feminine sex characteristics? The assumption is that female biology is a disadvantage in sports.

As always, class discussion returns to the premise that a female athlete can *play* like a man as long as she *looks* and dresses feminine—and if she does the latter, she is less likely to be harassed or investigated. Ironically, at fashion-conscious Georgetown, the athletes in their warm-up clothes constitute a separate and high-status social group: regardless of race or gender identity, serious athletes are distinguished by the dripping ice packs held to their sweat-suited ankles during class. However, some students confided feeling that female athletes were recruited based on their good looks, as well as their raw sports talent. One competitor shared that her coach had invited a gifted prospect to Georgetown, only to change his mind, telling the entire team that he "couldn't look at her face" for four years.

"But I like when women worry about looking good," said one young man in my Georgetown class, who was interning at the White House. "I like having female friends who change clothes seven or eight times before going out." This aspect of femininity was something he didn't want to see go away as women made inroads in professions that were still thought of as male. I pointed out that in my gay Dupont Circle neighborhood, there were also plenty of guys who changed clothes several times before going out. So does gender or sexuality govern concern about appearance? This led into a debate about the media's love affair, at that time, with tennis player Anna Kournikova, who enjoyed far more endorsements than players with more distinguished records. Several Georgetown males and at least one female rushed to defend the reward system of corporate goodies based on good looks; during this debate, I watched some very talented but less photogenic students cringe. Gradually, other women in class began making fun of the impossible beauty standards imposed on sweaty female athletes. One Georgetown runner asserted, "I think athleticism brings great freedom from the binds of femininity. While I'm running, I spit, pick wedgies, and blow snot rockets whenever I feel the need."

The importance of prettiness is not new in women's sports. We had discussed, at length, the World War II–era All-American Girls Professional Baseball League and owner Philip K. Wrigley's insistence on a "feminine" appearance, with strict rules of grooming and behavior for his players. Georgetown student Ashley Davis raised an interesting point in class, suggesting that there were certain transitional moments in history when women made small compromises for greater gain. She saw the players' dislike of their required short-skirt uniforms as a minor sacrifice in exchange for breakthrough professional opportunity in a more conservative time. "It may seem like a step backward because the league placed a lot of emphasis on appearance and image. I would argue, however, that it was a good transition step, because it would have been too radical, at the time, for women to play in men's baseball suits and spit tobacco. The league probably would not have been as big of a success without this transition phase."

What hasn't changed is assuming that women will value male attention and a wedding ring more than a championship victory. Courtship, not basketball courts, and weddings, not rankings, represent the essence of womanhood. These traditional role expectations appear in the casual language of sports talk. When the Duke University women's basketball team won their high seed in the March 2003 NCAA lineup, male sportscaster Rece Davis asked the players, "So, does it feel that you're finally going to be a bride instead of a bridesmaid?" Later, Boston College would be referred to over and over as the "Cinderella" team because of its first bid to the NCAA ball and its outstanding effort in reaching the Sweet Sixteen. Then Davis proclaimed on March 30, "That glass slipper you just heard shattering was Boston College." BC had gone back to being an ugly stepsister with big feet. But big feet can be an asset in playing hoops.

If star athletes are, metaphorically speaking, triumphant brides because they have been "chosen," or asked to the dance—in this case the NCAA—women's actual preparation for marriage is sometimes portrayed as a sport event akin to hunting and fishing. There is the chase, the "catching" of a man, and "hooking and landing" a reluctant prospect. This has been women's assigned game for centuries. Writing her memoir about convent-school life in the 1940s, businesswoman

Jane Trahey remembered boy-girl dances and popularity contests as the female equivalent of sports ranking: "During the alternate tea-dancing bouts with each other, we were being prepared for the big event—a championship tournament: the Senior Prom."[21] Often, girls internalize the message that in order to keep a boyfriend, it's wise not to best him athletically. One student said in class, "I was the star athlete of every sport I played. I started playing basketball with this guy at recess, and then we began dating. But I remember the phone call like it was yesterday. He said, 'We can't go out anymore. I just can't stand that you are better at me in basketball. My friends have been making fun of me.' And my heart sank." "Right," added another student athlete. "A woman can do everything a man can, provided she doesn't jeopardize his ultimate power or sacrifice her own femininity."

Though there is enormous pressure on gay athletes, male and female, not to come out, it is inaccurate to assume lesbian athletes are disinterested in love and commitment and a nice ring too. Regrettably, such aspects of their humanity are hidden from the press, and from sponsors, to shore up the presumed family-friendly wholesomeness women's sports offer in contrast to male athletes' violence or promiscuity. Greg Louganis (diving); Billy Bean (baseball); and David Kopay, Roy Simmons, and Esera Tuaolo (pro football) are some of the very few gay male athletes to come out formally in the media, and their books tell of their struggles for acceptance. Early in the twenty-first century, the *Chronicle of Higher Education* began to monitor the pulse of campus tolerance with essays like "Reflections of a Gay Athletics Director."[22] As more athletes and journalists began to write frank accounts of the unique pressure on gay high school students, my students expressed surprise and gratitude to see work in print about *their* world, their experiences. Conventional male football player / female cheerleader high school romances are validated by numberless Hollywood films, but lesbian athletes' courtships and partnerships remain invisible, often at coaches' requests. Several students who were team captains disapproved of their players dating one another during game season, arguing that couples upset team dynamics and that in principle this constituted a separate issue from homophobia per se. For all these reasons, it is difficult for the public to see the committed relationships that are part of many lesbian athletes' lives.

Although women's collegiate games desperately need more fan support, the lesbian fan base is a constant thorn in the side of women's sports promoters—television cameras don't linger on lesbian couples at games, as it's supposed to be "family" entertainment. The huge number of both affluent and working-class lesbians interested in women's sports and willing to spend their feminist dollars on season tickets remains a problem, rather than a solution, for public relations and marketing. At one top-level meeting on how to attract more fans to women's basketball games at a university where I was teaching, a booster said, "Let's all think hard now. Is there any group of fans or donors out there that we are failing to draw in through aggressive outreach?" And though dreading the awkward silence that I knew would greet my suggestion, I nonetheless cleared my throat to speak for my community, volunteering to put game-day flyers in every one of DC's women's bars.

Lesbian specificity is a hurdle itself in the current alphabet soup of queer identities. Many years after taking my class, a student wrote to me, "Thanks for loaning out your books. I found that *Strong Women, Deep Closets* answered a lot of my questions about how to manage my identity with my coaches and team. For so long I hated the fact that I am a lesbian. I wouldn't even use the L-word. But now, after coming out and realizing so many other women in sports are gay, I think it's both cool and exciting. There is a vibrant community just outside the gates of college." Although this student finished the semester comfortably using the L-word, even the LGBT sports media remains hesitant and inconsistent. *Out* magazine featured lesbian NFL coach Katie Sowers in its February/March 2021 issue but named her "the first out *gay* coach in the NFL" (emphasis added). The L-word appeared just once—ten paragraphs into the story—at which point Sowers offered the revealing quote "Without authenticity, you lose all credibility."[23]

After two or more weeks of deconstructing homophobia in sports, we move on to other social standards of physical presentation and body control, such as athletic fitness, the pressure on women to diet, and sports foods. Female students are under more pressure than any previous generation to look buff, and the accompanying eating disorders and levels of anxiety make up an acute problem at every school where I have taught. Each student knows someone anorexic or bulimic or has an anecdote about a friend obsessed with regulating weight and body fat. Feminist students well read in critical theory on body image are not immune to eating disorders. Student athletes recovering from injuries are particularly terrified of gaining weight and falling into disfavor; I met rowers, volleyball players, and cheerleaders whose coaches pressured them to lose weight or even subjected them to public weigh-ins.

The question of athletic fitness needs to be separated from the peculiarly American pressure on women to be a size 4. To get this discussion rolling, I show the *Frontline* television documentary "Fat," which includes profiles of large-size but physically active and self-satisfied adults. Ironically, the film's otherwise provocative stance in valorizing plus-size adults contains a sexist twist: We meet men who are athletically fit though overweight, such as a triathlon runner with a most impressive training regimen. However, the fat but self-confident women profiled in the film are not athletes. Instead, they are plus-size models and fashion designers. Their success is demonstrated by their ability to look great in nice clothes—they have defied societal standards by attaining well-dressed sexiness. Some of my female students are skeptical of the models' self-proclaimed happiness: "I don't believe they really like themselves." "I think they must *hate* how they look."

I gently suggest that the students have just demonstrated a painful reality—that oftentimes, women are one another's harshest critics, while men aren't quite as hard on women, or on one another, for exceeding size limits. "I *like* a woman with junk in the trunk!" one Georgetown athlete blurted out during this discussion, puzzled by his female classmates' cosmetic dieting. But it's women who bear the brunt of the backlash against feminism and social change in dialogues on nutrition. "I have the cure for obesity," says Richard Atkinson, cofounder of the American Obesity Association and head of the MedStar weight-control clinic at Washington Hospital Center. "Let's get all of the women out of the workforce, back cooking nutritious meals at home, and get all the men back in the fields behind the mules, working hard. . . . We were not a fat nation then. But unfortunately, we can't go backwards."[24]

African American students in particular raise eyebrows at this authority figure who longs for the good old days of kitchen and mule-plow work as a solution for medical weight issues, and the female students of all races resent the implication that Mom is to blame for going out to earn a living, thereby abandoning her family to fast food. Books such as Eric Schlosser's *Fast Food Nation* and Naomi Klein's *No Logo* reveal how public schools are complicit in making high-calorie snack foods and sodas available to young students throughout the school day.

For women, there's another size issue: height. A GWU volleyball player brought up the experience of being a tall woman in US society, stared at by children. "So I tell them, 'It's OK. I'm an athlete.'" For this student, a visible difference became acceptable through her athletic role, assuring the world that her physical gift was being put to good use. While we celebrate exceptionally tall men in basketball, rewarding them with lucrative contracts, women have only recently been invited to capitalize on height. My mother, a first-generation American, so outgrew her shorter immigrant relatives that at just five feet six she was nicknamed the Giant. Beauty, size, femininity standards—every student had a story to tell in class.

> Last night I saw the most recent *Sports Illustrated* "Swimsuit issue." I noticed that the models were terribly skinny, even anorexic, with "ten-year-old boy" bodies. Naturally, I asked my boyfriend if he thought these women were sexy (with my size 36D chest, I'm a tad biased), and he said, "Yes." I said, "But it looks like a guy could break her." And he said, "Honey, THAT'S the attraction."

> I didn't realize that second graders were on diets. That's crazy. You don't really see many minorities with eating disorders. "Have not, waste not." I mean, I've never been starving, but I've definitely wanted different kinds of food that were too expensive. But in general, I think that white people have more access, so food is not so important to them.

> I can blame my older team members for teaching me how to pop so many painkillers and ignore injuries for the sake of the team, or teaching me how to throw up and diet so I made that week's weight limit. But I can't get rid of the guilt, knowing that maybe I screwed some younger girl's life up or helped contribute to an injury by passing down the advice and coping techniques that are so rampant. . . . I was weighed every week. I was told each week how much I needed to lose, where I needed to lose it, and when I needed to lose it by.

> I work at Sports Club, and I was running a birthday party for an eight-year-old girl. She had a "get fit" aerobics party, full of exercise and crunches. Is this necessary? Is this fun for kids? To make it worse, the mother brought vegetable sticks and rice cakes as the party snacks.

> I stand in line at the store and get funny looks. I'm taller than all the women in heels and most of the men too. Then someone turns around and asks if I play basketball. That question is the one thing that gets to

me. What do I say? I am comfortable with my height, and I don't think that height really makes someone an athlete. When I graduate and no longer play, does that mean I am going to shrink? Will I lose my height when I stop playing sports?

My coach is notorious for making comments on girls' weight, especially when they aren't running well. As he picked up and dropped one of our sprinters on the floor, he said, "Did you feel the earth shake?"

I was so blinded by thinking that our coaches were looking out for us and wouldn't do anything to harm us. What finally opened my eyes were our nude weigh-ins. If someone wasn't losing weight, they were punished—these people were put in the back. Our coaches commended everyone who was losing weight and called out all those who still had "a ways to go." They'd chart our weight and display it. Teammates would cry. I'd hear them purging before games. It was the worst year of the team.

I hate the fact that women are expected to look perfect all the time, even at the gym. I hate even more that I give in to this societal pressure by packing in my gym bag a change of clothes (for after my workout), body spray and lotion, and . . . (shudder) . . . makeup. Not a lot, believe me, I used to go to the gym in a full face of makeup and leave with it all repainted on. Now I am much more low maintenance, just some powder, eye liner, and lip gloss. But still, I hate the fact that even after all of my women's studies classes I cannot seem to rid myself of these little beautification rituals that represent everything I am against. Most of all, I hate that no matter how many times people tell me I am beautiful, I simply cannot believe them.

"We have a 12 coming in this weekend." That is, a 12 on a scale of 1–10 attractiveness rating by my coach. This is what he tells us as we, thirteen young women clad in spandex and sports bras, sit down to stretch. We half smile, partly out of shock, more so out of self-consciousness. More than a few of us wonder what he's been thinking as he watched us do drills. What was I? Was I a 7?

Two days ago in the free weight room, a guy was teaching his girlfriend how to do bicep curls, but she seemed disinterested. Instead of helping her, he was getting nasty and frustrated. And then he flicked her arm so that her fat jiggled, and he poked her side, saying, "THIS is what we have to get rid of." It was public humiliation, an abusive relationship. I wanted to drop a dumbbell on his foot. They both knew I was watching.

So there I was at a collegiate athlete dinner—Division I NCAA water polo—and this guy refers to me as "a girl who could be a plus-size model"! The entire table went silent. As if I don't have enough body image issues. I am a size 8!

Listening to these discussions semester after semester taught me not to bring in snacks, which, though often appreciated by the tired and hungry athletes, made some students experience discomfort and self-consciousness about public snacking. Instead, I gave everyone sheets of stationery I'd designed with the heading "My women's studies professor thinks I'm perfect just the way I am."

Lastly, during this middle month of the semester when we focus on cultural definitions of masculinity and femininity, class discussions turn to the topic of aggression. Are males naturally more aggressive and competitive than females? Science-major students in class, intrigued by our assigned reading in Anne Fausto-Sterling's text *Myths of Gender*, point out the many, many examples of natural female aggression in the insect and animal kingdoms. One student comments that no one is going to call a female praying mantis or a stalking lioness "gay," despite sports books like Brian O'Donoghue's provocatively titled *My Lead Dog Was a Lesbian*, an account of the Alaskan Iditarod sled race.[25] We agree that anything a female can do *is* natural. Others jump on these analogies and point out that female aggression in the animal world is almost always directly connected to finding a mate or to feeding and protecting offspring, sex roles we'd qualify as feminine in *Homo sapiens*. It's females putting on football uniforms who create backlash.

Plenty of enlightened adults, able to dismiss old hunter-versus-gatherer distinctions and to model dual-career coupledom, still cheer at male football games while recoiling from acts of physical aggression by women athletes. Even when they win championships for town and nation, women who play hard, who play to score, face the unresolved problem of winning over fans and spectators ambivalent about female aggression. Complicating this picture are attitudes praising certain levels of social ambition in women. Many critics of female athleticism nonetheless accept female aggression as normal if a young woman is pursuing marriage—or competing for the lead in a drama production, a beauty contest, a spot in a top-ranked sorority, or, closer to sports, a place on the cheerleading squad. Ironically, these beauty arenas are hardly what one might call "safe" in terms of protecting young women from physical harm; one thinks of the long-unsolved murder of tiny pageant competitor JonBenét Ramsey. Campy Hollywood films such as

Showgirls capitalize on the public's titillation with ambitious, scantily clad performers deliberately injuring one another. The film *Miss Congeniality* skewered pageant preparation by having Sandra Bullock order pizza and beers for competitors, turning aside their protests with "It's light beer, and she's gonna throw it up anyway!" In the once staid world of Olympic ice-skating, the infamous Tonya Harding / Nancy Kerrigan rivalry and "kneecapping" incident led to an entire book of feminist essays, *Women on Ice*, edited by Cynthia Baughman. But playing contact sports, expressly to win, has always been perceived as antithetical to femininity or good womanhood; indeed, reform-minded physical educators of the early twentieth century actually forbade women's college teams from competing in varsity tournaments, instead hosting "play days" at the elite women's colleges.[26] Susan Cahn explains that the women's division of the National Amateur Athletic Federation, founded in 1923 and headed by Mrs. Herbert Hoover, primarily feared the commercial and sexual exploitation of female athletes at a time when male "stars" were first being sought out by greedy agents. But disdain for the profit motive mingled with a deeper message about the inappropriateness of competing to win: "The belief that commercial, highly competitive sport was inherently undemocratic reinforced such critiques. Women leaders condemned the elitist and exclusionary nature of male athletic culture, arguing that varsity teams, tournament play, and international competitions privileged the talented minority over the neglected minority. Such a system directed harmful publicity toward a few stars while appropriating resources from those who most needed athletic assistance."[27]

The concern about wasting resources on a star system certainly rings true today, when a teenage player like LeBron James commands a $90 million contract from Nike right out of high school. But as Colette Dowling suggests, "It's hard to know how much of the protest against the aggressive 'men's model' of sport had to do with the kinder, gentler philosophy of women's sport and how much had to do with female physical education teachers wanting to hang on to their turf."[28] Were educators in the women's division anticompetition because of concerns for democratic opportunity or because of fears of women's frailty? Cahn cites a 1923 article from the *Ladies' Home Journal*, Sarah Addington's "The Athletic Limitations of Women," concluding that "in her view the intense competition endangered the skilled few whose desire to win would inevitably lead them to exceed recommended restraints on physical exertion."[29] Today, in an America obsessed with winning, with being number one, many parents and educators are nonetheless deeply concerned that increasing girls' involvement in sports will encourage them to embrace behaviors once reserved for the roughest of men.

This is the old question: Are sports a healthy outlet for aggressive behavior, low self-esteem, and ADHD, or does involvement in an athletic subculture like rugby or football foster and normalize brutality? When we talk about aggression in girls, it's usually relational and social, as in Rachel Simmons's book *Odd Girl Out: The Hidden Culture of Aggression in Girls*. But in class, when we study the problem of aggression in male athletes who abuse women, we also look at when and where society teaches men to expect female deference or passivity. Hazing, in the subculture of men's athletic teams, can reveal traditional disdain for women and femaleness (see fig. 3.2).[30] When contact sports veer from group spirit into unbridled sadism, much of the responsibility lies with those coaches and adult mentors who are supposed to model athletic values for students: "I remember in junior high school, we were practicing football tackling, and the coach got upset that I wasn't knocking the other guy down and vice versa. The coach yelled, real loud and sarcastic, 'Hey! Fight each other—don't *love* each other!' It was meant to embarrass us, but I know that for me it suddenly made me aware of how perverted the adults' value system is and what a backward establishment we all have to live under."[31]

We are just beginning to accept that competitive play in "rough" sports may be, for many women, the same source of pleasure and confidence building that males enjoy. The sea change since Title IX's implementation means that several generations of women are grasping new opportunities at the same time—including my students, who accept equal opportunity as normative, and older women who were once denied access to contact sports but can participate in adult leagues now. In the years I taught class, college-age women steadily gained exposure to athletic female role models who were older than their mothers. In Washington, DC, this included the women's rugby and football confederations, featuring older women who were successful lawyers by day and tough competitors by night. The *City Paper* reported on the D.C. Divas football team, "[Gayle] Dilla was a 40-year-old financial adviser who, like most of her teammates, had never played a down of tackle football. Now she's a 42-year-old financial adviser and a hard-hitting football player. 'Never in my wildest dreams did I ever think I'd be proud of weighing 240 pounds,' says Dilla, the oldest Diva. 'But I am. This is a game for big girls. And I love it . . . I only wish the game was there for me sooner.'"[32]

In class, students reveal how much they admire and long for the confidence these older women have gained through masculine-labeled sports. Their writing speaks to the sheer athletic and nongendered context in which they operate on the field, track, or court, when concerns about feminine appearance are put aside in favor of skills, teamwork, and the pleasure of a demanding practice. For one Georgetown student, being able to train with the DC Furies women's rugby team was a milestone of confidence building and motivation, and she shared notes from one memorable workout, women mentoring women on the pitch.

> It is a Thursday night, and around fifteen Georgetown students are on the field in multiple layers, hopping up and down to keep warm. Then the Furies begin trickling in. These thirty-five women are fierce, tough cookies, and this is apparent from the outset. The newly elected captain belts out commands as we begin our pre-ball-handling plyometrics, which are quite possibly the most difficult exercises I have ever done, condemning weakness and "girly" faintness of heart and/or breath. "Come on, let's scare off some men!" she shouts, to the response of loud laughter and louder groans.

> Working with the Furies was interesting to me in another way—these women were some of the most confident and comfortable I have met since coming to Georgetown. What underlies their confidence? What combination of factors makes these fantastic women at ease with their bodies—able to take up space, be loud, and joke about their aggressiveness? I think that the answer to this question is that they are committed to their sport, and athletic involvement comes first. When you think about it, obsessions over "femininity" and "composure" are incompatible with contact sport.

> I have *missed* belonging to a team. There is something so fulfilling about knowing that your teammates are supporting you as you support them, that they see, hear, and are open to you. And even passing the ball, learning how to control the spin and aim; well, that was *great*. My arms felt engaged; they absolutely sang as they passed the oblong brown ball first to Julie. Then Bridget. Then Ellen. Oh, what a wonderful sensation. And the burning in my lungs after our relay had finished—the fact that I was able to catch my breath and continue sprinting forward, then backward, then forward, pushing up midfield, sprinting the whole length twice before tagging my teammate and hollering out support of her.

The middle month of class is when every student begins to talk back to the material we've covered so far. Next, we'll move on to the hot topic of Title IX, which so many critics believe is a female-quota victory at the expense of more-deserving males. That, too, will generate talkback about how far women athletes have come. But first, I need to know whether everyone's done the reading up to now. There's a midterm, which you'll find in the back of the book.

FROM LOCKER ROOM COMMENTS TO ONLINE ABUSE

A conversation about speech, violence, and culture featuring Dave Zirin, Bonnie Morris, Jessica Luther & Soraya Chemaly

The first 20 students will receive a copy of Jessica Luther's book, Unsportsmanlike Conduct: College Football and the Politics of Rape.

Wednesday, November 16 at 7:30pm
HFSC Social Room

For requests related to disability, please email lb1065@georgetown.edu

Fig. 3.2 Locker Room Talk event poster, Georgetown University, 2016.

Initiating Change
Adapting to Change

NWHM *&*
The George Washington University
INVITE YOU TO ATTEND
Game Changers: American Women & Sports

NATIONAL
WOMEN'S
HISTORY
MUSEUM

**THE GEORGE
WASHINGTON
UNIVERSITY**
WASHINGTON, DC

Title IX is considered a key factor in inspiring women to pursue equal opportunities in all of their endeavors. Furthermore, the ability to participate in organized sports has made a difference in the lives of women and girls who successfully applied the lessons learned in sports to other areas of their lives. Please join us for a fascinating discussion about women and sports before and since the passage of Title IX.

Jill Agostino   Dr. Bonnie Morris   Mariah Burton Nelson

Wednesday, February 19, 2014

Program: 5:30pm — Reception: 6:30pm

Jill Agostino (Moderator)

A current Editor at the Washington Bureau of the *New York Times*, Ms. Agostino has had a distinguished career as a sports editor for both regional and national newspapers and is the past president of the Association for Women in Sports Media.

Dr. Bonnie Morris, Ph.D.

A faculty member at both Georgetown and The George Washington Universities, Dr. Morris is a scholar who teaches women's studies including a course on gender and athletics.

Mariah Burton Nelson

A groundbreaking author, expert speaker, and former professional athlete, Ms. Burton-Nelson is a national authority on sports, success, and leadership.

The George Washington University
(Morton Auditorium)
805 21st Street, NW,
Washington D.C. 20052

TICKETS:
General Public ($10.00)
Students & Faculty (Free)
RSVP by Monday, February 17, 2014

http://nwhm.ticketleap.com/game-changers or (703) 461-1920

The National Women's History Museum educates, inspires, empowers, and shapes the future by integrating women's distinctive history into the culture and history of the United States.
www.nwhm.org

Check out NWHM's social media channels for fun facts and information!

Fig. 4.1 George Washington University / NWHM event poster, 2014.

FROM HALF-COURT TO FEDERAL COURT

Title IX and the American Playing Field

*F*air play is a key concept in sports culture. The expectation of fair play, on and off the field, holds meaning for everyone, not just athletes. In England, ideals of sport fairness found their way into common expressions such as "That's not sporting," "That isn't cricket," and "That's not playing the game." We use sports language in the United States, too, to affirm national values.

But *equality* is a different term, one with a gendered, racialized past. How do we make athletic opportunity fair and equal for men and women? In the experience of student athletes, does any school really measure up? This history is the focus in our third month of class as we begin to look at Title IX law in the United States.

When I began teaching in the 1990s, barely one generation into Title IX's benefits to women's sports, I found that students in my class either had no familiarity with Title IX at all or had accepted critics' complaints that the law constituted reverse discrimination—that it served only to hurt men and men's sports. These same very bright students at GWU and Georgetown were hard pressed to name the Thirteenth, Fourteenth, Fifteenth, Nineteenth, and Twenty-Sixth Amendments to the US Constitution and to identify how these marked turning points of citizenship. We thus begin the Title IX unit with a discussion of whether fairness, or equality, can be achieved by top-down legal directives when other paths to justice have failed. It's a peculiarly American dilemma, in a land where the Founding Fathers waxed poetically that "all men are created equal" while owning slaves and controlling women. The original US Constitution did not pledge equal rights for slaves, for women of any heritage, or for the continent's indigenous first peoples.

This is one week of class when I cover the entire chalkboard from top to bottom with timelines, and all that's heard for a while is the clicking of pens and computer keys. In 1868, the Fourteenth Amendment granted equality of citizenship rights to all persons born in the United States, followed by the Fifteenth Amendment in 1870, granting voting rights—on paper—to freed Black males. Still, Asian immigrants could not naturalize to gain citizenship, and Native Americans, too, were not considered citizens. The Nineteenth Amendment for women's suffrage was not passed until 1920. A Voting Rights Act passed in 1965 had to be introduced to dismantle overt barriers and threats to Black voters, and young people aged eighteen to twenty-one did not gain the right to vote until the Twenty-Sixth Amendment in 1971, although throughout the 1960s scores of young males under twenty-one were drafted and killed in the Vietnam conflict. The 1986 Supreme Court case *Bowers v. Hardwick* upheld criminalizing homosexuality even in the privacy of one's home, making it possible to jail longtime partners; in most states, gay and lesbian Americans remained felons under varying laws until *Lawrence v. Texas* in 2003.

Depending on one's identity, there was no guarantee of equality in this democracy, and for decades, these inconsistencies also shaped American sports. Who could play? Who could play together? Who could share a changing room, a bus ride, a motel, or a watercooler? Who could go to medical school to study sports injury? Forget about rowing crew; could women even attend Harvard, Yale, or Princeton? Were women able to study, publish, or present research on women's health? Which Olympic sports were off limits to women? And beyond the US borders, which countries sent no women to the Olympics at all?

Lingering, never ratified by enough states to become part of the US Constitution, was one proposal: the Equal Rights Amendment, introduced by suffragist Alice Paul in 1923. It reads, "Equality of rights under the law shall not be denied by the United States, or by any state, on account of sex." Tension over just which legal rights women should have, and how sex discrimination should be interpreted and corrected, characterized the entire second wave of American feminism in the 1960s and 1970s. Despite a long battle for ratification by the necessary thirty-eight states, the Equal Rights Amendment failed to be enshrined in the US Constitution, though many of my students believed it had passed. Campaigns to re-introduce the ERA are now emerging in states like Virginia.

But the 1970s did produce an equal rights law—Title IX of the Education Amendments, signed by President Nixon in 1972. Title IX banned sex discrimination in any educational activity or program supported by federal funding, and it quickly became the chief means of requiring most schools and colleges to equalize sports participation for women and girls. The law acknowledged and interrupted long-standing patterns that had disadvantaged women and girls from high school to higher education, from Ivy League quotas on female enrollment to outright no-women-allowed practices in STEM majors and magnet schools. It became illegal for institutions to deny women access to the engineering major or for law and medical schools to say to qualified female applicants, "Why should be admit *you*? You'll probably just wind up getting married and pregnant and dropping out. You do realize you'd be taking a space that rightfully should go to a male?" These once common practices are well documented and regrettably still occur. But Title IX remains best known for its impact on increased opportunities for girls and women in sports, where sex discrimination, often reflected in pitiful budgets and facilities, was most acute through the 1970s.

Though yoked with complex and ever-evolving "prongs" to measure compliance, Title IX is largely responsible for the rapid growth of women's sports in US athletic programs nationwide, bringing women's team funding, facility use, and coaching salaries more in line with how men's teams have traditionally been accommodated. Unfortunately, the requirement that women's teams receive a reasonable split of sports-program dollars was quickly perceived as a threat to men's sports. In retrospect, that's understandable: there had never been any plan to allocate equal funding to women's sports, particularly at schools where high-profile men's football teams enjoyed a preferential share of the entire athletics budget. Programs for women's sports would now compete for funding with all lower-profile, "non-revenue-producing" men's sports. At football schools, this race for leftover dollars pitted new women's soccer players against longtime male wrestlers and so forth, turning Title IX into a battle of the sexes and raising key questions about the expense of a football program, which often maintains one hundred scholarship athletes. At schools without a football program, such as George Washington

University, student athletes were more likely to examine ways in which women's basketball and men's basketball weren't equivalent, as these were the dominant programs on campus. At other colleges and high schools across the United States, as Sarah Fields explores in her book *Female Gladiators*, there were enormous challenges when, in the absence of a separate women's team, individual female athletes asserted their right to try out for a position on an existing men's team. The controversy over one girl playing with the boys, since few schools ever offered a complementary girls' football, baseball, or wrestling program, was also turned around as individual boys sought to play field hockey—a girls' sport in the United States though played by men in India and Pakistan. Too often, resentful schools and Little League communities punished the maverick athletes by forcing them to play in traditionally gender-specific apparel: skirts on the boys, athletic cups for the girls.

From 1972 on, the main challenge to Title IX concerned whether adding women's programs took important dollars away from existing men's programs. Mixed messages from both print and television media muddied the waters further. Here's a snapshot from my seventh year of teaching Athletics and Gender: Sunday, June 23, 2002. On that day, the thirtieth anniversary of Title IX, I opened up the *Washington Post* to find absolutely no mention of Title IX in the sports section. The day before, however, columnist Ellen Goodman had contributed a testimonial to Title IX on the editorial page: a reminder that women's advancement in sports was chiefly a political issue. Later that week, when ESPN broadcast a special on the Title IX anniversary, host Bob Levy began by declaring that the occasion called "not for a celebration, but an examination." In the same month, Secretary of Education Roderick Paige announced a National Commission on Opportunity in Athletics to "review" and "reform" Title IX. Fresh complaints that Title IX constituted a "quota system" unfairly hurting males came not only from coaches and wrestlers but from policy advocates such as Jessica Gavora, author of the 2002 book *Tilting the Playing Field*. Other female critics pointed to the dramatic statistic that women now made up more than 50 percent of the undergraduate enrollment in American colleges, suggesting that we had failed men and boys by allowing radical feminist change to privilege women and girls, with parity guidelines holding back the males, who were more likely to be interested in sports than females. With cries of reverse sex discrimination and "shrewish feminism," the stage was set in the second year of the George W. Bush administration to revisit and reform the controversial legislation. Any young athlete studying both television and print media during the week of Title IX's thirtieth anniversary would have been convinced that women had made gains in college sports not on their own merits but entirely at the expense of men's sports.

At issue is one of Title IX's three options for institutional compliance, which suggests maintaining a ratio of male and female university athletes proportionate to the ratio of male and female students enrolled overall. If women are 50 percent of undergraduates, then 50 percent of the sports budget should go to women's sports. This measure of fairness, however, was written at a time when female enrollment lagged far behind at most co-ed campuses. In fact, one intention of Title IX had been to challenge the cap on female enrollment at Ivy League schools that admitted three men for every two women. "Proportionality" at a school where women were historically just one-third of the students meant that an athletic program could satisfy Title IX compliance by giving female athletes one-third or less of a sports budget. No one could foresee the enormous success of women in academia; once the door was kicked open, women would be more than 55 percent of the students at many American colleges and medical schools in the twenty-first century. But no school enrolling both men and women was ready to give 55 percent of a sports budget to its female athletes. And, over the decades, as college men continued to receive millions more in athletic scholarship dollars than college women, the Office of Civil Rights never withheld funding from those colleges and universities clearly in violation of Title IX. Schools were far more likely to respond to student-led protests, lawsuits, and the threat of negative publicity than any fear of federal disciplinary penalty.

The backlash often came from those who argued that women simply weren't as interested in sports participation as men, or that lost athletic opportunities hurt males more profoundly. Title IX's critics eventually proposed sending "interest surveys" to college students to test just how many women really cared about athletic opportunities. This put the burden on women to justify equal access to funds traditionally favoring men. In one *Washington Post* feature, sportswriter Sally Jenkins quoted Curt Levey, director of the conservative Center for Individual Rights, as saying, "I don't think you should tell women they're interested when they're not," and Roger Clegg of the conservative Center for Equal

Opportunity added, "I don't think the best way to correct discrimination that is suffered by minorities and women is to have a program of institutionalized discrimination the other way."[1] In 2010, the interest survey was overturned by the Obama administration. Today, Title IX law is known by most college students and bureaucrats as a means for reporting sexual harassment on campus. At universities, the office of Title IX compliance is charged with managing multiple categories of sex discrimination—from a hostile environment created by faculty to homophobia and outright sexual assault. It's a shift from earlier decades of identifying Title IX with basic educational opportunity, as well as fairness from the classroom to the playing field. In 2021, serious effort to amend Title IX with transgender inclusion became a hallmark of the incoming Biden administration.

With so much changing from year to year, how did I teach about Title IX in class? While the law is easily misunderstood, it is also easily researched. With the touch of a keypad, my students could download thousands of articles, viewpoints, documents, depositions, and official statements from government offices and their own universities. I intended to introduce every opinion, offering students a range of sources as we plowed through the debates. We read Gavora's *Tilting the Playing Field*; Mariah Burton Nelson's "And Now They Tell Us Women Don't Really Like Sports?"; Lauren Kessler's account in *Full Court Press* of fighting for equal coaching pay at the University of Oregon; and editorials by male wrestlers charging that Title IX constituted reverse discrimination, such as "Wrestling with Title IX" by John Irving, author of *The World According to Garp* and *The Cider House Rules*. From our campus newspapers, we paired thoughtful student articles with opposing views. At Georgetown, we paired Meredith McCloskey's "On a Level Playing Field" in the *Hoya* with Ryan Wynn's "Why Title IX Is Bad for Georgetown" in the *Georgetown Academy*. Wynn argued, "Title IX's discriminatory rules prevent Georgetown from having an effective football [team], which could bring the school money and prestige."[2] McCloskey broke down raw numbers: "During the 1999–2000 school year, the undergraduate population at Georgetown was 46 percent male and 54 percent female. . . . The student-athlete population for the same year was 57 percent male and 43 percent female."[3] Ten years later, at Georgetown, we were reading Alex Lau's "Title IX's Beneficial Intent Becoming Discriminatory" and Matt Emch's "Title IX Causes Inequity," both published in the *Hoya*. Lau critiqued proportionality because Georgetown's women were at that point 57 percent of enrollment; he raised the idea of "discounting students ages 25 and older in proportionality tests. This age group, which makes up about 40 percent of the undergraduate population, will most likely not be partaking in varsity sports, and therefore shouldn't be counted."[4] Emch in turn suggested that "Title IX legislation was necessary, of course, when blatant sexism existed in college athletics," a view expressing confidence that those days were over and done with.[5]

We watched *A Hero for Daisy*, the film about Yale's female crew team whose frustrated rowers famously stripped to reveal the words "TITLE IX" painted across their bare chests, in protest of the lack of a women's boathouse. We heard guest speakers from the National Women's Law Center and other experts whose campus presentations I sometimes joined: see figure 4.1. In 2007, Susan Ware's handbook *Title IX: A Brief History with Documents* became an excellent go-to resource for multiple viewpoints, and I continually updated timelines and challenges in class, on the good old-fashioned chalkboard, for my students.

The enormous changes brought about in large part because of Title IX are best approached in a quick review of key turning points. Take a moment to read through the following sample timeline—which offers a sense of the cultural resistance to equal funding of women's sports over nearly fifty years:

A BRIEF TIMELINE OF TITLE IX

1971 Fewer than three hundred thousand girls participate in varsity athletics in US high schools. Fewer than thirty-two thousand women compete in college athletics; those who do receive less than 2 percent of the entire collegiate athletics budget. There are no college athletic scholarships for women.

June 23, 1972 Title IX of the Education Amendments is signed into law by President Richard Nixon. The bill's chief sponsor is Senator Birch Bayh (D-IN). The amendment states, "No person in the United States shall, on the basis of sex, be excluded from participation in, be denied the benefits of, or be subjected to discrimination under any education program or activity receiving federal financial assistance."

May 20, 1973 Senator John Tower (R-TX) proposes an additional amendment to exempt football, men's basketball, and so-called revenue-producing men's sports from Title IX law; his amendment is defeated.

1976 "Boys' rules" finally replace eighty years of "girls' rules" in basketball after varsity guard Victoria Ann Cape sues the Tennessee Secondary School Athletic Association.

December 11, 1979 The Office of Civil Rights establishes the infamous "three areas" under which a college program can be challenged. These areas are participation, scholarships, and equivalence. Percentages of men and women given varsity-sport roster spots must be "substantially" the same as the percentages of men and women enrolled as full-time undergraduates. A school that does not meet the proportionality test may satisfy either of two additional conditions showing a recent history of adding sports for the "underrepresented gender" or proving it is "fully and effectively accommodating the interests and abilities" of its students.

1982 The NCAA takes over the women's pre–Title IX women's athletic division, ending the female-headed Association for Intercollegiate Athletics for Women.

February 28, 1984 After attempting to eliminate the Department of Education, which enforced Title IX, the Reagan administration weakens Office of Civil Rights enforcement of Title IX with the Supreme Court ruling *Grove City College v. Bell*. This ruling declares that Title IX applies only to actual programs receiving federal dollars, which excludes most athletic departments.

March 22, 1988 The Civil Rights Restoration Act of 1987 overturns *Grove City College v. Bell*. The Office of Civil Rights resumes jurisdiction over Title IX only after Congress overrides President Reagan's veto of the 1987 act.

February 2, 1992 The Supreme Court rules that plaintiffs are entitled to punitive damages if they can prove intentional noncompliance with Title IX (*Franklin v. Gwinnett County Public Schools*).

1993 Howard University head women's basketball coach sues for sex discrimination under Title IX and the DC Human Rights Act. The subsequent award of $2.4 million in damages and back pay is the first such monetary award given by a jury for a Title IX suit.

March 1994 The University of North Carolina's final victory in the women's NCAA championship is sealed with an unprecedented three-point shot in the final seven-tenths of a second of play time. During commercial breaks, viewers heard the University of Oklahoma athletic director suggest dismantling their women's basketball program on the grounds that women's games weren't selling enough tickets; nineteen years before, Oklahoma coach Barry Switzer had gone on television to declare, "Women's sports will be non-revenue-producing."

November 8, 1995 Grant Teaff, executive director of the American Football Coaches Association and head football coach at fundamentalist Baylor University for twenty-one years, writes in *USA Today* that "capping participation opportunities in football discriminates against male student athletes."[6]

April 21, 1997 The Supreme Court lets stand a ruling against Brown University, which, in *Cohen v. Brown University*, lost a Title IX suit brought by gymnast Amy Cohen. The university had eliminated the women's gymnastics team while maintaining that it was meeting Title IX standards by "satisfactorily accommodating female athletes." Brown's defense was that fewer women than men were interested in sports.

2000 Nearly 2.8 million girls participate in high school sports. This represents an increase of 847 percent since Title IX's introduction in 1972. In both high school and college sports, women make up 42 percent of varsity athletes. However, in this same year, female students make up more than 54 percent of the student body at four-year colleges. Male students receive $146 million (36 percent) more than female athletes in terms of NCAA athletic scholarships.

2001–2 Women are head coaches for only 44 percent of women's college teams; this represents the lowest total since Title IX passed. More than 90 percent of head-coach positions in women's sports have gone to men since 2000. Women coaching women's basketball earn sixty-one cents to the dollar paid to men coaching men's basketball.

January 16, 2002 The National Wrestling Coaches Association and other men's groups sue the US Department of Education in federal district court, claiming that Title IX hurts men's teams and is fostering sex discrimination against men. The case, led by Mike Moyer, executive director of the association, includes charges that because of Title IX's focus on roster capping and proportionality, four hundred collegiate men's teams have been eliminated since 1972. Lead attorney Larry Joseph comments, "We feel Title IX is a great thing, as long as you remove the proportionality part of the equation."

June 2002 In a *Newsweek* article titled "A Train Wreck Called Title IX," conservative George Will declares, "Title IX fanatics start from the dogma—they ignore all that pesky evidence about different male and female patterns of cognitive abilities, and brain structure and function—that men and women are identical in abilities and inclinations."

June 22 and 23, 2002 In observation of Title IX's thirtieth anniversary, ESPN runs a full weekend of debates and "town meetings" on the law, as well as rebroadcasts the King-versus-Riggs tennis match of 1973 and the Women's World Cup championship game of 1999. At the ESPN town-meeting broadcast on June 22, eight-hundred-win women's basketball coach Pat Summit recalls of the olden days, "We sold doughnuts to buy uniforms."

June 2002 The Bush administration forms a commission to study Title IX, with hearings scheduled in cities throughout the United States. The Education Department's Commission on Opportunity in Athletics has until late February 2003 to issue its report.

Fall 2002 Insight Media mails out its usual catalog on educational videos in sports, and at least five videos debate the merits of Title IX. Promotional copy for one video incorrectly lists Billie Jean King's name as "Billy." A student's father visits my class and insists that Billie Jean King never defeated Bobby Riggs; in front of my students, he scolds and contradicts me, saying, "Look, I was there."

December 6, 2002 The *Chronicle of Higher Education* devotes its entire Review section to the Title IX debate, with editorials by six "experts." The lead column, from the men's wrestling coach at the University of Minnesota, begins, "The law was hijacked by feminist radicals. . . . Feminists want us to believe that men and women are interchangeable in every occupation."

December 2002 / January 2003 Mariah Burton Nelson publishes "And Now They Tell Us Women Don't Really Like Sports?" in *Ms.* magazine. She notes, "The Office of Civil Rights, which has the power to withhold federal funds from noncompliant institutions, has never done so."

January 28, 2003 Writer John Irving, whose novels *The World according to Garp* and *The Hotel New Hampshire* include nods to boys' prep school wrestling, weighs in with a lead editorial in the *New York Times*, warning feminists, "I *am* a women's advocate. I have long been active in the pro-choice movement. . . . But I'm also an advocate of fairness. . . . For every single NCAA sports opportunity for a woman, there are 17 high school athletes available to fill the spot; for a man, there are 18. Isn't that fair enough?"

January 29, 2003 The *Washington Post* publishes an editorial on proposed Title IX reforms that points out that "if there's any threat to wrestling and swimming teams, it's bloated football budgets. The NCAA allowance for 85 football scholarships for Division I football schools comes closer to an effective quota than anything in Title IX."

February 1, 2003 For the first time in the sixty-two-year history of Duke University's basketball program, a women's game is sold out: Duke versus the University of Connecticut. The 9,314-seat arena is packed as number one Duke loses to number two Connecticut. Five weeks later, in a historic upset, Connecticut's seventy-game winning streak comes to an end as Villanova defeats the shocked Huskies in the Big East championship. A friend calls me up and shouts into the phone, "David just met Goliath. Do you know what kind of psychological uplift this gives to all the other women's teams out there? *They* can do it too."

February 14, 2003 Ellen Staurowsky, chair of sports management and media at Ithaca College, blasts the commission report in the *Chronicle of Higher Education*: "The commissioners almost unanimously supported a recommendation encouraging the Department of Education to explore an antitrust exemption for college sports . . . which would trade institutional promises to cease discriminating against students on the basis of sex for a governmental promise to protect the financial interests of the football and men's basketball powers. . . . Nowhere in the application of civil-rights legislation has such a bargain ever been suggested, let alone considered reasonable."

February 22, 2003 Martin Henderson, staff writer for the *Los Angeles Times*, reports on an inner-city girls' basketball team forced to solicit sponsorship from a local restaurant chain to afford the shoes and gear routinely showered on the boys' team by Nike. "The Nike-sponsored Crenshaw High boys' team, for years one of the strongest in the city, had new shoes, warmups and gear. The girls had nothing. . . . While sizable sponsorship agreements between sports apparel companies and top boys' basketball teams are commonplace—there are hundreds of such deals nationwide and dozens in Southern California—they are rare in girls' basketball."

February 26, 2003 A Save Title IX website charges the commission with bias, based on the following there was no representation of Division II or III institutions, small colleges, or middle schools; opponents of Title IX outnumbered supporters by more than two to one; and members refused to read the 1996 Office of Civil Rights document on the three-prong test the commission seeks to overhaul. Other Title IX supporters complain that while commission members and Olympic gold medalists Julie Foudy and Donna de Varona issued a minority report recommending that Title IX go unchanged, Department of Education secretary Rod Paige refused to accept their recommendations or enter them into the record because they weren't "unanimous."

February 2003 Teresa Phillips of Tennessee State University becomes the first woman to coach a men's Division I basketball team.

June 2003 US district judge Emmet G. Sullivan rules against the National Wrestling Coaches Association, which sought to overturn the Department of Education's 1979 and 1996 Title IX policy interpretations. Sullivan's dismissal of the lawsuit against the Department of Education does not halt the department's own review of Title IX or its commission's recommendations for change.[7]

June 23, 2003 The thirty-first anniversary of Title IX includes a *60 Minutes* segment on CBS advertised with the misleading tagline "How did the lion's share of funding become the *lioness's share*? And what are the men going to do about it?" But on cable that night, girls (and boys) could watch the original *Bad News Bears* movie, remarkably enlightened for 1976; in one scene, Walter Matthau reminds reluctant Little League pitcher Tatum O'Neal, "It's not tomboy stuff. It's your nation's pastime."

March 17, 2005 "Additional Clarification" policy guidance from the Department of Education weakens Title IX by allowing schools to send an email survey asking female students which sports they're interested in. The interest survey is not sent to male students. If the women fail to respond, schools may interpret this as lack of interest and refuse to add or fund women's teams. It later turns out that most students automatically delete the survey, mistaking it as spam.

April 2, 2005 *Washington Post* sportswriter Sally Jenkins publishes "Not for Lack of Interest," arguing that

> if a university had catered solely to my "interests" as an 18-year-old undergraduate, the entire campus would have been converted into a giant bar offering cheap beer and free pool. . . . "Interest" is a word that dogs women's sports—it inherently suggests that, on some level, games are still not an entirely legitimate subject for females. . . . But the massive audience for this Final Four is plain evidence that interest follows opportunity. Last year's championship between Tennessee and Connecticut was ESPN's highest rated basketball game of the year at that time—male, female, or pro. . . . It rated higher than any NBA game on the network.

April 20, 2010 The Department of Education rescinds the "Additional Clarification" and the recommended survey. This change is announced and celebrated by Vice President Joe Biden at a formal event hosted in George Washington University's Smith Center gym, and I'm invited.

2011 New policy guidance highlights Title IX protections against sexual harassment and sexual violence. Schools gain new clarification in ways that athletic departments must use Title IX procedures to address sexual violence by and against student athletes.

June 28, 2012 In "Title IX at 40: Most Schools Still Aren't in Compliance," the *Christian Science Monitor* explains, "Here's the problem: 43 percent is not equality—especially when 57 percent of the undergraduates are women."

September 7, 2017 The US secretary of education announces there will be upcoming revisions to guidelines on campus sexual harassment and sexual violence cases under Title IX.

March 2020 A judge rules against the US women's national soccer team's sex-discrimination pay claim, asserting key differences between men's and women's soccer. Pro leagues for women are not covered by Title IX law, frustrating collegiate athletes who popularize the phrase "equality until graduation."

May 6, 2020 US Department of Education secretary Betsy DeVos issues changes to the interpretation of Title IX, requiring a live hearing with face-to-face cross-examination as part of any resolution in sexual assault charges. These changes are both abrupt and difficult to implement in the short window of time allocated. They are issued during a pandemic during which most schools have closed down, with neither students nor faculty on campus.

January 2021 Incoming president Joe Biden announces that Title IX includes protections for transgender athletes, ushering in a new era of debate.

March 19, 2021 *Washington Post* sportswriter Sally Jenkins creates a national uproar with her column revealing that the NCAA gives no payouts to whichever women's college basketball team wins the annual championship, while men's teams receive $2 million for winning a single game.

The timeline gives students the opportunity to approach the arc of change from multiple angles, depending on their interests and majors (prelaw, exercise science, journalism, gender and women's studies, and so forth). Because so much significant information can feel overwhelming, I begin the next class by personalizing some fine points of applied feminism. Having lived through the entire history of Title IX, which passed while I was an eleven-year-old, I share old headlines and stories with my students. In 1973, I watched the historic Billie Jean King / Bobby

Riggs tennis match on our tiny black-and-white family television set, and though a clumsy nonathlete myself, I was buoyed by knowledge that girls had a right to play. Transferring from a liberal private school to a more restrictive public junior high in 1974, I introduced myself to my new principal by waving a copy of Title IX and telling him that I knew my rights. I could play soccer and any other "boy" sports. When I moved on to the local high school in tenth grade, I took the mostly male PE unit in fencing. Feeling very much like Joan of Arc, I picked up a foil and learned to shout, "En garde!"

Almost twenty years later, I found myself teaching women's history at a private university in Upstate New York, where obvious inequities revived my dormant interest in women's sports and Title IX law. There was low attendance at the women's lacrosse games for the excellent reason that there were no seats for spectators, and, incredibly, the snow was never cleared off the designated women's field before an important match. Men's games, in contrast, were played in a stadium field supplied with bleachers, loudspeaker announcers, hot cocoa, and snowplow operators. When I shared this story with my classes in Washington, DC, there were mixed responses—from "No way," to "Typical," to "That happened to us." Anecdotes of discrimination in high school, in middle school, and all the way back to kindergarten poured out. Though every student I ever taught was born after Title IX became law and clear compliance guidelines were issued, almost all could report ways that girls' sports had been left behind, unfairly supported, and underfunded in schools required to be equitable.

These were some of our most heated class conversations. I made clear that all opinions were welcome in class but that written work had to be objective, well researched, and evidence based. To underscore the importance of scholarly work, I made a standard assignment of requiring students to submit a ten-page term paper on Title IX. As protests against the elimination of men's teams grew into a reform movement, I encouraged students to shift their paper to solutions and improvements in the application of existing Title IX law. I asked for and received permission to share any good ideas for improving Title IX with our athletic directors and the NCAA itself. The extraordinary range of responses—both personal and scholarly—made grading these finals a genuinely thrilling experience for me at the conclusion of each semester. For both prelaw students and those who hoped to work as coaches or in athletics administration, a quality research paper on Title IX's application since 1972 truly made the difference in a job interview. However, I also invited students to include personal reflections and opinions at the end of the paper, and these passionate paragraphs offered a range of insights. Here are but a few samples from twenty-five years:

> Last week, I attended a congressional hearing on the future of Title IX. The first things that struck me were the small size of the room and the enormous number of people who had come to watch. It occurred to me that my observations were symbolic of the Title IX struggle itself—lots of people, lots of interest, lack of accommodation. I had to sit on the floor!

> To be in compliance with Title IX, many universities have added women's crew. To me, crew always seemed like a man's sport; I never considered joining until one day my father and I went down to the boathouse to pick my brother up. I was greeted by an older gentleman whose first words were "You would be the perfect coxswain." I was this little, fragile, big-glasses girl about to start her freshman year of high school. From that point on, doors opened up for me; my first two years in high school, I was a coxswain for the men's team. Crew was my ticket to college.

> Hockey players were seen as heroes in my high school. Even the faculty and administration seemed to view them as special cases. Hockey players got special extensions, passed classes they almost never attended, and were constantly invited to perform important tasks for the school—speaking at assemblies, assisting the diocese with projects. The worst part was the principal. This man, who attended exactly one field hockey game in my four years, never missed a hockey game, in or out of season, at home or away. He found special tutors for hockey players, invited the team to his home for meals and to watch games on TV. Most of the hockey players got a kick out of the fact that I found their preferential treatment to be both unfair and sexist. They claimed that girls' sports simply aren't as exciting as boys'. The truth was, the principal just didn't know how to interact with women. When we would meet—I was president of the student senate—he always began by complimenting me on my appearance and leading the conversation to soap operas, which he thought I would find interesting. It would have felt nice to be respected. I would have settled, however, for more equally applied support and interest. He gave permission for people to see women's sports as unimportant. No matter how many powerful women attempt to change that view, sexism won't stop until men like our principal are out of office.

At my high school, all boys' junior varsity sports had nice uniforms—ones that fit. In four years, not once did *we* get new uniforms. It was hard to take us seriously when our uniforms clearly stated that we were not important; it made leaving the locker room a moment of torture—girls with skirts that barely covered their butts, softball pants that had to be rolled up, taped T-shirts proclaiming team #00. The field hockey team was forced to practice on an old elementary playground, a field so full of holes and garbage that it did not pass regulations for season games. The number of injuries from ankles twisted in rabbit holes or shin splints from running circuits around the block were countless. A teenager was found dead in the woods behind our practice "field." It wasn't a safe place.

While Title IX reads as a fair piece of legislation, it would indeed be difficult to tell a college wrestler that Title IX has provided an equal opportunity for him. . . . The result of the quota system has attempted to force females into things that they may not necessarily be interested in.

I was a high school sophomore the first time I heard "Title IX." No, I did not graduate from high school in 1975, and that is what alarms me most. It was not until my final semester here at Georgetown that I was enlightened to the dual athletic and academic purposes of Title IX legislation. But it is now tinted green with scholarship money and the envy of male athletes.

The GW women's rugby team, which has won its division four years in a row, receives less funding than the men's team, which has never even placed third. However, the fact that I can now view my favorite female soccer players on national television in the leisure of my own home is a direct, positive result of Title IX's impact.

Title IX is merely being used as a scapegoat for problems that would not exist if discrimination had not been formerly institutionalized.

When I was ten years old, I wanted to play Little League football. When I went to try out for the team, I received criticism from the parents and no support from the coaches. My mother spoke with the head of athletics in that region and had the coaches apologize to every female at the football field. Not only did I play football; I averaged two touchdowns a game. When I go to the same football field and I see other little girls playing football and scoring touchdowns, I think of the fight my mother faced and how it changed athletics for everyone.

My mother was a talented swimmer, but her (abusive) father would not pay for further training. My mother was the best on every swim team as a child and still has newspaper clippings from meets she won. Whereas my uncle, who would eventually become the New York State wrestling champ, attended private lessons, my mother and her sisters did not. Because of her disappointment as a child, she wanted to make sure I was afforded every opportunity she was not. Title IX gave me this ability.

People play sports not because a government bureaucrat tells them to but because they love sports. And whatever quotas can't be met by recruiting women have to be met by ditching men. My condolences go out to the men athletes who have lost their opportunity to play sports, the victims of quotas. It's not whether you win or lose; it's how the government plays the numbers game.

To say that a law ensuring equity in education is discriminating against men is comparable to saying that the women's rights movement is holding men back. Unfortunately, Title IX has been perceived as a hostile takeover strategy engineered by agitated feminists. The fact of the matter is that Title IX was passed by men in Congress.

There needs to be significantly more education, and at earlier ages. I played volleyball at a HUGE football school in Pennsylvania where women's sports and men's sports were definitely not equal. We were booted out of our gym countless times when the football team came in out of the rain, our practice canceled no matter how big our game the next day. And the court that we shared with the basketball boys was swept for them *every day*, but we had to beg for a broom so that *we* could sweep our courts before home games. I had no idea that I might be able to do something about this.

At well-endowed institutions, the "easy" solution to complying with Title IX has been to expand the range of athletic teams available to women. Unfortunately, this is simply not an economic option for urban public schools. Oakland schools cannot procure new facilities in order to meet sex equity requirements. Downtown Oakland's students, from diverse backgrounds, face daily biases, the breadth of which even the census bureau cannot capture. They live in a country where rules, laws, and values have been determined by white middle-class men. This has kept minority groups isolated and insulated from one another; the obstacles each group faces vary, as do cultural values and gender expectations. For this reason, appealing to *all* these groups on the basis of "gender equity" is a complicated, difficult task.

Reviewing my students' term papers, I learned a great deal about how their own sports had suffered or benefited under Title IX—and the unique role of athletic directors and school environment. At least half of every class looked back at the treatment of female athletes in their high schools, pointing out that few teenage girls understood that Title IX also served K–12 students. Though aware of bias, as high school students, most had been reluctant to charge powerful male administrators with unfair practices. One GWU soccer player who had been a confident high school athlete did confront her vice principal, asking why he attended every boys' soccer game but never came to see the girls play. For challenging him, she received a week of detention.

The study of Title IX took root in women's and gender studies at Georgetown, spilling over into other dedicated classes on law and attracting undergraduate majors to write theses and editorials. In the spring of 1999, a women's studies major named Liz Bent wrote her thirty-five-page senior thesis on how Title IX had evolved at Georgetown. At the time of her work, she was captain of the coed sailing team and aspiring to Olympic competition. Liz discovered that while Georgetown had become fully coeducational in 1969, seven years later, it still did not offer a single athletic scholarship to women, although by then Title IX was mandated by law and undergraduate enrollment showed women in the majority. The university claimed that there were certainly opportunities for women to compete, despite the lack of available scholarships, but the athletic program of 1976 included 350 male athletes and only 99 females. When the university then voluntarily reviewed its Title IX compliance, athletics director Frank Rienzo wrote the following report: "The Athletic Department of Georgetown University is committed to providing equal opportunity for women in athletics. The commitment creates a problem of finances. To ensure women a comparable status with men in athletics requires a rigid fiscal belt-tightening process. . . . The only recourse, which is not a solution, is to delete from the men's activities and give to the women. This is not a completely satisfactory alternative, but is the only visible alternative at present, without developing new sources of revenue outside the University."[8]

In her thesis, Liz pointed out that no law asked for existing men's activities to be cut: "Although the Athletic Department said it was committed to building the women's program, it also made a point of saying that the men's program was being disadvantaged." Her research revealed a classic pattern in resistance to Title IX: the presumption that equal opportunities for women mandated losses for men. However, Liz found that Frank Rienzo then went on to campaign successfully for women's athletic scholarships. A 1981 report showed enormous gains. Twenty years later, Georgetown boasted top-ranked women's basketball, soccer, and lacrosse teams, though assistant athletic director Patricia Thomas was still the only female administrator in the athletics department. Disparities in the number of female coaches and, in particular, their salaries compared to what coaches of men's teams earned remained the biggest equity gap on a campus where athletics were a visible priority. When Liz presented her research at the annual senior-thesis banquet for women's studies majors, a packed room of other students and faculty gained inspiration to do further scholarly detective work on the timeline of Title IX compliance in their own university workplace.

In DC, I enhanced class discussions on Title IX by bringing in guest speakers, including Georgetown administrator Pat Thomas and GWU senior associate athletic director Mary Jo Warner. Both women had been competitive athletes, in gymnastics and tennis, respectively, before embarking on careers as influential and popular administrators. Student athletes were well acquainted with these campus figureheads and felt free to ask them questions in class. With my nonexistent budget for guest speakers, I was barely able to offer the women an iced coffee as thanks after their always informative presentations. My gratitude for their availability—and years of dedicated service—was far greater than a medium-sized latte might suggest. Few GWU students in class would ever forget the sight of stoic Mary Jo struggling to hold back tears as she recounted how, when she was an elite tennis player, both the men's and the women's tennis teams at her college won their championships—but the athletic department presented congratulatory varsity letters only to the men. Decades later, at a ceremony honoring returning female athletes, the college finally gave the tennis women the letters they had earned. Such were the smallest yet most meaningful acts in righting the wrongs of past sex discrimination in women's sports.

Mary Jo Warner fielded some tough questions from GWU students, explaining the university's Title IX path of expanding and adding women's teams, like varsity softball and lacrosse, on the new fields at the Mount Vernon campus. Students from the new women's softball team at GWU subsequently began enrolling in my class the next fall. What made their presence poignant was that while their new team definitely represented a Title IX victory, the coaches and players felt pressure to prove their athletic worth to the larger GWU community—not hard to do, as one early softball recruit, Elana Meyers, went on to earn three medals in the bobsled events of the Winter Olympic Games. But GWU's male baseball players, who still lacked a university-operated field, bitterly resented the construction of a state-of-the-art softball facility for women. And when I taught the exact same class three hours later over at Georgetown University, GWU's crosstown rival, I encountered bitterness from female softball players frustrated that GWU, and not Georgetown, had acquired the Mount Vernon junior college campus, the deal that had made possible the construction of GWU's softball space. In urban DC, just finding open fields that could accommodate women's team sports was a struggle; putting crew teams on the Potomac River became a solution for some schools. However, as a sport traditionally associated with elite White institutions, crew attracted and recruited very few women of color, noted in a critical 2003 study by the Women's Sports Foundation.[9]

What really worked to bring all women into better athletic options? From my stance behind the lectern, I watched these tense dynamics play out on each campus. During the month when Title IX dominates class discussion, students frequently talk about parents' roles in monitoring their daughters' opportunities. There's great hope pinned on fathers of daughters: the assumption is that, having played sports, older men wield more influence over other male critics and can make headway where female activists fail. One news story posted by the Women's Sports Foundation spotlighted a father who challenged the discrepancies between girls' and boys' fitness rooms at GAR High School in Wilkes-Barre, Pennsylvania. Richard Wren's son, not his daughter, attended GAR, thus increasing the aura of his heroism for acting on girls' equal opportunity. But my students also question why we always focus on the father-son or father-daughter connection: Don't mothers make a difference? Will mothers protect the legacy of Title IX for their daughters? Whatever happened to the battling PTA mom? Is her voice ineffective on sports issues? We still accept the cultural trope of Dad, not Mom, taking a daughter to a ball game and explaining the game as the more expert parent; few television ads or movies portray a mom with seasoned expertise coaching her daughter. How many generations of girls benefiting from the opportunities accelerated by Title IX or other sports expansions will it take until Americans accept the critical mass of grown-up, retired elite female athletes with wisdom to pass on as mentors and coaches? This is also an issue in the labor force. Where expertise is a commodity, the assumption that men will be more sports literate, with more of a lifetime of playing experience, leads to fewer organizations hiring women as referees, athletic directors, and sports commissioners.

One student tells me, "Although there are a lot of feminist moms who demand that Title IX be enforced, I don't see those women putting their behinds on a bleacher to watch *my* games." Another student shudders and adds that when we do see TV and film clips of mothers involved with competitive daughters, it's usually in the "mean mommy" role—the program *Dance Moms*; the film *I, Tonya*; or the sensationalist case of Wanda Webb Holloway, who in 1991 attempted to hire a hitman to kill the mother of her daughter's junior high cheerleading rival. Inevitably someone in class makes the point that men and male-headed companies have more money invested in sports, whereas feminists and "soccer moms" are perceived as occupying social spaces or donating to causes well outside the sports industry itself. At Georgetown, which saw many years of campus backlash against the women's studies major, some students feel that women in and out of governance are consulted on matters of policy only if they advance conservative viewpoints; they see many critiques of women in sports or in the military citing the Independent Women's Forum and Concerned Women for America. Activist mothers of all political stripes are also mothers of sons, as well as daughters, and too often the Title IX debate has been framed as a battle of the sexes for sports dollars. In DC, many Georgetown and GWU students worked as interns on Capitol Hill for representatives with strong traditional views. In those offices, my students might hear that collegiate women athletes are not really as invested in sports as men. Hearings on Capitol Hill included testimonials that Title IX was more damaging to sons than uplifting to daughters. As Mariah Burton Nelson put it, "Opponents no longer express worry about damage to women's delicate internal organs, as they did in the late 1800s, nor claim that women lack the endurance to sprint full court, as they did in the 1950s, nor fret that sports make women unfeminine, unattractive, or gay, as they did as recently as the 1990s. The twenty-first century argument goes like this: Title IX has 'gone too far.' It must be reformed because women's equality is hurting men."[10]

By 2011, policy guidelines for Title IX included addressing sexual harassment on campus. This shifted what most students knew about the law, as not all women played sports for a university team but many more had experienced some form of harassment. Some came to class already familiar with the Title IX compliance office as a place to report stalking, harassment, and inappropriate advances by faculty or staff. This range of concerns might seem very far away from equal funding of women's sports, until we remember that the original intention of Title IX law was to eliminate discrimination in all educational activities. The creation of a "hostile climate" at a school constitutes sex discrimination at its most daily and pervasive level: in one case, a family used Title IX to complain about the sexual harassment their young daughter experienced every day on her bus ride to school. Fear of entering a school bus, a classroom, a faculty mentor's office, or a training room affects the learning environment and a student's academic performance. As I observed personally through years of teaching at different institutions, some male professors evaluated female students' class presentations based on their looks, invited them to share hotel rooms at conferences, approached them romantically, and sent them inappropriate texts or emails. In class, we studied sexual harassment as a pervasive problem in different contexts: the film *The Invisible War* offered a sobering look at soldier-on-soldier rape in the US military, and *The Hunting Ground* shocked some viewers with its documentary candor on the subject of campus rape. The role of popular student athletes in sexual assault dominated headlines after Stanford swimmer Brock Turner was handed a light sentence for violating an unconscious classmate, from a judge who felt Turner had a promising future as an athlete. There were also homophobic coaches who made practice miserable for LGBT athletes and, certainly, female coaches who initiated inappropriate relationships with female athletes. These situations required support, confidence, and clear directives on process for any student athlete to initiate a Title IX complaint against a coach.

At the high school level, students who saw inappropriate behavior by a coach or teammate might experience retaliation if they reported it, but without action, the behavior continued.

On my high school baseball team, we had a true-blue collar coach straight out of East Baltimore who would tell us stories about strippers and drinking and crotch grabs that I'm sure some of the priests overheard at my Catholic high school. We would line up for sprints around the bases, and the last guy around, or whoever got on coach's nerves most in practice, had to suffer the indignity of running the entire field with a bra on. "BRING OUT THE BRASSIERE," he'd scream. I'm sure if I went to a coed high school, this guy would have been fired in the first week. I felt bad for the players who were freshmen—or unpopular—because the humiliation did not roll off them too easily. It insinuated that to be a girl on a baseball field was as embarrassing as it can get.

While I was reporting on [a certain abusive player], he came to my office twice: once to threaten me personally and once to threaten to burn the office down.

Title IX protections are also limited to educational institutions that receive federal funding. More and more university coaches and trainers are being held accountable for ongoing or past abuse of student athletes, but in the larger public sphere, just off campus, students find abusive attitudes expressed quite openly by men in positions of authority, as one young woman told me:

I work at a sports bar where the police eat and drink at a huge discount. It's a big police hangout, an atmosphere of unchecked hegemonic masculinity, a "safe" place for men to "be men." It seems like there's this enormous connection between that behavior and sports—and it's so much worse on game days. I've never felt the need to speak up until last night. As I was delivering drinks to the bar, one policeman said, "What do 10,000 abused women have in common?" The answer: "They don't know how to fucking listen." Wow. The bartender thought it was so funny he retold it to a couple of guys. The policeman saw the look on my face and went, "What? Are you offended or something?" I know people have gotten fired for upsetting the "regulars." But I told him I thought it was a disgusting joke, not at all funny, and to please remember that there were women here. The scary thing is that this is the group of men I'm supposed to call if my partner abuses me.

With my advance warning that these discussions might be triggering for those still battling posttraumatic stress from sexual assault, some students skip class on the days we look at athletes and abuse. Others plunge into the heart of the problem: How does sports culture create disrespect for women? Does it begin when coaches put down anything female, using the female anatomy as an insult to goad male players, cursing them as playing "like ladies," and other misogyny? We read Jessica Luther's text *Unsportsmanlike Conduct*, which looks at how the NCAA and media handle college football players charged with assault. Among the most chilling contributions in class come from student athletes who say they feel assaults on female athletes are "payback" for Title IX and should be expected. Making room for women in sports, some students believe, cost men too dearly.

The zero-sum game spilled over into campus discussion. In the CNN series *First Ladies*, Georgetown University history professor Marcia Chatelain spoke to White Americans' fear of diversity, citing the racist backlash directed toward Barack and Michelle Obama as the nation's first African American occupants of the White House. Chatelain saw the struggle for Black visibility as threatening to many White Americans, some of whom equated the ascent of a few people of color into national roles with White disappearance. A similar theory may be applied to the backlash against women's sports, symbolized by Title IX. The specter of women's athletic access causing men's programs to disappear became a rallying cry against legitimate equal access. Donna Lopiano, executive director of the Women's Sports Foundation, once told *Time* magazine that "the attitude for too long was that it was O.K. for women to have equal opportunity only after every boy who wants to has the right to play and never loses that right."[11] Not all men experience equality as a loss. But Title IX has also drawn criticism from conservatives simply for being a government program. At Georgetown, a proudly conservative student athlete in my class wrote her Title IX paper on what she saw as the immorality of benefiting from any government handout. While she recognized that she was a beneficiary of Title IX in terms of the allocation of women's athletic scholarships, she remained ambivalent. She added that of course she saw the irony in her politics, because so many male athletes she knew had enjoyed preferential admissions status at their colleges nationwide *as athletes*, some avidly recruited regardless of their academic preparedness.

In her article "Where Are All the Women Coaches?," *New York Times* author Lindsay Crouse commented, "Now the United States produces many of the best female athletes in the world. But that equality stops at graduation. . . . Today we raise our little girls to follow their dreams and to excel. That is, until they become women and expect to be paid for it."[12] Title IX originally expanded and protected women's access to education. Athletic scholarships put thousands on the path to college, and a college education put graduates on the path to better employment opportunities. Still unresolved is the pay scale awaiting most women in the workforce. But editorializing only goes so far in America's culture wars; more often, opinions are shaped by personal encounters—such as seeing how a daughter's second-rate facilities affect the outcome of her game. Here's a memory.

One year, staying late on campus to grade midterm exams, I skipped dinner and took in a Georgetown women's game. It was a bitterly cold and snowy night at the end of regular basketball season, just before the NCAA championships, with Georgetown's women playing a Big East home game against Connecticut—the number one seed in the country at that moment. McDonough Arena was packed to the rafters with women's basketball fans. I was lucky to find a seat close to the court.

I watched UConn's star player, Diana Taurasi, warm up. Arms akimbo, she let the player ahead of her take a shot, clapped her hands twice, lowered her head, and charged through the pregame drill. A dozen little girls clutching bright yellow disposable cameras hovered at the edge, snapping photos, until one mom dragged her daughter away and up into the high bleachers. "No! No!" the kid cried. "You ruined it! I wanna be down there—I wanna watch it from there." *Flick. Whoosh. Flick.* Diana Taurasi slapped the outstretched palm of a teammate on crutches who was unable to play this game, so I went over to greet my own Georgetown student, Joi Irby, also sidelined by recent ACL surgery.

I watched woman after woman pour into the old gym until no space was left for any fan to wedge onto the cramped plastic bleachers. Why weren't we playing in the Verizon Center, like the Georgetown men's team, where some of us old grown-ups, exhausted from weeks of shoveling snow and walking to campus on ice, could lean back in actual seats? But here we were, at the second-rate facility, midwinter backache and papers to grade be damned, as my Georgetown students took on the best team in the land. My worlds collided when UConn coach Geno Auriemma came over to shake Joi Irby's hand. And the game began.

Oh, the beautiful use of space, the side shots, the drive down the court, the release of the ball like a spray of fountain water, a perfect arc through the air. Taurasi shot from behind her back, across the court, and my Georgetown Athletics and Gender student Nok Duany sank a three-point shot. It was 22–40 at halftime, Georgetown heads still held high. The Hoya team was global feminism in action, fielding student athletes I knew had been recruited from Cameroon, Sudan, Hungary, and the Caribbean islands.

And then the ancient scoreboard quit. There, at peak drama, with the object in motion preferring to stay in motion, all action had to be halted, and an uncomfortable long break followed as officials worked desperately to fix the old electrical connection. The players cooled down; their bodies chilled and began cramping; they glared at the wall. The score disappeared, feebly came back to life, disappeared again. There, in our nation's capital, a whiff of "separate but unequal" lingered in the old "women's gym." It was at that moment that I heard a frustrated, tuition-paying Georgetown dad call out loudly, "What's the score?" giving me the eventual title for this book. And just behind me, another man whispered to his wife, "Well! I can certainly see why the *men* don't play here."

Fig. 5.1 Author atop Dragon's Back Trail, Hong Kong,
Semester at Sea, 2019. *Photo by Kinsey Holloway.*

GLOBAL ENCOUNTERS WITH WOMEN'S SPORTS

Teaching Students at Sea

As an ambassador of global feminism, on three occasions I took my student athletes and my Athletics and Gender curriculum around the world. The world revealed to us both the far-reaching impact of American-brand marketing and the limits on female athleticism imposed by cultures with strict customs of sex segregation. But we also attended games, learned new disciplines of health and wellness, and pushed the limits of our own physical endurance as travelers.

Our physical appearances, clothing, and gestures frequently signaled or symbolized American power, sexuality, and wealth to those we met. For women particularly, acts of public fitness taken for granted at home, such as morning jogs in running shorts, were transgressive and culturally offensive, depending on the political landscape. But where individual workout displays clashed with local sensibilities, communal exercises with local community members beckoned us to authentic participation: Tai chi in the parks of Shanghai and Beijing. Yoga retreats in Myanmar and India. Hiking Dragon's Back Trail high above Hong Kong (see fig. 5.1.). Joining unexpectedly hardy elders in ascending Mount Huangshan in China's Yellow Mountains. Camel treks in Morocco, capoeira in Brazil. And for the young women students in my care, travel far beyond the United States sparked new questions and experiences of the body: In countries with stricter codes of modesty and dress, why were so many older women able to relax without self-consciousness in traditional women's bathhouses?

Our learning curve grew by latitude and longitude.

How did I adapt the women's sports seminar to include a more global focus? For an American professor like myself, with a purposeful but largely US history syllabus, it hardly sufficed to start by throwing a few international athletes into our class conversations. That sort of limited lens, spotlighting global athletic celebrity with no context, is familiar and comfortable, an approach constructed for American viewers through decades of Olympic Games coverage. I wanted to challenge my class and myself to go beyond the collectible-Olympic-fashion-dolls model of sports diversity.

In the digital era, merely having access to online resources of international sports journalism did not make our understanding or our politics more regional, no matter how many of my assignments required a variety of global perspectives or extended our discussions of discrimination at home to include challenges for women and girls around the globe. In and beyond the United Nations, most countries have no equivalent to Title IX and no comparable platform guaranteeing female athletes' opportunities while they are enrolled in school. Moreover, holding up American policy as a benchmark for female athletic opportunity avoided holding our home country accountable for its own brand of ongoing race and sex discrimination in sports. Looking at sports as quasi-religious rituals, as sacred games, brought us closer to the cross-cultural origins of athletic performance, but it also tempted my students to view unfamiliar practices as "exotic." Like everything else about the class, the international component evolved over time, informed by world events—which in our own US society built on intersecting responses to war, communism, feminism, terrorism, globalization, and Olympic spectacle.

In preparation for a more international focus, I began by asking the class to consider how often athletic identity and *American* identity are used interchangeably. Our national culture is based on winning—the West, the Super Bowl, the world wars. I shared that in the thousands of college papers and Advanced Placement exams in US history I've evaluated, I often found students describing American heritage as a giant sports event: "Then George Washington stepped up to the plate," "Democracy came into play," "You could say this general was not a team player." We returned to the sports metaphors we had listed on the first day of class, the telltale idioms of American slang, up to and including

"Three strikes, and you're out," a phrase now emblematic of racial bias in prison sentencing. In American writing, there's an easy association between male athleticism and leadership, or power, but that is not the same measure of manhood in all cultures. What about American slang for women in sports? Students jumped in with the very US-specific nickname "soccer mom." How many times had that phrase been used to describe a social address or even a haircut rather than a sports role? At rallies around Washington, DC, my students observed women holding up colorful signs that stated "Soccer Mom for Peace," while policemen patrolling these events grumbled that such assignments forced them out into the cold when they could be at home watching Sunday football. Soccer moms were making more of a statement about being a serious voting bloc than about athleticism. And America's politicians might court soccer moms for a particular kind of vote yet fail to bring American women to the policy table as leaders—medical, political, or educational—making decisions on athletics.

I soon identified key biases in the outlook of my American students. First, the twentieth century had set up certain foreign countries as our rivals in sports glory, and these rivalries were nourished by US foreign policy. For more than seventy years, communist regimes were the enemy, and during the Cold War, American athletes met with these Eastern counterparts only on the playing field. Because socialist governments vastly outpaced the United States in training young female athletes to compete on the world stage, such as in China, East Germany, North Korea, the Soviet Union, Romania, Czechoslovakia, and more, female strength and muscularity became markers of the possibly doped womanhood of enemy regimes, not levels of conditioning all athletes might aspire to. These politics exacerbated pressure on American women athletes to present an outer gloss of commercialized Western femininity. In the 1970s, doping scandals and defection to the United States by talents such as Martina Navratilova and Nadia Comăneci reinforced self-serving American narratives about the costs of having one's athletic career and body controlled by a totalitarian state.

As critic Cynthia Enloe demonstrates in her research, globalization in the 1980s and 1990s meant that in places like Vietnam, the Philippines, the Mariana Islands, and rural China, more girls were making Nike sneakers than competing in them. By the 1990s, when the Cold War ended and the Berlin Wall came down, US political interests shifted to identifying terrorism rather than communism, and a new Islamophobic discourse flavored Olympic contests. Both right-wing and feminist organizations critiqued Muslim-majority nations where laws discouraged or prohibited women from competing at the Olympics; Saudi Arabia, with the strictest controls over public display of women's bodies, did not include a female athlete on its team until the London 2012 Olympic Games. Frustration with the slow pace of change made uneasy bedfellows of feminist groups and conservative think tanks looking to demonize Islam, but few Americans, including my students, could list the many Muslim women athletes who had already won gold medals.

We looked carefully at the select foreign news headlines steering Western readers to critique Muslim, Arab, and African countries in terms of women's sports. From Iran: "Promiscuous Women Cause Earthquakes, Iran Cleric Says."[1] From Turkey: "Womanhood Is Dying at the Olympics."[2] From Nigeria: "Sponsors Avoid Funding Women's Teams over Fears of Lesbianism."[3] It is easy to find voices such as these in the global press. Yet similar biases are also found in American history and American journalism. In 2001, prominent clergymen Jerry Falwell and Pat Robertson blamed gays and lesbians for bringing down God's punishment on the United States in the form of the 9/11 attacks. A cowboy cookbook popular during my father's young adulthood warned that the mere presence of a menstruating woman in the kitchen would cause homemade mayonnaise to curdle. I suggested to my students that anyone might pull random examples from America's biased opinion makers and proceed to generalize about the limited status of women in the United States. Instead, we could discover what different women worldwide were achieving as national athletes.

If politics and religion were responsible for many ingrained biases, there were also Hollywood film stereotypes to unlearn. On that first day of class, when we shared our own preconceived sports stereotypes, some students had suggested that Asian athletes were usually found in the martial arts. The big-screen and TV movies popularized during the 1970s, featuring Bruce Lee, and then the 1980s' Karate Kid franchise gave American viewers a superficial knowledge of karate, kung fu, and Asian culture. The mid-1970s also offered Americans a television series called *Kung Fu*, with the lead role played by a White actor, David Carradine, portraying a Chinese American warrior. There followed the 1974 disco hit "Kung Fu Fighting," and other pop-culture swipes at Asian athleticism appeared in references to President Nixon's "Ping-Pong diplomacy" with China. A more disturbing personal memory from my own third-grade classroom of 1970 is how my Japanese American best friend suffered the pejorative nickname "Karate Chop" from White boys on the playground. In 2020, Americans heard President Donald Trump refer to the COVID-19 virus as "the kung flu," disparaging its presumed Chinese origins; a surge in hate crimes against Asian Americans followed in 2021. Likewise, dramatic sword fights and facial scars designating *the bad guy* have long characterized Middle Eastern men on-screen. These aspects associate "foreign" masculinity with aggressive weaponry or sudden-attack cunning, familiar tropes for an enemy. But ironically, that stereotyped scariness factor could be appropriated for athletic purposes: Southern California's Coachella Valley High School has used an "Arab" mascot for its football team since the 1920s, complete with a beard and headscarf, as well as belly dancers at halftime.[4]

To balance these lingering images of war, enemy, and weaponry, I had to familiarize my students not only with a range of international sports but also with the possibilities of sports as diplomacy. Some diplomatic initiatives are sponsored by the US Department of State, which uses popular athletes as global goodwill ambassadors, as historian Ashley Brown addresses in her research on Black tennis champion Althea Gibson. There is a State Department initiative called Empowering Women and Girls through Sports, and UNESCO's home page states that "UNESCO, as the United Nations lead agency for Physical Education and Sport (PES), considers and adopts sports as a vital medium for Peace and Development." But I also began enhancing my syllabus with information and guests from organizations like Seeds of Peace, PeacePlayers International, and Sport 4 Peace. These successful programs bring together children from opposing communities to play sports: Israelis, Palestinians, and Egyptians; Protestant and Catholic youth in Northern Ireland; conflicting tribal groups in South Sudan; Greek and Turkish-affiliated children in divided Cyprus; and those of postapartheid South Africa.

Administrators of these excellent initiatives often find that it's difficult for girls in troubled communities, especially refugee camps, to participate in sports programs. Girls not only are culturally forbidden to mix with boys but are also often responsible for fetching water and kindling, preparing food, and caring for younger siblings. Sports equipment donated to villages and refugee camps usually ends up in the possession of boys. To foster gender equity, the Sport 4 Peace program sent women athletes with pop-up travel "gyms" into Iraq and Afghanistan, offering free basketball and volleyball clinics that preserve customs of sex segregation and modesty while training a new generation of girls. Sport 4 Peace staff also ran a Sport for Life Peace Camp for Palestinian and Israeli girls. We learned how Afghan women were able to represent national team fandom in accepted, if vicarious, athletic roles as television sports reporters.

In class, we watched films like *Thin Ice*, *Chak De! India*, and *Zanzibar Soccer Queens*, celebrating women and girls whose talents helped them excel in athletic events traditionally reserved for men and boys. *Thin Ice* looks at a Himalayan women's ice hockey team, which depends on recruiting girls from Muslim, Hindu, and Buddhist villages and succeeds by having women's village councils prevail on male village elders for permission and support. *Chak De! India* is the story of an unemployed men's soccer coach in India who agrees to take over a women's team, creating a champion group from girls representing every national culture, language, and tradition, including girls whose families pressure them to quit and accept arranged marriages just before the championship game. *Zanzibar Soccer Queens* explores an adult women's league on the conservative Muslim island east of Tanzania, showing that while some husbands oppose their wives participating in recreational sports, for the women on the team, soccer is a means for staying healthy, getting off drugs, leaving sex work, and bringing pride and income to their community. And we were learning that for many talented young girls across the African continent, the real barrier to participation in a sports workout—or a school day—was lack of access to affordable sanitary napkins.

The unit on international sports was a gateway for us to talk about how and why soccer, in the United States, is seen as a sport played by White girls, whereas in the rest of the world that is hardly the case. Soccer's relatively late arrival in the United States meant that its status as a masculine sport in much of Europe and South America competed with already established American football, baseball, and basketball. During one of our class discussions, I heard a member of the men's basketball team jeer that in *his* Atlanta community, soccer players were called "grass fairies." As youth soccer was introduced to the United States in the 1970s, the decade of Title IX feminism, many young American women like myself learned soccer at the same time we were learning about our own rights. This combination produced two generations of World Cup victors who were also articulate spokeswomen for girls' athletic opportunities. However, with most colleges' facilities constructed for sports like football, track, and basketball, adding a soccer field was an expensive prospect, particularly for landlocked urban schools. In this way, soccer became identified with affluent suburbs that boasted more green spaces, where girls, often White, began youth competition with a "safe" contact sport. Politicians soon courted the soccer mom, whose socioeconomic address in a higher tax bracket might mean a vote to protect property values. This of course contrasts ironically with the role of a "soccer mom" in, say, a Guatemalan or Palestinian village. But in the United States, as suburban soccer teams grew, college-bound young women soon expected to continue playing on athletic scholarships. To be in compliance with Title IX, expanding women's opportunities based on interest, some schools added women's soccer as a Division I sport yet did not add men's, arguing that male students were more interested in basketball, football, and baseball. For some of these reasons, women's soccer in America became more successful and high profile than men's, if woefully underfunded professionally. At the same time, in some parts of the world, like Brazil, women weren't allowed to play the game at all.

But it was one thing to bring *in* global women's sports narratives. The real shift in viewpoint and awareness required me to take my class around the world. In addition to many years teaching women's sports history stateside at George Washington University, Georgetown, Saint Mary's College, and UC Berkeley, I also taught it at sea. And I hope to do so again.

On three different voyages, I was a women's studies professor aboard the global Semester at Sea program, which since 1963 has taken college students and faculty around the world every semester for an experiential learning voyage: ten or twelve countries over one hundred days. I first taught on Semester at Sea as a young professor in the fall of 1993, when I was barely ten years older than the students in my classes on board. Then I returned in 2004 and again in 2019, older and wiser, and adapted my women's sports course to our international itinerary. Passport, visas, malaria medication, and water bottles in my battered backpack, I took American student athletes through Brazil, Cambodia, China, Cuba, Egypt, Ghana, Greece, Hong Kong, Japan, India, Malaysia, Mauritius, Morocco, Myanmar, Russia, South Africa, South Korea, Taiwan, Turkey, and Vietnam.

For each semester at sea, preparing syllabi and coordinating in-country dialogues and field programs took up to a year and a half of planning. Moreover, the shifting geopolitical landscape and US foreign policies made travel to certain regions unwelcome, unpredictable, or just plain banned, although that could change in an instant: the key word with Semester at Sea was always *flexibility*. For me, crucial experiences on my first voyage in 1993 informed my opportunity to introduce Athletics and Gender aboard Semester at Sea in 2004 and 2019. I knew from that initial journey to assign shorter, succinct readings specific to the ports on our itinerary and to accept that the combination of a rough sea and malaria medication would limit homework focus even in the most studious of students. I also knew there was a dedicated place for a course on sports culture in a community of young Americans far from home. I saw how, cut off from their usual campus spaces, taking leave from teams and practices and the comfort of working out at the gym or sports club, students grew panicky about staying in shape as they traveled the world—especially when the open buffet at mealtimes and special banquet events permitted easy weight gain, no matter how many rigorous land hikes we completed. Geopolitically, that Global North / First World self-consciousness about gaining weight or maintaining a "bikini body" in a student community that was 75 percent female contrasted starkly with the poverty and famine we encountered in the Global South. For too many of the working poor in urban and agricultural cultures we saw, *exercise* was the built-in daily demand of hard labor under the hot sun, not the privilege of leisure time in a country club. Yet every community had its games and recreation, whether for the very rich or the very poor. What my students noticed was that while elite daughters often had access to private sports facilities and might play certain games like squash, laboring daughters didn't join in the street-soccer games organized by their brothers. Girls had double duty of factory work and housework. However, girls, as well as boys, were often raised to know and perform the traditional, sacred dances of their heritage, and we attended these skilled performances. Instead of soccer, traditional dance movement was the activity most likely to be part of women's and girls' lives, and it was often the most accessible event for us to attend as guests and participants.

Traveling on Semester at Sea, American student athletes saw first-hand how national teams and international sports competitions up to and including the Olympics and the World Cup offered a way out of poverty—and into funded acclaim on the world stage. But how did custom and culture shape ideals of international sports glory for girls? Could women athletes succeed as respected mediators between warring nations? In refugee camps where so many of the world's displaced children struggle to survive, were global health and development funds for youth distributed so that sports opportunities, training, and equipment reached girls, as well as boys? We saw how the comportment of a female champion could break barriers for those who followed—or create a perception of dishonor with deadly repercussions back home. Chaperoning and housing, media attention and team uniforms all shaped a woman's reputation if and when she left home for international competition. As in the United States, sports also offered a way for isolated youth to travel abroad and bring resources back home to family and community, generating pride. The potential for success as a national symbol gave women and girls new agency in regions where poverty—plus cultural preference for sons—too often led desperate families to choose female infanticide. When female wrestler Sakshi Malik won India's first medal at the 2016 Olympic Games, Indian cricket icon Virender Sehwag tweeted, "#SakshiMalik is a reminder of what cn happen if u don't kill a girl child."[5]

The biggest challenge for some American students on Semester at Sea was seeing and negotiating limitations on female roles. They'd been raised to believe or at least discuss the impact of second-wave feminism on female opportunity in America, and they now struggled to take in the reality that women were far from liberated. In most of the regions we visited, gender roles reinforced a rigid binary of male versus female behavior codes, dress, and honor. Entire villages or city streets might appear to be populated only by men and boys, with women and girls shielded behind house walls or, if venturing into public life, covered from head to toe. Children at play were almost always boys, kicking a soccer ball or cane ball made out of anything from duct tape to coconut fibers. Small girls of four were already busy tending even younger children or assisting mothers with housework and chores. Our Westernized concepts of play, sports, workouts, and sportswear were all challenged as soon as we left the ship. Here were the communities where our casual, affordable American workout clothes were manufactured, usually by very young and underpaid women.

We, however, were no strangers to our hosts, as American sports media had reached into nearly every corner worldwide, setting up expectations of what Americans and American athletes were like. The media-manufactured popularity of Black sports figures meant that all too often, the few African American males in my Semester at Sea classes were mobbed by children shouting, "Michael Jordan!" and "Kobe!"

For my students, one surprise was discovering how much dance played a role in men's and women's lives across the world. Village mothers who had never taken PE or joined a sports team, octogenarians bent from a life span of toil, and female toddlers alike hurried forward to initiate us in traditional women's dances. These often strenuous, long-lasting performances—in India, China, Japan, South Korea, Ghana, Malaysia, and Morocco—were not tourist-level routines; stripped of the gratuitous sexuality found in movies meant for men's eyes, authentic women's dances spoke to community, tribal and national identity, village pride, and female life rituals. Many were the pulled muscles in our group as we struggled to keep up with energetic female elders who demanded that we join in for hours. How could we resist, when, on one memorable occasion, the sacred dance was a celebration of having received government funds to build safe housing for women? Our female hosts in Kerala, India, had just shown skeptics a thing or two by completing a challenge to build a house in twenty-five days with twenty-five women laborers; their collective had dashed from the shining work site to join in the celebratory dance gathering. Tears and sweat streaming down our faces, my students and I humbly accepted the honor of lighting an oil lamp to bless female power as the village leader offered prayers of gratitude—and then we rejoined the ecstatic dance floor. Back in the United States, I had observed similar athleticism from otherwise traditional matriarchs at ultra-Orthodox Jewish weddings, where male-only circle dances or whirling aunts and sisters celebrate a marriage, as the chaste bride and groom may not dance together. On Semester at Sea, my student voyagers could see in action the concepts we had already studied in American sports history: women's muscular performance is allowed and even approved if it is somehow linked back to family roles and ritual life stages.

Intense discussion of these issues was particularly intimate on my first voyage in 1993, when I sailed with 550 students and faculty aboard the old SS *Universe*. It was a preinternet voyage; my students and I recorded our impressions in journals and on predigital cameras. We were completely cut off from family and friends and home for weeks at a time, with unreliable mail delivery in most ports. The built-up need to share feelings and describe encounters spilled over into class discussions more immediately than in later voyages. These experiences resulted in lessons and materials on gendered sports culture that I later used to construct a shipboard sports class in 2004 and 2019.

It was thrilling to travel with students who chose to look at sports and gender across cultures. In Japan, we encountered kindergarten class sandpits that were not recess sandboxes but serious practice circles for future sumo wrestlers. We attended baseball games where young men, not women, were the section cheerleaders and the stadium snack was squid on a stick. In China, a thoughtful young man named Ocean told us that his country's one-child policy for population control had unintentionally resulted in a surplus of overprotected boys. Ocean longed to learn how to swim, bike, and box, but the aging parents who relied on his support feared he might get hurt—so no sports. And when I took my students into the jungles of Sarawak on Borneo, as guests of a traditional tribe, we learned a most surprising Athletics and Gender lesson. Because I was the leader of our group and an unmarried woman, I was made "an honorary man" and taught to hunt with a blowpipe. In a country with many complex practices of cross-dressing and transgender performance, I was casually welcomed as an athlete and warrior, invited to sit beside the tribe's medicine man at night and instructed in manly arts of hunting by day.

Handed an enormous blowpipe about three or four feet long, I aimed at the tree target and with my second dart hit the bull's-eye—greatly impressing the male students in my group, who complained, "You made it look easy." The Iban men offered me a live piglet as a prize, a touching gesture I had to decline, but I left with my own *sumpit* and *temilah* blow-dart gear. As we prepared to depart, I pressed the warm hands of as many women as possible, and they nodded at me: the he/she, the woman who played men's games, the woman who hit the mark, the childless warrior who took no husband.

What followed was yet another lesson in cultural ideas about female strength. As our tour guide drove us back to the airport, late for our flight, there was no time for a rest stop. I had certainly planned to change back into the long dress and clean headscarf I had donned at the start of this field program. Walking into Kuching International Airport, I looked so fierce and grimy that I was instantly stopped by security police, separated from my class, patted down and frisked, and taken to a detention chamber. As I'd not seen a mirror in two days, I was mystified by so much fuss. Then I realized I was still wearing a blowpipe and poison darts strapped around my hips.

I nervously explained to the officials that I had just escorted twenty students to a traditional longhouse visit and that the darts were merely a gift from our kind hosts. No, they were not poison tipped. In fact, they weren't even sharp enough to puncture a piece of paper, if they'd allow me to demonstrate; this was a souvenir set, not a real quiver of darts. Finally, one official interrupted me with a challenge: "So. You seem to like the cultures of Malaysia. Will you root for Malaysia in the World Cup?"

With all my heart, I gave thanks for those adolescent summers at Rainbow Soccer Camp in Chapel Hill, North Carolina. I told my detainers that not only would I cheer for Malaysia, but I had played soccer too. "No," they all responded at once. "Women don't play soccer." This was 1993, six years before global broadcasts of the winning US women's team. Right there in that airport office, I demonstrated on a handy grapefruit a few fancy moves I'd learned at age fourteen, juggling off my knee and ankle, and the officials were so impressed I was let go. Once again, proficiency in a male skill had raised my stature and served me well. I nuanced interrogation at customs by invoking the universal language of sports, a language connecting men in a brotherhood of soccer across borders. A different woman, unfamiliar with "the beautiful game," would have been shut out of that friendly conversation—and missed her plane. So do sports, gender, and politics intersect: the main theme of our class.

The 1993 and 2004 voyages brought us to baseball games in countries both capitalist (Japan) and communist (Cuba). By 2004, incoming students were better prepared to analyze gender as it applied to sports worldwide, but they were less nuanced in approaching racism and colonization, particularly when we arrived in South Africa. Only nine or ten years old when apartheid was overthrown and Nelson Mandela liberated from prisoner to president of a new South Africa, my American students had no context for the long years of antiapartheid activism familiar to many of their professors. My class toured the District Six Museum of Cape Town, then hosting an exhibit titled *(Dis)playing the Game: A Celebration of More Than a Century of Sport*. This included photographs of the many Black and "coloured" teams from the apartheid era, explaining to visitors that people of color had "developed sport as a site of political resistance, particularly . . . when political organizations were banned." These rare club-sport images represented women and girls, as well as men and boys, as local, indigenous, successful, and "banned" athletes, depending.

More than in any other port on Semester at Sea's itinerary, South Africa compelled students to compare separation by race. In South Africa, we juxtaposed apartheid with Jim Crow law, Negro League baseball, and other segregated games and facilities in US history. The Hollywood film *Invictus* and John Carlin's book *Playing the Enemy* are popular sources showing how men's rugby helped heal postapartheid South Africa, but first, I immersed my class in the 1980s global boycott of South Africa's White-only teams. *Arms Linked: Women against the Tour* is one unique book of poetry and prose by women in New Zealand who rallied in opposition to their nation hosting the 1981 Springbok Tour. The book speaks to the gender divide in New Zealand sports diplomacy at the time, as athletes weighed whether or not to play against an apartheid team. Male sports fans, both Pakeha (White) and Maori, loudly favored meeting and beating South Africa's Springbok team on the field. Women demanded a boycott and faulted men for wanting the show to go on. Some Maori men believed the traditional performance of the haka warrior dance as a game-opening team ritual made their politics clearer than any paper statement. These readings and conversations, which we held with staff at the District Six Museum, energized student athletes on Semester at Sea to look at the unfinished dismantling of racism in their home sports communities. We also visited the gender studies program at the University of Cape Town and discussed the 1984 Olympic Games, where White runner Zola Budd, banned from representing apartheid South Africa, had competed under the British flag and in a much-debated incident accidentally tripped American runner Mary Decker. When American fans booed and hissed Zola Budd, were they booing apartheid; showing

US loyalty to Decker; or enjoying the classic "catfight" encouraged by Western media, which so often set up good girl / bad girl rivalries at the Olympics?

The stark contrast between affluent White Cape Town and its gleaming luxury beaches, packed with recreational facilities, and the poverty of townships just out of sight presented a clear challenge to some Semester at Sea students. A few who wanted to avoid engaging in any sociopolitical analysis did so by opting out of more-serious field programs and instead literally jumping into kinetic recreation: hang gliding, bungee jumping, parasailing, and swimming with sharks—activities that cost hundreds or thousands of dollars and circumvented meetings with township residents and other cultural exchanges. In group discussions after we left South Africa, some Semester at Sea staff, as well as students, defended their choices in athletic terms—that after weeks of having been cooped up on board with limited gym equipment, they simply craved a physical workout adventure on land. However, some of the best writing that my sports and gender students handed in addressed head-on the ways that sports functioned as a handily escapist, apolitical space for those with privilege to avoid other concerns. In 2004, Black students on our voyage convened a panel on race and racism for the shipboard community in the wake of the South Africa visit. In the voyage video made by staff filmmaker Greg Ritchie, one of my students from spring 2004 speaks directly into the camera, saying that what sparked so much feeling for her was seeing the mistreatment of "people who looked like me."

For the female majority on Semester at Sea, ambivalence about the body appeared both in research papers and in field-trip journals. Many young women were brand new to world travel. All students were free to dress quite casually aboard the ship, and with a ratio of three females to every one male student, swimwear-clad flirtation marked time at sea in between classes. And a friendly rivalry among the shipboard residence halls, or "seas," culminated in the much-anticipated Sea Olympics midpoint in the voyage. Pool games, dance contests, and tug-of-war on deck added physical intimacy, as well as opportunities to show off beachwear and suntans. The daily dean's memo and various signs around the ship implored, "Please do not wear wet bathing suits into the Dining Room." This freedom to reveal curves and skin then ended abruptly each time we entered ports with strict standards of dress, where young women might be sent back on board if they disembarked in cleavage-exposing tank tops. "But it's so hot here!" was a common protest by some students who weren't fully prepared to emulate the practices or dignified stoicism of our cloth-swathed female guides. At the same time that American students demanded the right to expose their shoulders, knees, and necklines, when given the opportunity to undress altogether in the company of local women, many recoiled.

In three different ports, South Korea, Turkey, and Morocco, I took female students with me to a women's bathhouse: the traditional hammam or the modern Korean spa, a site for steaming, soaking, singing, exfoliating, and exchanging gossip, where relaxed nudity beckoned beyond the closed doors of women-only space. Although the student athletes were accustomed to female gym changing rooms associated with sports-club spaces or women's team locker rooms, getting naked with three generations of local families for a scrub and soak proved intimidating. The vulnerability of physical nakedness brought up every student's anxiety about her perceived imperfections. Embarrassment, physical competitiveness, distorted body image, and complex eating disorders made it difficult for anyone to admit to liking her own body. "I hated it," the students wrote later. "I feel so fat in my own skin." "Why can't I have the peaceful self-acceptance of these wrinkled old ladies?"

Though it was not easy, we soon spent hours in class talking about the mixed messages of American culture: be fit and sexy, always measuring yourself against other women's bodies while remaining at war with your own through diet and low self-esteem. It was clear that we could hardly expect to jump into dialogues with women from different cultures when we often resisted discussing the differences among ourselves. Had sports opportunities improved any of these issues for my students' generation? Who was happier in her body—the exposed American or the well-covered Moroccan matron? Athletes who were young women of color took the lead in these discussions, quick to point out that in fact *White* beauty standards were part of what we'd all packed in our travel baggage from America. Students identifying as Tamil (Sri Lankan) and African American offered these comments:

> In the baths, where everyone was equal in dress (or lack thereof), those who felt comfortable with their bodies enjoyed the massage, while those who were not as comfortable felt violated and ashamed. Several seasons of aquatic sports in high school prepared me for personal exposure. I

reminded myself that I had no need for shame. I see how competition and obsession with fashion and fitness has made the American woman fear her own body, and I'm not sure what kind of statement that makes about sisterhood in the United States.

Why do we have false modesty in the company of other women? If a woman had shown up in a miniskirt in Puritan days, she would have been flogged or called sinful, even called a witch. Yet in our lifetimes, on TV the *Brady Bunch* girls wore miniskirts to school and were considered America's purest daughters.

Predictably, back on board, we moved into debates about the veil and the burka, as well as the Western association of "liberation" with more-revealing styles of dress. By 2019, this included discussion of the fashion "burkini," a more modest swimwear that Aheda Zanetti had designed for active Muslim women. Although the burkini made it possible for more religious women and girls to take part in athletic pursuits, ranging from lifeguard work to competitive swimming, the adapted swimsuit had already been banned on at least one beach in France. In remarkable contrast, the all-body swimsuit for women had become controversial just as Olympic men began competing in streamlined bodysuits—for elite male swimmers, the new and must-have expensive racing uniform. Additionally, there was not any *one* Muslim cultural response to the female body in a state of private exposure or exercise: Women might be cheerfully naked in the traditional bathhouses of Turkey and Morocco, but in 2013, when I spoke at the Gathering of All Leaders in Sport conference in Doha, Qatar, I found a different mood in the ultramodern women's sport club. There, locker-room signs informed patrons that a naked body was offensive and that women should cover up quickly when changing.

For students invested in looking good in sportswear, Semester at Sea offered multiple approaches to the politics of global manufacturing. Both business courses and women's studies included perspectives on women's labor in the free-trade zones, sometimes with actual tours of Nike companies and other brand sites in China, Vietnam, and elsewhere. However, while student activism around sportswear sweatshop conditions dominated Georgetown University in 2001, with campus sit-ins demanding accountability from the campus bookshop for purchases from offshore suppliers, there was less visible protest on this issue among Semester at Sea students. Most took advantage of the inexpensive sportswear stocked near our port in Vietnam, lured by assertive saleswomen who met our ship with the call "Nike, one dollar!" The conditions in factories producing low-cost gear were not always revealed to us, or if so, groups permitted to visit were likely to receive a presanitized public-relations tour. The idea that it was a feminist victory for a top female athlete to have a shoe named after her in the manner of Sheryl Swoopes changed to concerns for workplace safety once we reached the neighborhoods producing those shoes. I used the classroom exercise developed by globalism professor Cynthia Enloe, inviting students to look at the labels in one another's shirts and shoes. How many were American made? Most were made in China, Vietnam, Pakistan, El Salvador, Mexico, and Haiti. To outfit American families with affordable brand names assembled overseas, how did companies keep those costs low? By now, my Semester at Sea students knew that their stylish poolside bikinis had been named after US atomic-bomb tests on Bikini Atoll in the South Pacific. But few were familiar with the modern geopolitical leapfrogging where Filipina workers headed to free-trade zones in the Mariana Islands, a US territory since World War II, in order to assemble clothes that later left Saipan with the technicality "Made in the USA."

My third voyage with Semester at Sea was one of the best in terms of smooth sailing and wise students. For the sports class, our main outing in China introduced us to a national boxing champion, and we had a tough training session in his gym. But this rougher aspect of athletic masculinity was balanced with an equally challenging session with a tai chi master in a local park. There were abundant opportunities for the 2019 class to indulge in low-cost sportswear, brand-name sneakers, and bags and caps in the markets of China and Vietnam, but on this trip, we also plunged in to manufacture sports gear ourselves—for young players in Ghana, through the program Alive and Kicking. We stitched soccer balls together with long needles and then enjoyed a scrimmage at a local school, playing on broken glass under a steaming sun. Proud images of Ghana's male soccer athletes appeared on items from tissue boxes to candy bars, but images of girls in sport uniforms were also to be found, in the ubiquitous milk ads promoting healthy childhood. The shy young women who taught us how to sew soccer balls (much more difficult than it looks) soon outmaneuvered us during a friendly match on the local school field, making me think back to my first Semester at Sea voyage, when that airport official had informed me that women did not play soccer, after all.

As I adapted and updated the issues covered in class, memorizing the words for "Thank you" and "We are honored to be your guests" in a different language every six days, I had infinite support from the caring and sensitive Semester at Sea staff. The administration, experienced in setting up every type of global field practica its faculty proposed, was always more than helpful in arranging our outings to ball fields, sports companies, and dance theaters. Through such experiences, students fortunate enough to join a voyage could see for themselves the challenges facing women in the larger world, where child marriage, hunger, and customs of physical modesty kept many girls from participating in sports. Through bus windows or on foot, we saw girls hand-laundering their brothers' soccer jerseys on riverbanks, wringing and hanging them out to dry—urban laundry lines flapping the names of men who went from poverty to fame.

Fig. 6.1 Author with WNBA All-Star Layshia Clarendon, University of California at UC Berkeley, 2019. *Photographer unknown, from the author's collection.*

CHALLENGES FOR A WOMEN'S SPORTS PROFESSOR

Evaluating Twenty-Five Years of Class

After fourteen weeks together, my students and I reach the last day of class. Time for a party, evaluations, some last-minute advice and small gifts for graduating seniors, and a good discussion on what the future holds for women and men who play sports. What's the score? What do we need, as a democratic society, to assure genuine equality of opportunity?

We revisit some of the key themes of the course: We've examined past barriers and demystified the historical origins—religious, medical, social—of objections to women in sports. We've critiqued the media's erasure of female achievement and noted how it limits female solidarity, as women's sports literacy is based on men's sports. Male athletes are still negatively compared to women when they fail, and female champions are still paid less than men, so women continue to be devalued on two fronts. Women athletes continue to be ranked on their femininity and commercial appeal one hundred years after the reformers of Mrs. Herbert Hoover's Women's Division warned that this could occur if women went pro. In sports, achieving fame and manifesting feminist change are not always the same thing; moreover, a student points out, the cruelty of social media has normalized body-shaming all over again, allowing men to rate women in new ways, such as the Harvard men's soccer team caught rating individual members of the women's team in 2015.[1] Students who have pursued internships at domestic violence organizations also question whether male athletes who abuse women are truly held accountable, especially during a winning season in which their physical aggressiveness has an athletic value. We discuss a quote from Lindsay Mapp at Raliance, an organization studying domestic violence policy: "What would a theory of change look like—to shape a sports system and culture where violence against women did not exist?"[2] Another student points out that while two generations of Title IX–era dads have been public advocates for their athletic daughters, American women don't always attend women's events in large numbers. And while sports remain a key route from poverty to affluence, from underserved inner-city schoolyards to the realm of corporate power, it's primarily when the talented young athlete is male. No girl has yet been offered the $90 million Nike contract once extended to a high school–aged LeBron James. No college women's program enjoys the sort of donor gift recently pledged to Binghamton University: $60 million from an anonymous family to fund a new men's baseball stadium on campus, with a training facility and clubhouse. Will this change? "No," says one young woman in class. "Society's expectations for women's actions never align with how sports allow women to act. And society's expectations for the female body don't align with an athlete's body." She suggests that top female athletes, while admired, will remain anomalies, limiting their reach and their rewards. Others disagree.

There are simply too many insights to share in our last hour and fifteen minutes together, so during the final class each semester, I distribute a handout inviting students to list what they see as *good news* for women athletes, points that are clear and significant gains in recent years, and *problem areas*, including stereotypes and practical challenges continuing to limit female athletes. Across twenty-five years, student responses have been remarkably consistent. Here is a representative sampling of their comments since the late 1990s:

THE GOOD NEWS

- The popularity of women's soccer and basketball in terms of spectators.
- Recognition that women athletes are no longer considered deviant for their excellence and achievements.
- Expansion into the professional realm.
- Greater inclusion in media, advertising, endorsements, and even Wheaties boxes.

- A whole generation of girls is growing up with female sports stars as heroes.

- Title IX functions as leverage for gaining equality.

- Medical and scientific research reminds women and girls that it is healthy and good for you to participate in sports.

- It is feminine to be fit; women's sports has seen an uprising of stars who are great athletes and also admired as feminine.

- Every game of the women's Division I NCAA tournament appeared on ESPN.

- There are successful female basketball coaches and administrators, not only players, at the college level.

- Women increasingly hold executive positions in the sports business world.

- The US women's soccer team has paved a path to higher pay.

- Girls are participating in sports and sports clubs at younger ages.

- The fact that there are female announcers covering male sports is a huge gain.

- There is increased support for those who want to participate in male-dominated sports like ice hockey, football, wrestling, and boxing.

- There is huge coverage of women in the Olympics; women bring home a significant amount of the gold.

- Nike commercials have a positive image of women athletes.

- Women are viewed as more competitive, out to win.

- Female athletes now use their muscles to throw old myths out the window.

- Women athletes "are just bigger, badder, and stronger than ever."

THE PROBLEM AREAS

- Male insecurity. Basically, women athletes challenge manhood. Society must change the view that women in sport infringe on the role of men.

- Women need to gain more publicity for more recognition. But the way the Nike ads try to make a positive point seems wrong: "I'm a boxer—but I still wear a dress and paint my nails!"

- Women need to obtain funding equal to men's for scholarships and equipment.

- People don't pay attention to women's sports because they believe women do not possess the skills men have.

- A woman's sport is seen as a temporary job until the "real" profession of motherhood; she should give up the sport to have a family.

- Women shouldn't be "too muscular."

- There is pressure to be both beautiful and talented in order to receive media attention.

- Stereotypes: all women athletes are mannish lesbians.

- Male audiences don't take female athletes seriously.

- Not enough female coaches—a bias toward male coaches.

- WNBA salaries are far less than NBA salaries.

- Title IX is ignored; funds are never withheld for violations.

- Girls need to be encouraged as equals with boys on the field, kindergarten through high school.

- Women need to be taken seriously—showing the ability to balance life, sports, and being feminine or sexual without society disrespecting the athlete.

- Women have different rules and restrictions in some sports.

- Not enough good sponsor ads that *do not* focus on sexuality.

- Beyond college, there are few opportunities for women to continue playing.

- Women are expected to have "ideal" bodies while still performing at high levels. And society allows for great accomplishments only if women's behavior stays in line with femininity.

- African American women are still faced with the disparaging stereotype that views them as less womanly, less feminine, and sometimes even subhuman.

- In some ways, the image of the female athlete has changed for the worse—seen as an intruder into traditional male preserves.

- *Women* box other women into categories, calling each other fat, gay, and so forth; women don't necessarily support women's sports or go to events.

- Football is still the "third gender" whose budget is never cut.

- Women's sports are generally not perceived as generating big revenues for colleges (and, with no dunking in basketball, for example, sports are viewed as less exciting for spectators).

- Women cannot coach top male athletic teams, and the number of female athletic directors is nowhere near the number of male athletic directors.

- Sexual harassment and comments belittling women's sports knowledge are common in the sports business workplace.

One GWU student, Courtney Brooks, wrote a long response:

I was thinking back about some of our class discussions, and something kept bothering me. When we talked about today's female athletes and how they are expected to play both the athletic role and, afterwards, the feminine role, I didn't think that this was necessarily so bad. And, to go even further out on a limb, I am not bothered by the fact that men are now being held to these same high standards. Instead of being upset about the fact that we are supposed to be compassionate, caring, and nurturing and then the next minute aggressive athletes and victorious champions, I think we should look upon these qualities with pride. I think it's great that women have "broken the mold" and gained acceptance in aggressive, competitive sports. I don't think, however, that we should be trying to rid ourselves of other qualities that we are glorified for. Instead, let women be nurturing but powerful, compassionate but aggressive, sweaty but beautiful. And, while we are being superhumans, have men look up to and strive for the standards we have set. Men are slowly being expected to be caretakers, sensitive, and nurturing. In my opinion, these are human qualities that should be revered. It should be seen in a positive light that women can be both breadwinners and moms, champion athletes and fresh-and-presentable ladies. Slipping on a dress and squirting on some perfume after a game should be something we admire. I would rather see a football player clean of sweat and in a button-down shirt after a game; this is something men should feel pressure towards as well. As women grow to accept, and love, and cherish all the qualities that we encompass, then I think men would soon strive to be both football champs *and stay-at-home dads as well.*

Another student, George Washington University soccer player Jessica Sultzer, concurred: "Title IX gave women the license to compete like men, and everything women are doing to become equal to men means that women are becoming like men, rather than becoming equal on their own ground. Although the implementation of Title IX created conditions for women to have equal access to sport, along with positive consequences, such as increased participation and improved performance, many of these benefits have come with pretty heavy costs. Application of the male model of sport and the male value system as the standard for women's programs has created an environment with increased potential for conflict."

On our last day together, we also revisit ways that women are catching up to men, in defiance of critic Arthur Daley, who wrote in the *New York Times* that "any self-respecting schoolboy can achieve superior performances to a woman champion." He wrote these words in 1953, on the heels of the 1952 Olympics Games, where Maria Gorokhovskaya had won seven medals in gymnastics. But superior performances would eventually be in reach for millions of women, with the gradual introduction of better training, shoes, and vitamins. Women readily broke records set by "schoolboys" of earlier times when *all* people, regardless of gender, began to benefit from some of the better human progress of the twentieth century—and we make a group list.

Changes benefiting all people to live longer, active, healthy lives: Better food; clean water; toothpaste; water bottles for transportable hydration; insulin, antidepressants, and penicillin; ice; orthopedic shoe inserts; asthma inhalers; sunscreen; early-detection campaigns and cancer studies; x-rays; content labels on food and drug packaging; HIV treatment; vaccines; hot tubs; Alcoholics Anonymous and Narcotics Anonymous support groups; contact lenses; surgery; advocacy awareness around asbestos and lead-based paint; the Americans with Disabilities Act; LGBTQ rights; birth control; mammograms; activity-tracker watches; good footwear; sports bras; and tampons.

Changes benefiting athletes in particular: Personal trainers, sports foods, state-of-the-art shoes, home gym equipment, weight training in public facilities, video replay to study games and event performances, global networking with other athletes and teams via social media, and improved pathways for reporting coach and sex abuse.

In making this last list, the students show all the ways that *human* evolution (with help from technology and medicine) has enabled women to catch up to men. But one premed student shared that despite her own athletic prowess in high school, visiting military recruiters still expected girls to be less fit than boys:

I was a competitive gymnast all my life and throughout high school was stronger than most of the boys in my class. The army came to my high school to recruit, setting up a table in the lunchroom. The two officers who sat there, both male, offered boys who could do 50 push-ups in a row a free army cup. All these boys tried, and the officers would correct their form, and the boys just couldn't hit 50. So I went up to the officers, and I said, "Can I take a shot?" They looked at each other, smirked, looked at me, laughed, and said, "You can do 40, if you'd like." I said, "No, that's okay," got down on the ground, and pumped out 50 perfect push-ups—a walk in the park, when I compared it to my gymnastics workouts. I stood up, smiled, and their faces were priceless. They were completely dumbfounded as they handed over my free cup. It was very interesting to see their disbelief—that I could complete a task the boys could not.

We also still portray women's athletic potential as temporary until motherhood. Female athletes' careers are physically interrupted by motherhood in ways that most male athletes' bodies aren't altered by fatherhood. But more and more students are also open to understanding that athletic *identity* is lifelong, no matter who you are, and that all people *without* disabilities are "temporarily able-bodied" persons (TABs), a phrase I learned at a disability-rights workshop. Gender is but one factor in human athletic potential and experience. And we return, as always, to the cultural discomfort some feel in seeing women join men in the public arena of high-status roles. GWU student Ayu Tanaka suggested, "To claim that male athletes are suddenly being disadvantaged, just because women are finally finding success and presence in a domain that was historically male, is just another example of men's masculinity being threatened—by the unfamiliar presence of women in their delegated spheres."

We traditionally end class with a short film clip: I'm partial to that powerful crossing-the-finish-line conclusion from *Personal Best*, which leaves students either weeping openly or ready to run up a mountain. After I shake everyone's hand and find myself engulfed in bear hugs from big football guys, all that remains is for me to collect the Title IX term papers and plunge into the grading process—a process made slow by my own enjoyment and my frequent pauses to earmark smart or moving paragraphs, such as those I've quoted in these pages.

After I submit grades, I'm allowed to read the course evaluation forms, and I am keenly interested in what my actual students have to say about this classroom experience. How do they rate our semester? What did it mean to them? Over the years, anonymous course-evaluation forms yielded these comments:

> I enjoyed this class so much. It is because of this class that I am going to minor in women's studies. I love being involved in a class discussion, as heated as it could get at times. Now when people say stuff like "It's so unfair that Title IX takes away good male varsity teams," or "Women's basketball just isn't as interesting or as profitable as men's," I can not only intelligently tell them they are an ass—I can prove them wrong with valid facts.

> I decided that Women's Studies was essential to my education, as I have been socialized into femininity and did not choose it for myself. I wanted to learn how and why women's roles are culturally created so I can learn to analyze the behaviors that I have believed to be innate. Women athletes are particularly interesting to me because they have moved into a predominately male sphere and made it their own. I attended a small girls' school for my entire pre-college education, and we were encouraged to participate in sports throughout our school careers. It was

not until high school, when I began interacting with peers from coed schools, that I encountered women-athlete stereotypes.

I can't underscore how much your class meant to me and changed my thinking for the better. I showed up in Washington, D.C. in 2004, having spent the previous 18 years living in rural Oklahoma. When I arrived, my framework of understanding seemed to explode. Suddenly I was facing realities I'd been sheltered from my entire life and was questioning everything that I'd always taken for granted. To call it culture shock is an understatement. Through Women's Studies and your class, I developed ways of thinking about and making sense of everything that had me feeling at odds with my new reality. Most importantly, I learned that my progressive thinking and progressive action didn't have to remain separate. Your cause had implications far beyond my academic career—it has informed my passion and activism in a way I never could have imagined, and I can't thank you enough for that.

I have never learned so much that I can apply to my life as I did in this class. I truly look to you as a mentor and role model as I venture into the sports industry as a woman. I hope to one day facilitate change and equality in every aspect of sports, especially in agency work. Seeing your passion for women's equality and that "can do" attitude showed me that I too can do it and never back down!

It felt a little weird being the only male in the class. I am really here to learn about how sports has interacted with the broadening role of women in our society. One girl came up to me and said she thought it was great that I was "comfortable enough with my sexuality" to discuss the issues in this class. I don't know if this is good or bad!

This class has been directly responsible for enhancing my awareness of gender issues and has challenged me to be more sensitive not only toward female athletes but toward all women. Remarks like "Girls that get athletic scholarships are undeserving" reek of arrogance. And declarations such as "I hate Title IX" hardly seem constructive. Perhaps if more men would listen to what women have to say, then their opinions would be more geared toward a common goal of building stronger sports programs for both men and women.

I honestly expected that there would be more guys in the class than just myself. I must say it was interesting to hear the things the girls in the class had to say about men in general. I definitely learned a lot by spending two and a half hours each week with twenty women. At times I felt a little alone, and I felt like people looked at me to give the explanation defending all mankind for one or more of the dumb things that we have done. Other times I felt like I might be crucified for something or other that I said. But most of the time Dr. Bon thanked me for bringing up a point not yet considered. I think this saved me more than once. Overall, however, I think that I learned more from the girls than they learned from me. In the end I think I'm a better person. I wish that the class wasn't over.

And from one Georgetown football player, who I'll never forget: "You truly have opened my eyes and have given me a new perspective on gender issues in the athletics department. Your class played a large role in my decision to write my senior thesis on athletics and gender. I will be forever grateful for your help and teachings."

As campus policy dictates, I'm never allowed to read these faculty evaluation forms until most students have left campus for winter or summer vacation, or have graduated and are gone forever. But many, many students elect to write me a more personal note on the last page of their term papers or final exams, and some leave touching letters or even gifts of team jerseys in my mailbox, describing how the course has changed them. These are genuine friendships that have lasted, allowing me the incomparable pleasure of keeping in touch with graduates who are now Title IX lawyers, coaches, sports trainers, health professionals, Olympics staff—and pro athletes. Often, I receive messages like these:

> Aloha from Hawaii. I know that you are always up for a good pro-women story . . . and I have just rebroken the mold for sports in Hawaii. I was the only female rugby player on the island this past summer, and I did play against the Marine squad, multiple times. I have earned their respect and received kudos on my level of skill. Another girl proved herself out there in the world of sports . . . and beat the boys. "When in doubt, ruck over!"

> I'm watching "The Today Show," and Billie Jean King just appeared, so I wanted to send you a note about how much Athletics and Gender opened my eyes. Through that course, I confirmed that I want a career serving women in sports. Now I am coaching an 8th grade lacrosse team, interviewing for Division I coaching jobs, and interning with the "Let's Move" campaign. My goal as a rising college coach is to create a team environment free of homophobia. Did you know that this year the men's NCAA final four was televised, and the women's final four was not?! As a coach, I want to raise this point with the NCAA and demand that next year's final four is televised, receiving equal media coverage.

One of my former students from the GWU women's softball team became the head softball coach at a university where I myself had been a visiting history professor. She introduced a new research class on sports and gender in the same gym building where once upon a time, early in my own teaching career, I had worked out between classes. When she wrote to me asking for advice in assigning current books, I saw my syllabus in action: graduates from the sports class were now enlightening new generations.

Increasingly, my graduates' involvement in women's sports is international in scope, transcending borders. One wrote me from Georgetown's satellite campus in Doha, Qatar: "I am now confident and ready to submit my application to the Sports Industry Management Program!" Another wrote from Bahrain asking for help in creating a pilot model for recording the history of women's sports, in order to highlight the successes of the Bahrain women's swim team. With decades of Athletics and Gender graduates emailing me articles on Title IX reform and other pertinent women's sports issues, I've found it easy to keep up with new research. Almost daily, I find my email in-box jammed with messages from past students, usually beginning with "Hi, Dr. Bon. I miss our class. What do you think of this recent news article?"

Looking over my students' words from nearly a quarter century of classroom interactions, I revisit how sports culture and athletic identity shape ideals of equal opportunity in America. Almost always, the focus of the class was a positive experience for the students and for me as well. But what worked and what didn't work over the years in my personal classroom odyssey may be instructive now to others navigating their careers as teachers or coaches. In the interests of complete transparency, over the next few pages, I'll identify some challenges I faced as the teacher who developed this course. I found that some challenges were the same on every campus: critics who felt women's sports were laughable or that women's history was not a "real" academic subject; the vulnerability of athletes who confided serious abuses they'd experienced; and my own vulnerability as an untenured, underpaid adjunct professor who could not guarantee continuity as a mentor. Since 1995, there has been progress in two of the three preceding problem areas.

First of all, *backlash*. This class serves multiple different majors and pre-professional interests. Prelaw students, policy interns, women's and gender studies majors, future health and wellness counselors, youth fitness advocates, and kinesiology and education majors all benefit from hearing the scholarship athletes, walk-ons, and club players dish some home truths about sexism in sports. However, despite an uptick in the importance placed on gender awareness for the workplace, academic distrust of women's studies remains. Students choosing to enroll in such a class continue to experience backlash from friends and family. Throughout the years, I experienced backlash too, typically from critics who had never met me, never read a copy of my syllabus, never visited a class, and never looked at the regularly assigned textbooks we used.

The first vehement editorial about my course appeared in a conservative student newspaper, *Independence Magazine*, distributed on campus at George Washington University but funded by the same off-campus benefactors behind the *Dartmouth Review* and similar enterprises. The editor in chief's front-page attack on my class, nicely timed during March Madness of 1996, listed one of my course textbooks in a "Rogues' Gallery" of subversive "p.c. material" and alleged that the cover photo of a woman holding a softball bat was "suggestive of a phallus." During the 1997/98 academic year, it was the *Georgetown Independent*'s turn, with a student writer charging that "the knowledge, if it can be called that, acquired in . . . Athletics and Gender . . . does little to make you a productive citizen. You might say, 'Wow, this crap we make up as we go along is really interesting.'" That an undergraduate who had neither interviewed me about my curriculum and publications nor visited my class would call my academic expertise "crap" was a new low and, in my experience as Georgetown faculty, a style of disrespect atypical of Georgetown students. Still, at least once a year, something similar floated up from the depths to remind me that merely creating a regular forum for talking about the history of women athletes was threatening to some or considered educationally subversive.

The evolution of my role from teacher and facilitator to a more public persona as Title IX advocate and women's sports booster grew apace during the 2002/3 academic year, when the George W. Bush administration's Commission on Opportunity in Athletics actively recommended reforms to Title IX law that would weaken the scope of its application and enforcement. Teaching Athletics and Gender at both Georgetown and George Washington University that year, in the shadow of the White House, I frequently exchanged my academic mortarboard for the clip-on mic of advocacy. I appeared on *NBC Nightly News* in a nationally broadcast segment, addressing how Americans might better encourage young women's athletic participation. Basketball season began, and I encouraged student fans to attend women's at-home games more consistently. During winter break, I wrote my regularly appearing column in a local paper, urging male readers to consider what Title IX reform might mean for the many female athletes in our community. My editor at *Metro Weekly* forwarded an angry letter from one reader:

> Bonnie Morris winds down her disorganized screed ["Gender Battles on Title IX," January 9, 2003] by wishing for more attendees at "womyn's" sporting events (the women's studies equivalent of clapping for Tinkerbell), while overlooking the obvious: fans vote with their feet. There is more interest in professional football than women's basketball. For Dr. Morris, freedom of choice only applies to sexual and reproductive freedoms. The rights of men to attend sporting events of their choosing or to play male-only sports is a sin . . . and all who dissent with this ambitious agenda are stereotyped as violent, sexist homophobes. Hey, Dr. Morris: "Keep your hands off my football."[3]

To be clear, nowhere in my column had I threatened freedom of choice, asked fans to clap for Tinkerbell, addressed reproductive rights, spelled *women* with a *y*, or charged dissenters with violence and sin. This was just one example of a pro-women's sports viewpoint being equated, instantly, with man hating—and taking football away from guys.

Another media challenge emerged in the spring of 2003, when a young woman representing a conservative campus group asked whether I'd serve on the Title IX panel she was organizing. She explained that she had also invited a speaker from an antifeminist and anti–Title IX lobby group, the Independent Women's Forum. Knowing the group's stance on Title IX, I declined the invitation to debate them. Although this meant I would miss an opportunity to defend Title IX with facts, I felt I could not agree to a debate that suggested female equality in federally funded institutions was preferential and debate worthy. In the same way, throughout my career, I have maintained that participating in *debates* on gay rights is problematic; the premise is that my rights are debatable or require an opposing view. Instead of debating, I gave a more thorough and personal interview about Title IX policy to a student reporter for the GWU newspaper, the *Hatchet*, and accompanied students from both Georgetown and GWU to Title IX hearings at the Capitol, where they were able to meet soccer champion Mia Hamm and a variety of congresswomen. Then, on March 31, 2003, the infamous April Fools' Day issue of the *Hatchet* served up a satirical attack on Title IX and female athletes.

> After 30 years of butch girls vainly attempting to play sports, young women at universities throughout the nation are finally heading back to the kitchen. . . . Athletic Director [name deleted] said the repeal of Title IX will revitalize the school's men's teams. "Quite frankly, most of our female athletes were ugly, uncoordinated, and generally useless," he said. "With less of these she-men running around here, the school will have more room to accept hotter, sluttier girls for our hard-working male athletes." . . . While the school cannot legally force female students to perform sexual favors to male athletes, such activity would be strongly encouraged. "Regular sexual favors will keep them in shape, give them their protein and give them new opportunities to contribute." Some, however, were not as supportive of the repeal, chiefly women's rights leaders such as noted sandy vagina Martha Burk: "We are on a crusade for ugly girls and lesbians everywhere, and we will prevail."

Clearly presented as sophomoric humor, it ends with the dare "Feminists, send rants to domylaundry@gwbonghit.com." But this column hit too many nerves to be ignored. It was distributed to the doorsteps of all campus buildings—from student residence halls, to the Smith Center athletic department, to the popular student deli—during the very week that GWU's best female athletes were about to depart for spring NCAA championships. The writer reinforced two competing stereotypes— the ugly, presumed lesbian athletes versus the "hotter girls" willing to perform oral sex on male athletes—and then dismissed older women's sports advocates as "sandy" and sexually unappealing altogether. Aware these were insulting words, the satirist anticipated protest but placed limits on serious objections by pre-identifying these as "feminist rants."

College sexism in any form can and does intimidate students from enrolling in women's studies classes. An athlete struggling to please coach, parents, teachers, boyfriend or girlfriend, teammates, and recruiters, balancing hours of practice with academics, may not want the additional headache of being teased for taking a women's history course. Students with real grievances about the climate for female athletes often found that they became targets simply by coming forward to identify problem areas. In her own book, *More Than a Game*, Title IX advocate Cynthia Pemberton noted, "The reality was that there was nothing inflammatory about what I'd done or how I'd done it. What I'd done was confront long-standing traditions, norms, and values, which was controversial by nature."[4] I had to be mindful of not using too much class time to discuss how each of us handled backlash. But we did not ignore the climate of scorn for women in sports. We looked at it historically.

Because of the backlash that often lurked just outside the door, ensuring students' comfort to speak freely in the classroom became my absolute top priority. For that reason alone, I rebuffed many, many approaches from assistant coaches, trainers, and occasionally local journalists who begged to audit the class: "Just let me sit in—you won't even know I'm there!" Even without the intimidating presence of athletic department staff, I found that when several student athletes from the same team enrolled together, each stayed silent for fear of saying anything disloyal to team, coach, or school. Entire teams or, more often, starting lineups sat in clusters, self-segregating into geographic zones in the classroom. On one campus, I watched lacrosse women glaring at crew, baseball simmering at basketball, and soccer women openly mocking the cheerleaders—and a near fistfight broke out when a member of the dance team informed women's volleyball, "We work out more and are in better shape than *you all*." Because I saw the peer pressure silencing otherwise vibrant contributions in class, I offered journal writing as a safe space for sharing broader reflections. For years, those individual sports journals were the most important assignment required of Athletics and Gender students. Weekly entries were ungraded but had to be turned in for credit, addressing that week's class topics in some way.

I was amazed by how enthusiastically these overworked, tightly scheduled Division I student athletes accepted an extra writing assignment. Students who were alternatingly boisterous, sullen, and exhausted in class became thoughtful, political, and poetic in the private confines of a journal. They seized the invitation to explore their past and present experiences in sports, releasing astonishing material. Some talked about being controlled by a society that demands winners, about trying to make their parents proud, about seeing a long-missing "deadbeat" father show up in the bleachers for that championship game. There were moving stories about racist referees and triumph over injury or addiction to painkillers. Every page was a tearjerker. A silent young woman revealed to me, "They told me I was good enough to go to the Olympics. But when I broke my arm a second time . . ." or, most wistfully of all, "I wanted to

play, and I was *good*. But it was considered unacceptable in my culture."
A male baseball player who in class expressed open contempt toward
women in pro sports confessed his own limitations as an athlete and recorded his grudging admiration for the emerging female players whose
careers would outlast his own. A young man confided actually feeling
grateful when he sustained a serious head injury, effectively ending his
football career; it was a way out, for him, from a lifetime of answering
to his forceful father's ambitions.

The opportunity to keep a journal of reflections about athletic stereotypes led student writers to personalize their notebooks. I received
journals as thick as dictionaries, stuffed with news clippings, slick magazine ads, and even a birthday-party plate printed with themes of girls in
sports. There was a cocktail napkin printed with Charles Schulz's cartoon heroine Peppermint Patty hitting a baseball: *WHACK!!* Such found
material was pasted in without any prompting or suggestion on my part,
an infinite variety of collages and commentary. Two women who were
walk-on athletes without scholarships, paying their way through college
as waitstaff in noisy sports bars, regularly wrote entries on bar napkins
during work breaks, jotting down the sexist comments they overheard
while serving male customers; I'd open up their notebooks to find fray-
ing but legible bar coasters and peeled-off beer labels. Each journal itself,
as a tool of witness, was always carefully selected, revealing a great deal
about the author. A few students wrote haphazardly on any old page or
ripped sheets from plain campus notebooks they already owned, but a
startling majority picked out expensive leather journals from top-of-the-
line stationers at the mall, with all the dignity of shopping for a senior
class ring. One timid student spent a small fortune on an art-portfolio
diary for her sports journal, emblazoning it with glue-on gems and the
word "VICTORY" spelled out in gold, silver, and bronze glitter—the col-
ors of Olympic medals. Inside, she pasted images of strong women on
each facing page. Another memorable notebook announced, "THIS IS
MY SPORTS JOURNAL FOR DR. MORRIS" in computer-generated Goth
typeface. No one typed their entries on laptop computers in the years
1996–2004, though I would have of course permitted it; no, this was a
journal, handwritten.

Students on the road with their teams during spring or fall competition wrote in their journals while on the bus or plane, prioritizing the
sports diary over all other homework. Those entries showed me the arc

of the season: the victories, the sometimes hostile towns, and glimpses through bus or train windows of roadside signs and billboards mocking women's bodies. Class sports journals thus traveled around America and abroad, too, to spring-break meets, athletic domes in Texas and Georgia, crew regattas, overseas training camps, Bronx gyms, doctors' offices, waiting rooms, airport security lounges, boyfriends' cars, and health-food stores. When the GWU women's basketball team traveled to the NCAA Elite Eight, top three-point shooter Lisa Cermignano made sure her class journal was more than a scrapbook of victories. Tucked into the back cover was a letter of support from another GWU faculty member, esteemed English professor Faye Moskowitz, who had handwritten to the entire women's team, "I wish to express my thanks and appreciation for all you have done for us here at G.W. this year. Your grit, your guts, your refusal to reach for anything but the stars has inspired this university. I've always been proud to be a woman, but lately I've been carrying my head a little higher than usual. Good luck to you all."

The most common themes, which appeared over and over, boiled down to five categories: (1) childhood memories of youth sports and family attitudes; (2) present college conditions for scholarship athletes and fans; (3) issues of gender, sexuality, and sexual harassment; (4) body image and eating disorders; and (5) media coverage of women versus men in sports. The journals also sketched out a landscape of pressure and work controlled by ambitious coaches, NCAA recruiters, and gym managers, as well as, in a few childhood memories, priests and nuns who were way out of line as disciplinarians. Each semester, I settled in with interest and a little trepidation for what was always the most honest student writing, the most authentic testimony of athletic experience, that I would ever read.

The journals also served as an outlet for the unexpected stresses in these young athletes' lives, as when scheduled sports events were canceled for weeks following the September 11, 2001, attacks. Students living through the period of time after Washington, DC, was attacked used the journals to write about their personal fears, their frustration with the interrupted playing season, and their guilty feelings over longing to play sports when so many lives had been lost. Muslim student athletes confided their experiences of airport searches and harassment, strangers' displaced blame, and instances in which people pelted them with garbage while on fields of play.

Inevitably, students reluctant to speak up about coach abuse or off-campus gay bashing in front of their classmates or teammates used the journal project to sketch their real concerns in stark, honest language. One African American student documented the open racism of her coach, who, in preparation for the campus visit of a blonde White athlete he wanted to recruit, had told his majority-Black team, "We finally have a ten coming to join us." I also found heartrending contrasts in the journals. During the spring semester at one college, a male student's journal began with this glowing tribute to baseball: "Everything is all right with the world. Why, you ask? Spring training is underway, and the neatest thing in the world for me has started. All my ideas of responsibility, leadership, courage, magic, respect, and happiness come from this game. It's yet another reminder of how sports brings people together." The very next journal I opened came from a female student in the same class. Her writing spoke to the memory of being assaulted by a baseball player during her first week of arrival at college. There could be no greater contrast than these two journals' assessments of how baseball informed their lived experiences. And that was only the beginning of many years reading journals that were nothing less than testimonials to abuse in sports culture. What were my legal, ethical, and academic responsibilities in receiving such confidences?

In my own life, I use personal journal writing for a trinity of purposes—as comfort, as witness to the era I live in, and as a space for trying out a narrative memoir I might edit and publish later. I assumed most of my students' entries would offer commentary on social stereotypes toward female athletes. After all, this was a *women's studies* class, and the assigned course readings were historical accounts of how far female athletes had come. I had encouraged all my students to see that they, too, could be sports historians—to think in terms of publication, for I hoped I might assist, in particular, those whose athletic careers would terminate at graduation but who could go on to maintain their athletic identities through sports journalism. In short, I envisioned helping interested athletes edit their true-story observations and critiques into marketable memoirs about the climate for college athletes. But much of the writing was so personal it was clearly not meant for public disclosure. These journals offered a settling of accounts. They were, in the intense subculture of athletes' lives, in which games were seldom fair, a means of *keeping score*. And there were grudges aplenty, some of which addressed the limited opportunities for talented women. During one semester, I learned that our star senior female athlete had accepted a $20,000 offer to play in Europe; our star senior male athlete, whose grades were much lower, graduated directly into a six-figure contract.

I confronted these dynamics of journal writing for class at a time when an excellent guidebook was available. *Public Works: Student Writing as Public Text*, edited by Emily J. Isaacs and Phoebe Jackson, offered advice from other instructors who dealt with the public/private boundaries of student journals. The book also featured a terrific chapter written by professors and students at George Washington University, where I was teaching. Many of the book's reflections addressed the dilemma of assigning grades to personal or intimate material, and the opening sentence, from English professor Andrea Stover, set the tone: "My main goal as a teacher is to promote the desire to write. In my experience as both a writer and a teacher, this desire is fragile because it requires a delicate balance between privacy and exposure."[5] Other contributors examined how students are "silenced" even when class assignments invite private submissions of material. Angela Hewitt and Robert McRuer addressed "the pressure to produce knowledge as a commodity. . . . Clearly, the last thing our students need is another competitive public space to demonstrate and market their 'skills.' . . . 'Skill' may have been reduced to signaling a slick ability to pick up, try out, and apply the newest, most marketable scholarly framework."[6] These words reminded me that my athletes had enough on their plates without their risking their scholarships through narratives like "How I'm Surviving a Sexist Coach." No matter how much I wanted to help survivors reach closure by airing grievances, few students wanted their accounts to go further than my ear. Litigation? Paperwork? Publicity? Backlash from the teammates who loved Coach? No, thanks. For a student, it was relief enough to share with a sympathetic teacher the bumps in the long road to becoming a twenty-year-old track star.

For all the preceding reasons, after several years, I discontinued the sports journal assignment. It was an ethical quagmire, being entrusted with so much information I thought required legal action. Many were the journal entries that also revealed abusive practices in students' high schools, early youth teams, and, saddest of all, their own families. The Title IX violations alone were staggering—as were the accounts of eating disorders triggered by coaches who had pushed female athletes to lose weight. My compromise was to announce that I would continue helping *interested* students transform personal writing into good sports journalism, while also extending office hours for those who wished to discuss taking action in clear cases of abuse.

All of this coincided with an explosion in new sources for self-expression: blogging, Facebook, Twitter, and other social media gave my students additional outlets for sharing the most intimate outrages of their lives. So instead of turning in their own handwritten journals to me alone, by 2003, the students in my class regularly critiqued other college athletes' sports journals posted online—posts that were now called *blogs*. From a safe distance, we had gained a wealth of internet diaries to study and relate to. The rapid normalization of online blogging also made my athletes more willing to be correspondent diarists whenever they left the campus world for grander opportunities. When GWU softball player Elana Meyers went to the 2010 Winter Olympics in Vancouver and took a bronze medal in bobsled, we followed her journey via her online diary. Private and public writing quickly overlapped in new ways, with few guidelines.

After I had taught the sports class for a number of years, universities also began introducing new protocols for faculty's and university employees' responses to student reports of sexual harassment and assault. When I halted the journal assignment, I rebuilt the syllabus with formal reporting rubrics and counseling information, and I directed students to public resources in the wake of fresh media coverage on abusive coaches and team physicians. With support, students began to feel comfortable taking the lead in holding authorities accountable for unchecked abuse.[7] Instead of assigning journals as a class exercise, I taught methods for interviewing and oral history, encouraging students to seek out and tape-record or film adults in their lives who had been pathbreakers in sports. This served multiple purposes: we all grew more engaged in documenting the positive role models around us; students who grew tongue-tied when interviewed as campus athletes learned to turn the tables as patient interviewers themselves; and, most important of all, students with learning disabilities or writing challenges embraced *oral history* and documentary film as alternative academic skills. But I do miss those journals, the glitter pens saved for writing on bus trips heading home from a game victory, those whip-smart feminist diatribes scrawled, during a work break, on wet bar napkins.

Anyone who has ever been a student or a teacher knows that the makeup of a class will have considerable bearing on the climate for open discussion, which is one reason I suggested journaling. There's no way to predict when, where, or why a particularly difficult student may enroll. In a course purporting to look at changing gender roles in sports, I put every effort into ensuring all viewpoints were welcome, whether a student identified as male or female, transgender or nonbinary. There were one or two semesters where I ended up with all-female enrollment, and occasionally, I had a class with only one to three male students in a group of thirty or thirty-five. Critics of women's studies have often alleged that genuine dialogue cannot occur unless both men and women are present in comparable numbers, but on those occasions when our male enrollment was three out of thirty, or 10 percent, Georgetown women in particular were swift to share experiences of being the only female in a Georgetown class, noting that it was interesting to have the tables turned. Sheer numbers of women did not automatically manufacture a feminist political climate: at Georgetown, more-conservative women students frequently took the lead in our discussions, raising incisive questions.

Over many years of refereeing class dialogue, I challenged intentional *and* unintentional racism more frequently than overt and antagonistic sexism. This was particularly acute when we discussed the potential offensiveness of Native American mascots; many students admitted they did not know "a real American Indian" and were startled when the daughter of a prominent tribal chief seated among them raised her hand to signify membership. I had become a sponsor of the All Native Basketball Tournament in Canada and was able to bring in materials from the very active Haida Gwaii team on which a mother-daughter duo played together. By 2020, students were far more sensitive to racism in sport and were alert to the concerns of trans athletes as well. However, once in a while, a male student did make generalized remarks about women that were clearly "triggering," in today's terminology. One student asserted in class, "First, it is undeniable that men's sports carry a greater tradition, and it can be argued that men have more talent. Second, I feel that the inherent physiological makeup of men and women make sports more interesting and appealing to men." Both male and female classmates challenged him to a lively debate. But other incidents could be painful, as I recorded in my own journal, early in the twenty-first century:

One male student in my class this term, who has repeatedly attacked Title IX, today declared, "Women who get raped bring it on themselves." Every female athlete in the room got the fixed look on her face that signaled more clearly than words, *I am a survivor*. Tension mounted as I waded in to interrupt/control a very unexpected situation. I told him briskly that his comments were not the thoughtful contribution I hoped for in our discussion of sexual assault on women athletes. The way the women's faces took in and reflected what I said helped me to wrap up class without further incident, but not before several women walked out. These students waited outside to speak with me once class had ended. Several explained that this same male student had a practice of making provocative remarks to and about women in their other classes and that he seemed to relish goading feminists. I know that I have an opportunity (and an obligation) to educate this young man, yet he seems determined to provoke me—and others—in order to see if "the feminist professor" will "attack" him with a predictably antimale response he can then report. Because we have extended him the ordinary and appropriate courtesy of free speech, particularly mindful that he should feel welcome as a male student in class, he freely hurt every woman in the room today. What can help a student like this become open to *hearing* the viewpoints of women? In a majority African American classroom, populated with Black studies majors, do we ever hear a White student declare that racist lynchings were brought on by the victims? Perhaps a terrible analogy, but I observe that even the *discussion* of equal opportunity for women in sports continues to evoke astounding backlash. And now off I go, after this exhausting teaching day, to women's rugby practice, where I am faculty adviser. What can I possibly advise, tonight?

When I had a rare day like this, I sought refuge in my scrapbooks of thank-you notes from past students. This favorite letter, from a 1997 male graduate, always reminded me to keep at it:

I would like to take this opportunity to thank you personally for opening my eyes. I must tell you, I had doubts about your curriculum. I went into this whole experience with less than an open mind, but your humor and persona persuaded me into paying attention. And believe me, that is not an easy task. I just wanted to tell you that I did listen to what you had to say and I realized that my own pre-misconceptions were just that, and it wasn't until I was forced to look at the issue that I started to visualize a woman's viewpoint. I became much more aware of my own attitude, not only towards women, but everyone in general. Thank you for helping me. You are an asset to all of us. And thanks for not picking on me. I was outnumbered, ya know.

Honestly, this is why a women's history professor gets out of bed in the morning. I hope he went on to raise both daughters and sons.

And one more, from another young man:

Dr. Morris, you may be proud to know that one of your Women and Athletics students (me) helped produce a piece on potential changes of Title IX for CBS News. I got to interview a player on the Washington Freedom, and I also helped interview Eric Pearson, chairman of the College Sports Council, who is seeking reforms to Title IX (and a guy I actually quoted in my final paper; weird, huh?). I think he was impressed with my knowledge on the subject and my ability to hold an intelligent conversation about it. Anyway, the piece aired this past Sunday on the CBS Weekend News, opposite the Super Bowl, which means absolutely no one saw it. But it aired nonetheless. When it comes to Title IX, I'm wicked smaht!

I had not only created a course, but as the students' own notes suggest, I filled a very public role on campus. My role was being a visible, approachable friend to college athletes. Plenty of professors followed college sports while refusing to excuse absences for the actual student athletes traveling to a championship; it's a bigger commitment altogether to *care about the human being in the uniform*. For the student athletes at any school where I taught, just knowing a teacher who was an advocate for their concerns and who attended their games, encouraged them to write about their experiences for publication, or connected them to relevant professional networks made all the difference in a healthy undergraduate experience and an on-time graduation. For me, the rewards were many: meeting families at games and being invited to serve as an honorary coach or to attend end-of-year athletic banquets. I met celebrity athletes and sportswriters, appeared on local and national news, and accepted invitations to talk about my class at conferences (see fig. 6.2). On one occasion, during a historic snowstorm that grounded air travel and stranded many of us at DC's airports just before the holidays, my long delay was made bearable as members of GWU's men's basketball team, similarly stranded, recognized me and took me under their wing. Another time, when I dined at a Georgetown restaurant with a friend and discovered to my horror that I had left my wallet at home, members of the Georgetown men's basketball team who were dining out at the next table simply reached over and paid my bill.

However, a close relationship with any university's athletic department and students is a political balancing act. I knew a great deal about the athletes' personal lives, fears, and frustrations, and as a result, I was appointed to GWU's athletes' council to weigh in on academic concerns. This of course bound me to GWU's brand, yet I was simultaneously teaching at GWU's rival, Georgetown, where I also had an embedded role as a faculty member who sat on the honorary-coach bench. Sports is based on rivalries—long-lasting, colorful rivalries. Teaching for more than one school was my livelihood, but I had to be careful where I sat, what I said, and what color shirt I wore on any given day, not to mention which ball cap I wore for a television interview. This was also true of my recent years in California, when I simultaneously taught at UC Berkeley and at its athletic rival, Saint Mary's College.

In expressing sensitivity to the unique concerns for college athletes, I hope I have also affirmed the wide variety of students enrolled in this course—not all of whom played sports. Over time, more and more were young men committed to social-justice issues beyond athletics. At every school, I had to be mindful not to seem *too* devoted to the needs of working athletes in class, especially when we hotly debated editorials proposing that student athletes be paid as employees of the university.

Few of my students knew that as part-time faculty, I might be visible, fully enrolled with a wait list, and involved with their concerns on campus but also so underpaid compared to my tenured colleagues that I juggled several adjunct positions and routinely taught four courses per semester. On the East Coast, I carried an overload for more than ten years. I could write three other books about my experiences teaching the three other courses I designed and taught to capacity. As long as my classes sold out, indeed overfilled until the fire chief himself paid a stern visit to one of my crowded classrooms, I enjoyed the continuity of being renewed every year, and I planned and plotted my guest speakers, game appearances, and office hours well ahead of time with confidence for each new semester. I boldly promised to see each student through to his, her, or their graduation.

This familiar routine of working with my beloved students in Washington, DC, came to an end in 2016, when George Washington University made sweeping budget cuts in the humanities, abruptly eliminating the regular half-time appointment I'd held for so long. I had taught Athletics and Gender almost every semester for twenty years and had been elected Professor of the Year by vote of the student-athlete community; that award, a framed varsity letter, hung on the wall of an office I now had to pack up and abandon. It was devastating to explain to my current class that I would not be on campus to attend their future Senior Day ceremonies or commencements. As an influential grown-up in my students' lives, I was put in the awkward position of reassuring *them* as I brokenheartedly peeled their autographed team-championships posters off my longtime office walls. To compound my loss further, in the haste of clearing out my office, a staff member threw away a large box of my sports class notes and treasured student letters. While expressing sincere appreciation for my decades of teaching, neither GWU's nor Georgetown's women's and gender studies program had enough allocated resources to keep me on its faculty with a full-time salary. This had everything to do with the tiered structure of using contingent faculty, who have no security, to teach the majority of college courses as long as it pleases the current administration. Thousands of dedicated professors throughout academia, the 75 percent of university faculty who are not tenure track, are simply *not renewed* annually, regardless of teaching evaluations, service, and record of publications, though these are the standards for promotion and tenure for others. And as a program and not a department at most colleges, women's studies does not have funded, tenure-track faculty positions and instead relies on part-time instructors or faculty tenured in other departments. Becca Rothfeld wrote in a 2020 article, "The real enemy is at-will employment, which manifests in the academy as the absence of institutional protections for contingent faculty."[8] Georgetown acknowledged my twenty-plus years of service by making me a silver vicennial medalist at a dignified ceremony overseen by President John DeGioia, and at GWU, I was honored with the title at the tender age of fifty-six of emeritus professor—though unfortunately without any corresponding pension. I could no longer afford to live in Washington, DC, in the apartment I had called home for twenty-two years. So where to next?

With many years of teaching energy remaining, I accepted a thrilling invitation to teach at UC Berkeley, driving across the United States with my women's sports teaching notes in the summer of 2017. In line with UC Berkeley's mission to "desegregate the curriculum," I began teaching Sports and Gender in US History to the largest and most racially diverse class I'd ever had. We were still exploring how Black athletic bodies have

resisted or been exploited through political control and commercializa-
tion, but now student papers incorporated present-day controversies,
from Colin Kaepernick taking a knee to Serena Williams enduring tennis
officials' disdainful treatment. Should college athletes be paid to play?
Was there still a plantation system of promoting young Black bodies as
performers for the White audiences who could afford expensive season
tickets?[9] I brought in guest speaker Layshia Clarendon, WNBA All-Star
and Cal alum, who addressed homophobia and racism in pro sports (see
fig. 6.1). Because the class was so large, I offered to take every student
out for coffee or boba tea at least once, in groups of five or six at a time.
In this way, I introduced myself as an ally to many East Asian and South
Asian international students, who were often the first in their families to
attend college and anxious to succeed. Some had parents who had never
learned to read. Others were unsure how writing a paper on discrimination in sports would serve their competitive engineering or computer
science major. To this last point, a young man in class stood up one day
and directly addressed his own cohort of STEM students. He shared how
I had directed him to a local exhibit in the Berkeley Public Library on
the Paralympic Games; having a disabled brother, the student wished
to design innovative prosthetics for Paralympic athletes. He'd met the
exhibit photographer at the library reception and now had introductions
to several top sports companies that wanted to see his engineering designs for adaptive gear. Suddenly, all the students in class could picture
themselves as webmasters for the Paralympics or as the heroes who
designed new running legs for former athletes wounded by war-era land
mines. It made a huge difference to have this perspective reinforced by a
student, living proof that one did not have to be an athlete or a political
activist to level the playing field in sports. The discussion that day was
also meaningful for some athletes in class who had sustained injuries
early in their college careers and were exploring different ways to work
in sports professionally.

Nothing could have made me happier than introducing women's
sports history into the University of California catalog. By establishing
a credit-granting class at Cal, I hoped that students who studied women's
sports history in high schools and community colleges across the state
would be able to transfer their work to Berkeley later on. In California, I
was soon approached by two other area schools, and I ended up teaching
women's sports history at both Santa Clara University and Saint Mary's

College of California. Now I was simultaneously a Golden Bear, a Gael, and a Bronco and was vying for a spot in continuing studies at Stanford as well. These commitments involved endless hours of driving, on either terrifying Highway 880 or gorgeous Pacific Coast Highway, sipping from Cal Bear, Gael, and Bronco coffee travel mugs while plotting course lectures during stalled bumper-to-bumper madness. The first time I saw whales on my way to work, I forgave GWU for eliminating my teaching position, but three years later, as wildfires consumed my redwoods and the air above turned orange with toxic roasted particulates, the whales and I exchanged nervous looks about California's future.

I share these insider peeks at specialized teaching because, as we continue to reshape the way college teaching functions, there are those who question the need for women's history in any scaled-back budget. Often, these are critics who do support the full funding of college sports, especially football, as revenue-producing enterprises that underwrite other campus operations. But the football player who takes women's history is not an anomaly. And the feminist who coaches football isn't either. A history of women in sports is far more than a bridge builder for a college; it can be—and, I argue, should be—*the* supportive and accessible environment for talking about enormous issues of athletic pay scales, racial justice, sex equity, and school spirit. The only real problem seems to be figuring out the instructor's rank.

The course remains sizzlingly relevant. When I began teaching the first week of class in the spring semester of 2020 at Saint Mary's College of California, students were abuzz with interest in two news features. First, there was the ongoing college-admissions scandal, a long investigation revealing that many wealthy celebrity parents had paid and bribed officials to have their children admitted to top universities. The fact that daughters were as likely as sons to be set up as desirable team recruits, complete with false narratives and backstories about their supposed athletic value, interested my class: it was now normal to assume that colleges looked for and prized women who had bankable athletic talent. But the other issue immediately brought up in class was the US women's national soccer team pay dispute. For years, the Women's Sports Foundation had circulated reports with titles like "Winners on the Field . . . Losers at the Bank," pointing to wild disparities in World Cup pay between the men's and women's teams. Although the women outplayed the men, their wages and bonuses lagged far behind. By 2020, lawyers for US Soccer were arguing in court that under the Equal Pay Act, male players simply had more responsibility and that according to "indisputable science," the men's team required "a higher level of skill." My students argued about whether the soccer wage debate was about scarcity of resources or outright bias.

The frustration expressed by many of the women soccer players collided with some critics' arguments that they should be happy to be playing at all. Writer Brad Polumbo called Megan Rapinoe a bad role model for girls: "They look up to her and see not a disciplined, respectful sports icon, but a groundlessly bitter, petulant celebrity who is totally ungrateful for the opportunities she's had."[10] I mentioned in class that we had come full circle: when my course was first offered in 1996, sportswriters had been sidelined by a men's baseball strike, the players demanding millions more dollars. With no World Series to report on, journalists looking for a more upbeat sports story were "discovering" women's teams, praising the underpaid heroines. Now, a woman like Rapinoe could be charged with acting like a male player in the boardroom, though considering the women's pay scale, it seemed a stretch to label her bitterness "groundless." Twenty years earlier, our star soccer player at George Washington University, later a member of the Canadian women's national team, had suggested in class, "Women who play sports have just started to realize this can be a moneymaking business. Men's pro sports has lost the love of the game, with everything about dollar figures and the desire to win overshadowed by the seven-figure paycheck. The fact is, women's sports are still pure. They have not been tainted by enormous paychecks." Had that changed?

The pay gap wasn't much prettier in basketball. We found, popularly circulating on the internet, an image comparing the career highs of Sue Bird and LeBron James. Both had seventeen seasons in pro basketball. Both had won four championships. Bird's 2020 salary was $215,000 and a $11,356 bonus for winning in the finals. James's 2020 salary was $37.44 million, with a finals bonus of $370,000. Ironically, a key complaint about bringing women into equal participation with men is that women cost more, with organizations needing to accommodate pregnancy leave or add a women's locker room to facilities that had never anticipated hosting women's teams. A favorite story on the Georgetown campus noted that when women were first admitted as undergraduates, there were no women's bathrooms in the science building, for it was assumed women would not major in the sciences. Other students, looking at the professional pay gap, reminded me of the situation at their high schools: girls forced to play on substandard fields littered with trash and even discarded needles, the school district having argued there just wasn't enough funding to upgrade for the girls' teams. Stereotypical concerns about women getting hurt in sports don't apply when actual hazards might be resolved with greater investment of dollars.

The issues that drive my course—gender stereotypes and sports policy—are as fresh and fierce as they ever were. And while today's students are more prepared to dive into race and gender as intersecting categories of oppression, I have found that most young Americans are barely more familiar with the heritage of Black women in sports than my first college students of the 1990s were. No one in my UC Berkeley classes in 2018 or 2019 had heard of the Don Imus controversy or knew that we had briefly experienced a national dialogue on Black women athletes and race-baiting in 2007. In seeking powerful role models, my students could not name the first African American woman to win gold at the Olympics (Alice Coachman), the first Black African woman to win gold (Derartu Tulu, South Africa), or the first North African Muslim woman to medal at the Olympics (Nawal El Moutawakel, Morocco). They didn't know Sheryl Swoopes, the first US woman to have a signature basketball shoe marketed to other female athletes. All were shocked by the film I showed in class, *Playing for the World*, a history of the Fort Shaw Indian School women's basketball team who dominated the 1904 World's Fair in St. Louis and then were staged in zoo-like exhibits, sewing and ironing when not in competition, demonstrating competence in feminine domestic skills valued by White society. But after being introduced to the historical background in class, students at Cal produced remarkable analysis in their work, such as this insight from Zirui Zeng: "Sports, in the eye of the economist, is essentially a presentation of bodies in front of a paying audience."

Most students still need or can benefit from accessible, posted history timelines on the dates of world wars, the introduction of differing media technologies each decade, the progression of Native Americans in sports, the social and legal climate for LGBTQ athletes, and turning points of desegregation by race and gender. It can be a trap, however, to situate this information as purely *historical* rather than ongoing: I've had students thoughtfully respond to readings about the women of color who in the 1950s and 1960s graduated from a championship team into a life of domestic service, few professional sports opportunities being open to them. These same students were shocked when their Mexican American classmate shared that right then, in her first year at college, she had already been typecast as a future maid. Referred to a local specialist for her sports injury, she was asked, while undressed and exposed on his examining table, whether she wanted a job as his family's house cleaner. Her poignant anecdote led to a raging class discussion about ways in which our media presents discrimination in terms that create an unhelpful split: Black male athletes as victims of racism, female athletes as victims of sexism. When are women of color, who confront intersecting biases, centered and heard from in dialogues on sports?

And so the syllabus is updated over and over and over—for the small college classroom, the huge lecture hall, the high seas, the flagship state university, the Jesuit campus, and the adult education seminar. In 2021, women continue to deal with questions of how they differ from men not just physically but in their approach to playing. As one of my students pointed out, if we don't recognize women's differences, do we ignore women's unique strengths? Echoing classic nineteenth-century ideals, today's fans and social reformers hope that women's increasingly visible roles will "clean up" sports business corruption or athletic lawbreaking by modeling a "pure" example of sportswomen untainted by greed, cheating, and sexual violence. I place quotations around such terms to isolate meanings historically attached to women's role in US society. The same arguments that haunt women's emerging role in sports were once heard in the suffrage movement. Both then and now, there are plenty of American men who don't want women to "clean up" their good time or to enter their masculine arenas—whether as voters or as athletic competitors and rule makers. And women aren't angels or hired to play that position.

My student athletes note that while we valorize female difference as a moral beacon when it's handy to do so, we continue to equate athletic importance with men, and as Celia Brackenridge has written, denial about the abuse of women in sport stems from "a characteristic set of beliefs . . . that sport is a site of justifiable male privilege over females."[11] We accept the giant revenues paid to men or generated by a male fan base. We equate commercial opportunity in sports with male physical ability—and female good looks. And we continue to permit transgressive and transgender female sports performance and bodies only insofar as male commercial interests and arousal follow along.

What's at stake for American women, particularly young women of color, as female athletes fight for their 50 percent of sports funding? Equality feminism argues that women, as citizens, taxpayers, breadwinners, and students, should be legally equal with men in terms of rights and opportunities and that, in a democracy, women have the right to compete for existing jobs and salary rewards that were once male only. Today this means professional sports, and true equality includes the opportunity to box; wrestle; play football; and even profit from controversial endorsements, such as athletic shoes known to be made in overseas sweatshops, or from events sponsored by tobacco and alcohol brands. For many young female athletes fighting their way out of urban or rural poverty and into the limelight, there is no reason not to pursue the same material rewards showered on their sometimes less-talented male peers in sports. Women, too, would like to make money, and it's a mistake to assume all feminists are anticapitalism or antiprofit. Billie Jean King began her own activism fighting for fairness in women's tennis prizes; today Serena Williams asserts, "We should have equal prize money, especially nowadays that people are really focusing more on women's tennis, as opposed to men's."[12] Today's educated and affluent fans of women's sports can pressure institutions such as golf clubs that limit female members despite hosting top public tournaments. So many business deals are conducted informally on those links, effectively shutting women athletes and executives out of the old boys' network—and there is no women-only equivalent backed with the same money, landscaping, and recognizable prestige. A very popular argument for women's participation in sports is, in the words of finance columnist Nancy Dunne, "greater opportunities in athletics have helped to boost the number of highly skilled female executives. . . . Those developments are now paying off in the business world, where women trained by coaches in goal-setting, teamwork and leadership are shattering glass ceilings with confidence."[13] Dunne's essay in the *Financial Times* made clear the connection between sports and business skills such as time management, quick and confident decision-making, and a strong work ethic.

But another kind of feminism assumes that women can, and should, transcend corporate interests and excesses and bring different values to venues increasingly marked by for-profit greed, corruption, and materialism. When I began teaching in the 1990s, social scientists saw clear gender divisions in consumer and voting roles. Women did most of the back-to-school shopping for high-status, brand-name athletic jackets and sneakers they often couldn't afford to buy for their kids, influencing not only the display decisions at Niketown but also the decisions of some public schools to introduce non-athletic-brand school uniforms as an equalizer. For some mothers, doing what was best for healthy children included supporting youth sports and organizing resistance to gun violence. Some feminists weren't completely comfortable promoting the inclusion of women in pro boxing, or they expressed similar misgivings as women advanced into combat roles in the US military. Debate about violence and militarism aside, middle-class feminist reformers have often made enemies of working-class women by criticizing "rough" job categories as distasteful or harmful and attempting to regulate or limit work opportunities through protective labor laws. By dictating what sort of work and profit motives are desirable, altruistic, or progressive for other women, too many White feminists have ignored the economic conditions and lack of choices driving other women into jobs they might not choose for themselves. This history is important because the notion that all women are imbued with nobler motives and higher standards than men has real potential to slow women's gains in the sports world.

Yes, male athletes' salaries may indeed be bloated, especially when compared with the take-home pay of female ER nurses and schoolteachers, but that's no reason to suggest that women are naturally willing to accept less pay for more work, especially when they are the ones most likely to be raising kids—alone. Female players and coaches pushing for higher salaries and better media publicity are weary of being portrayed as selfish or angry, but a society shaped by unpaid slave labor and adult women's volunteer work still resents paying women what White men earn. In early 2021, resistance in the US Senate to raising the minimum wage from $7.25, where it had languished since 2009, is a case in point; there's an expectation that working women can somehow stretch those dollars and live on less. This includes women athletes. As one student told me, "My dad uses that word—*purity*. He wants to know what happened to the purity of women just playing for the love of the game. He'd like to have the women's game stay pure, which means untainted by money." Daughters now expect equal pay for equal effort. But pay equity lags behind women's demonstrated and enthusiastic success in skilled contact sports (authentic dialogue overheard at the Cherry Blossom women's rugby tournament: "But, Mom, I *had* to tackle her!").

Traditional gender roles aren't the only obstacles to women's advancement in sports. By the twenty-first century, schools all over the United States had cut physical education time to make room for standardized test preparation.[14] In some districts, school funding and teachers' contracts depended on improved test scores, hence the ubiquitous news stories on teachers caught "helping" students to do well by providing the answers for standardized tests ahead of time. Inner-city schools have long contended with limited funding and poor equipment. All of these are issues affecting girls' early access to sports training in their school day, but authorities tend to see sports as recreational or monetary rather than educational. In class, we read an essay by John Gerdy, a visiting professor in sports administration at Ohio University and the author of "Competition at What Price? Rethinking the Role of Athletics in Our Schools." Gerdy suggests that the United States look to the European model of private sports clubs rather than burden secondary schools with elite programs, which he contended were rarely fair to the interests or abilities of all kids:

> Although a football or basketball program can unite a high school in a way that an English department cannot, the primary purpose of the institution remains, as it always has been, educational. In short, a winning football team does not make a high-quality educational institution.

> For example, the vast majority of health, physical education, and athletic related extracurricular school spending goes to fund football. It is a sport in which the final high school game is the last time that 99 percent of the participants ever play football. Yet football flourishes while high school gym requirements are reduced. . . . In short, an official policy of encouraging students to pursue a healthy life through exercise is simply no longer a priority for our nation's schools—this, while increasing numbers of Americans become obese.[15]

Football's power to rally school spirit, as Gerdy suggests, made women's sports a low priority in many small towns. By the 1990s, the decision to eliminate other school sport activities such as gymnastics and swimming sometimes resulted from litigation or insurance concerns. In my day, one could not pass ninth-grade girls' PE without completing the terrifying gymnastics unit, which mandated individual routines on the uneven parallel bars, trampoline, and balance beam. Several times in that winter of 1976, ambulances took unskilled girls with sprained necks directly from my PE class to the emergency room. Similar concerns have taken diving boards from public pools and halted pole-vaulting for varsity high school boys. As a youthful pole-vaulter, my father broke his wrist while following the directions of his coach, recalling that it was the only time ever he swore at a teacher. By the late 1980s, public-awareness campaigns around HIV transmission in the era of AIDS meant that coaches and referees also had to stop games when any player evidenced even minor bleeding. Critics soon scoffed that Americans had lost their "no pain, no gain" ethic because of lawyers, weaklings, and the nanny state, but placing legal limits around injury to children was a significant social change. It opened up new public dialogue on sexual and physical abuse of both boys and girls by coaches, trainers, and team physicians. It also redistributed the old-fashioned concerns about girls getting hurt into realistic protections for all children, which in turn helped normalize training practices and education for professional women athletes. Each of these transformations in cultural values and law made my Athletics and Gender course relevant for prelaw, premed, and nursing and business students, as well as those who were already working as managers at sports clubs.

The history of women competing in sports, and their struggle to be funded and publicized fairly, is also the history of gradual equality in public life. We continue to uncover the ways that women heroically contributed to national strength in fields considered so masculine that female talent, though useful at the time, went unpublicized. Witness the recent popularity of books such as *Hidden Figures*, *Code Girls*, *Fly Girls*, and *The Girls of Atomic City*. This much-needed unmasking of past strength is emerging in other national histories too—one example is Margaret Willson's *Seawomen of Iceland*. We can hand each successive generation of students the tools to understand and dismantle barriers to equal opportunity by honoring the women of the past. We ought to know their names: the women who brought their game, who taught us to keep trying.

WOMEN'S SPORTS HISTORY: FROM STRENGTH TO RESISTANCE

IN HONOR OF WOMEN'S HISTORY MONTH

MONDAY, MARCH 13, 2017
4-5.30PM, THE GREAT HALL

Join us for a lecture by **Dr Bonnie J. Morris,** Professor at Georgetown and George Washington University, on how women have handled stereotypes, discrimination and limited ideas about the female body to achieve record-breaking triumph in the athletic world.

www.gph.ucsd.edu/cgeh
Twitter: @GEH_UCSD

Fig. 6.2 Women's History Month poster, University of California–San Diego, 2017.

Fig. C.1 Author with Olympic bobsled medalist Elana Meyers Taylor, George Washington University, 2014. *Photograph by Patrick Nero.*

CONCLUSION

When the Scoreboard Went Dark in 2020

The year 2020 should have been the year of womanpower. We were celebrating the centennial of American women's suffrage: one hundred years of the right to vote. On my own calendar, every month was packed with women's history celebrations and speaking engagements, reminders of the hard-won suffrage struggle. Women's History Month of course overlapped with March Madness basketball—we could anticipate seeing image after image of women's teams, profiles of coaches and legacies, and tributes to top-scoring University of Oregon player Sabrina Ionescu, who had just set a record in points, assists, and steals unmatched by any Division I player, male or female. Halftime reports might have included the usual well-placed public service announcements about breast cancer and domestic violence, issues affecting so many women. The buildup to the summer Olympic Games in Tokyo would, finally, culminate in weeks of media attention to the best female athletes in the world, and 2020's media would also bristle with the controversies women had dared to raise, such as equal pay, spearheaded by the US women's championship soccer team, and the Me Too movement, naming sexual harassment and abuse. Across social media, eye-catching charts drew attention to pay disparities. The year crackled with promise for women.

Then, to use a sports metaphor, the virus threw us a curveball.

The planned montage of female power, athleticism, public demands for equality, and increasing rectification of past harassment skidded to a halt as 2020 ushered in *real* March madness: a global pandemic no one had foreseen and for which the United States seemed particularly unprepared, in terms of hospital equipment. Schools closed, and athletic seasons were postponed. The NBA and March collegiate basketball tournaments were swiftly canceled. Worried investors watched a stock market plummet as questions about the Tokyo Olympic Games were finally answered with the first-ever peacetime decision to postpone the Summer Olympics for one year.

This was the shifting outlook for my spring 2020 class of Women in Sports students at Saint Mary's College of California, then in the fifth week of our semester together. Their immediate concerns were practical: Would classes go online? (Yes.) Would students have to leave their dorms, vacate campus, and go home? (Yes.) Assuring them we would proceed through the midterm and the rest of the term online, I invited our group to consider the opportunity fate had presented to us. We could write, as a class, about how the pandemic was affecting women's sports. What were the students seeing?

Foremost in my student's observations was that so many Americans kept working out—running, jogging, cycling, and playing hoops games until playgrounds, trails, and stricter social-distance rules cut back group activities that weren't family members only. Here in California, warnings to restrict all recreational activity and workouts to the home were soon resisted. Athletic identity and fitness, for both men and women, had long been linked to public activity and display of the fit body. This attitude itself was a change from earlier twentieth-century views on the public female. As we had seen in the class film *Pumping Iron II: The Women*, even gym culture remained heavily male through the 1980s, with sports-club memberships normalizing for women by the 1990s. Now women were desperate not to lose ground in fitness training. Those with a home gym, a rowing machine, a stationary bike, or an elliptical track would fare well during quarantine, but owning such gear made a clear distinction of affluence and privilege, often along lines of race, as well as class.

The interruption of actual NCAA season play at my students' own college campus and beyond was another matter. I noticed a similarity to the angst that my students in Washington, DC, had expressed just after the events of September 11, 2001. Both then and now, college athletes on scholarship or in their first year of eligibility, poised to explode into their long-awaited career of college play, were terribly frustrated—but also racked with guilt for feeling frustrated. How dare they have such selfish feelings when people were dying and first responders were begging everyone to stay home? When would life go back to normal? Was there any sort of guaranteed date for that? How could they stay in shape until then? What about the kids being recruited for the next year? Why now, when they'd only be eighteen once? With so many people suddenly forced to self-isolate at home, becoming more sedentary and eating based on what was available, could parents model ideals of fitness and self-control for their children? Did those isolated children, now homeschooled, still have access to books or videos that supported women and girls as athletes?

My spring 2020 class operated within these awkward parentheses, aware that women's sports and NCAA championship concerns were very low on the list of global survival priorities but nonetheless charged by our college to stay on track with planned coursework. To "act normal" meant continuing with studies in women's sports history, just online for the very first time, still asking the hard questions about ongoing sex discrimination.

I invited the Saint Mary's class to study the various ways that women's issues get pushed aside in times of national crisis or revolution. Which women's issues or aspects of sex discrimination might turn out to be important in the COVID-19 pandemic? As kinesiology majors, several students were quick to identify with underpaid nurses and underpaid nursing-home staff and to ponder why traditional—a.k.a. female—caregiver roles of service to others' bodies stay low waged. They understood from the class readings that in the American past, the state argued for compelling interest in the maternal health of women, and thus potential injury to the womb, the developing fetus, or fertility was used to bar women from rough sports and certain higher-paid jobs (although the history of women in slavery told another story). But during the 2020 pandemic, nurses were exposed to lethal viral loads daily; "protection" of adult women's health was inconsistently defined and applied. Society expected women to exhaust themselves in caregiver roles, either professionally, in hospitals and assisted-living facilities, where COVID-19 spread quickly, or in re-created school spaces in the home environment, regardless of income, support, and training.

Some students saw a silver lining in fresh job opportunities presented by quarantine. As personal trainers and part-time fitness instructors, they could deliver the product of a home workout via internet platforms.

Would we go back to early twentieth-century ideals of women work-ing out privately in the home? They were now equipped historically to see such shifts across generations. I reminded them how Jack LaL-anne's popular television program in the early 1960s had revolution-ized workout culture for housewives—including my own mother, who went on to practice modern dance exercises in our living room and later ran her own after-school dance classes for children from our basement in Maryland. Women have long found creative and socially sanctioned ways to combine domesticity and exercise culture. In the recent past, that was done not to avoid a virus but to operate within the sanctioned domestic sphere. However, mandatory self-isolation at home in 2020 was no great equalizer for all who experienced it. Those with better home gym equipment flourished. Those now isolated with abusive or homophobic family members lost public sanctuaries, workplace alli-ances, and long-anticipated departure for college life. Sports served as a confidence builder and a social support network for women leaving domestic violence, but now some women not only lost access to those workout communities, but their carefully laid plans to move out and start new lives were interrupted.

And this brought us back to the stalled women's revolution. We'd been examining sports opportunities for women in societies in which public leadership and exercise remained limited. The 2020 Olympics, we had hoped, might accelerate the representation and success of female ath-letes from Iran, Afghanistan, Saudi Arabia, and Yemen. What Americans were experiencing now was the obligatory homestay, the private-only display of the body, which in strictly sex-segregated cultures was no temporary crisis but a total way of life for women.

I gave my class the option of changing their final term paper topic from Title IX to "How is the COVID-19 pandemic affecting women's sports?" Students also submitted weekly journal entries about the pan-demic, which we shared and discussed online, and in the final week of class during April 2020, these journals were revised and reshaped into thematic papers. The project, as we called it, grew apace. There was no shortage of material in the mainstream media: headlines offered us food for thought such as "How Will Coronavirus Impact Women's Sport?";[1] "Coronavirus Threatens All Women's Sports—U.S. Women's Soccer Is Just the Tip of the Iceberg";[2] "Coronavirus Compounds Financial Con-cerns in Women's Sports";[3] "How Covid-19 Is Affecting Female Athletes,

Women's Sports Leagues";[4] and "Covid-19 and Women's Sports: Another Casualty of Gender Inequity?"[5] But what my class had to say turned into a living document of the spring we all experienced together—a document, I hope, that will prove useful to future sports historians.

Let's see what these students had to say.

> There is a struggle between the pursuit of national glory and human safety during this pandemic.

> Before the pandemic, women would get paid less, and even receive less from sponsors, which is a problem in itself. Of course male athletes will be affected by the lack of pay, but women already struggle. Because the Olympics were set back a year, soccer player Carli Lloyd has also postponed her retirement to play in the Olympics one last time.

> Any athlete can tell you the dangers of quitting, stopping once, makes it much harder to return, and if these athletes had to leave for 6–7 months in order to find paying jobs, they would hardly be in any condition to return to the sport. With the current state of the Covid-19 pandemic, all professional sports are suspended, but less publicized is the cancellation of all youth sports across the country. . . . While this measure is certainly necessary, I am scared of what its repercussions will be.

> There has been a desire to keep women out of harm's way throughout American history and the history of most countries. Despite this, 91% of American nurses are women. In this pandemic, it is largely women who are dealing with the disease. But God forbid these same women play baseball: that's far too dangerous. In times of war and turmoil, it is quite surprising that things we would normally scold, we then permit, such as letting women stand in the crossfire.

> Will everything just go back to normal? Will women have the fight and motivation to continue doing the sport they love? The NCAA instituted a "dead period" where college coaches around the country can't sign any players or take any recruiting visits right now until April 30th, and who knows if that's subject to change. How is this going to affect high school teams and college teams after this pandemic is over? Around the world, there are empty fields and arenas losing millions of dollars with tournaments being cancelled or postponed. Thousands of youth leagues are on hold with many sponsors hit by the economic slowdown and the hope of nervous parents looking for refunds. . . . These parents are key in any question of a recovery.

> Men in the NBA can survive without being paid for a few months, but the players in the WNBA, on the other hand, are not as prepared. . . .

The growth of financial instability that most professional female sports experience due to the Coronavirus also leads to a decrease of world recognition. For example, women's softball was supposed to debut in the 2020 Olympic Games for the first time since 2008, which could ultimately be put on hold for women in the National Pro Fastpitch League.

Coronavirus has exaggerated many of the stereotypes that women have been fighting so long to reverse. The gender gap may not seem at the top of the list of priorities during this pandemic, but it is one of the many long-term impacts that Coronavirus will have on society. The virus has exponentially increased the need for care not only in hospitals but also in the household.

Will more women than men get laid off? Will any? And who decides what team gets a financial cut? It would be interesting to see if women's teams take a cut before men's teams do.

During World War II, people used sports as a way to escape the reality of the world they were living in. But now we can't even do that. . . . The Coronavirus isn't allowing us to have an escape from the constant bad news that we hear on TV.

Some [women athletes] may not make enough to support themselves or their families, and that could risk their needing to have *two* jobs, which puts them even more at risk for getting the virus themselves—and passing it on to their families.

One day, athletes were competing normally, the next, they were forced to accept the new reality presented to them without sport. Athletes, families, and fans across the world rely on sports for entertainment, as a physical escape, and even as a sense of identity. This unpredictable pandemic has left many individuals with questions about their eligibility, scholarships, and even recruitment for high school athletes. Without oversexualization in female sport coverage during the enforcement of the shelter-in-place law, will women return to the sport world with less media attention, fan attendance, and recognition than before?

Many people believe that they [the US women's soccer team] "chose the wrong time to fight for equal pay" and "those women should be grateful to even compete." How ironic is it that women have been told to *wait* for decades. Finally, when a powerful group of female athletes make national history, bringing in more revenue than the U.S. men's national team, and ultimately gathering the courage to fight for equal pay for themselves and generations to come, they are told again to *wait*, it's not the right time to fight.

My younger sister had just had tryouts for high school lacrosse right before this quarantine, and made varsity as a freshman. Throughout this shelter in place, she has voiced her frustration about how her hard work was for "nothing." She and so many young women are inside, unable to practice the skills required for their sport.

The Olympic Channel now airs reruns of Olympic performances, but I have noticed while many Olympic men have a variety of rerun sports, I have mostly only seen reruns of figure skating, gymnastics, and track for the female Olympic athletes. Little to no attention has been shown to female Olympic victors in sports such as weightlifting, swimming, and field events, where women have achieved numerous athletic victories. ESPN shows reruns of historical athletic performances in the NFL, NBA, MLB, and AHL, yet the U.S. Women's Soccer team, which had TREMENDOUS success last summer, rarely has their accomplishments highlighted.

While it is hard to look on a positive note, there are some positive trends. The WNBA draft was held virtually on April 17th and drew its highest television audience in 16 years. Some experts explain this is due to many sports fanatics being hungry for any coverage of live sports during the shelter in place. [But] increased desire for sport can drive revenue and finally give women's sports the revenue they deserve.

I saw these, all over the media, for days: "Men's March Madness," "NBA," "MLB Opening Day," even news about the men's state basketball championship being cancelled at my old high school. What do all of these have in common? They all revolve around the male athlete.

A while back, Nike decided to suspend any financial penalty for pregnant athletes for the next year, because of all the complaints and allegations. This is a big deal, because many female athletes struggle with juggling their career and pregnancy. . . . I can only wonder if the same policy will uphold throughout the next year. Will the pandemic erase this policy? According to the U.S. Census Bureau, 76% of health care jobs are occupied by women. To go along with this, 85% of nursing and home health aid jobs are held by women. These women are sacrificing their own health and time with their families. What happens if a nurse/doctor is a single mom? What if their kids need help being home-schooled during this time? How are they keeping their kids active without youth sports leagues?

Athletes perform for a living, and with the inability to do so now, it may be hard for some of them to continue to live comfortably. If female athletes did not have a contract to begin with, how are they supposed to be supporting themselves and/or family during this time of the unknown?

The recent debate for gender equity internationally promoted the development and support of women's sports before the emergence of Coronavirus. However, the pandemic has had adverse effects on women's sports—the sector is not equipped to handle the current recess in the sports world. More so, women's sports will suffer as many sports organizations have suspended the contracts of women players, whereas men's teams only receive pay cuts. There have been cases of emotional, physical, and sexual abuse of women players by their coaches and male players. Many of the cases have never resolved, and the affected sportswomen have not received justice for the pain inflicted. The Covid-19 pandemic increases the existing inequalities experienced by women players. Women may face threats to their safety and liberty, as they could be confined at home with their abusers.

Just focusing on Saint Mary's, it is inevitable that the senior male athletes would secure that additional year of eligibility because they have a chance to get drafted into professional play; however, it could be a more difficult decision for senior female athletes because there is not a "next step" in softball following their collegiate career—other than the USA National team. This state of contemplation can put people in a position to either worsen or better their mental health, which is something that hasn't really been talked about that often during this crisis. . . . An athlete's mental health is constantly being tested because of their dual lifestyle of being an athlete and a working individual within society. But women athletes around the world are already used to having their mental health tested, since for years, male athletes were seen as superior.

Politicians are taking advantage of our focus on the virus by passing bills that would negatively impact marginalized populations. In the past few weeks, the Justice Department has been involved in a Connecticut court case regarding transgender athletes. A trend I've noticed throughout the history of sports is the constant message that athletes need to "prove" their gender, though it manifests differently for men and women. Now, if a female athlete is given attention, it mostly focuses on her role as a caretaker or mother during the quarantine, as if trying to separate her identity as an athlete from being a mother. In contrast, male athletes are questioned about the impact the pandemic has on their exercising routines.

I have never seen more people walking around, running, biking, and even rollerblading in my neighborhood and in Sacramento in general . . . and I saw more women than men enjoying outdoor activities. This is truly a hard time for the women who are in sports, especially those who need to be stronger and whose workout sessions usually include a resistance training in the weight room.

Our summer camps not only help young women from all over the state come experience what it would be like to be a part of the Saint Mary's Gaels soccer team; it also helps us raise money for team expenses for the following season. But in light of this pandemic, we are no longer going to hold the camps this year. Since 16 is the age to become eligible to participate in the Olympics, many young women who could not make the cut due to their birth dates would not have been able to be Olympians. Now that the games are being held in the summer of 2021, Sophia Butler, who turns 16 on the sixth of June this year, is technically able to be a part of the U.S. team. But is this morally right for the athletes that were already set to be part of the team for this summer?

Zoom does not give the feeling of doing the exercise in person. And in some cases, Zoom class isn't an option for the instructors or the people who participate in the class. It is hard for people in this current time to come across a stationary bike to set up in their homes, one, being too expensive and two, most retailers have little to none in stock. Both parties are suffering during this time of isolation.

I think if we were all together in class, our discussion on this court case [the U.S. National Women's Soccer Team and their claim for equal pay] would have been amazing. However, I was stuck in my kitchen reading the news. And I think many people are in the same situations, being at home, not being able to show their emotions toward the verdict. This pandemic has fortified us in our homes, and the reactions to this verdict, in my opinion, have not been as significant as they would have been if we were not in the middle of an outbreak.

My older sister Tracey and my father are head coaches for the girls varsity softball team at the high school in my hometown, Rancho Cotate. My parents coached a women's slow-pitch softball travel team, the Rohnert Park Pirates. Essentially, I was raised on the softball diamond, and by the age of twelve, I had the fortunate opportunity to visit close to seventy-five percent of the states in the country. Now all sports have been postponed until further noted. My heart goes out to all the afflicted, from the nationally affected to the internationally distressed.

I would imagine that just about all "scandals" within the professional sports world will take a back-burner position due to the impact of the pandemic. Energy is required to fight the still existing injustices, whether the conversation is on gender pay-gap highlighted largely by the US Soccer WNT or the Houston Astros sign-stealing scandal.

It makes me so proud to see a fellow Orinda Matador, Sabrina Ionescu, setting records in women's basketball and creating an amazing legacy the world will never forget. Sabrina not only had a triple-double but became the first player, man or woman, to reach 2,000 points, 1,000 assists, and 1,000 rebounds in NCAA play. She just made history!

A group of soccer moms are buying and giving meals to frontline work-ers. These moms connected on the sidelines of their children's games and used that bond to start something amazing—donating 1,700 meals to police officers, firefighters, and other workers who are helping during the pandemic. A pub down the street was about to close, and the owner is one of the soccer moms herself. It just shows how sports not only bring the players close together, but the moms behind the scenes as well.

With shelter in place, those with eating disorders are at higher risk of relapsing or experiencing an increase in the severity of their disorder. Stress from the pandemic can also worsen this. The lockdown has caused a shortage of mental health treatments available. . . . Staying at home and being exposed to food constantly poses a threat to those who binge, and due to limits on physical exercise, others increase their dietary restriction.

Many Americans are being laid off, bringing less and less money into their households. Because of limited funds, when sports open up again, parents are less likely to put money into sports for their children. My concern is that the possible financial crisis in youth sports could cause an unhealthy divide of class and gender.

This week, I learned a new phrase: Zoom fatigue. Although it is a blessing to be able to dance at all during these times, I find myself upset during Zoom dance classes. Zoom eliminated the energy of the room, the emotional and physical energy released, the laughs, the hugs. Over Zoom, that depth of connection is lost. . . . And while there are thousands of free online workouts available for people to do at home, women may not have enough time or energy to participate in them. In the pandemic, women make up the majority of health care workers, and, as schools close, working mothers have to take on childcare.

Although we are going through a pandemic, we still have the power to speak out about social justice and fight for the rights of those who are being discriminated against, like the wage discrimination case of U.S. women's soccer. I wonder if things would turn out differently if deci-sions were not overshadowed by this pandemic.

Family planning is such a huge topic for female Olympic athletes, as there are a guaranteed four years between each Olympiad. Now, with this postponement, any such planning for these women is pushed back, and what if they are reaching the end of their reproductive years? Do these women retire from sport into an entirely new phase of their lives, motherhood, or do they continue with their athletic identity for just another year?

With the huge strides that have been made over the last several years for eliminating the sports gap, will the pandemic set all of these progressions back? I raise this question because women seem to be returning to their traditional roles . . . they are forced to be back in the kitchen, being the caregiver and the loving wife. This isn't to say that they were not doing this before the pandemic with their athletic identity, but with that identity out of the picture for now, I wonder if this pandemic will put a hold on the evolution of women in sport. . . . Every time I have ventured out to the grocery store, I see that the shelves are all out of flour, sugar, and most other baking ingredients. If women now have the time to embrace their historic roles as women, is the present societal norm of the athletic, career-driven modern woman going to revert to a "traditional" woman?

I can imagine the frustration of those with great athletic potential coming from low socioeconomic status backgrounds. There is no level playing field anymore. Training centers are closed, and access to the same quality equipment or facilities has vanished. What about age? Can some younger athletes utilize this extra year and beat out their older, more seasoned counterparts?

It's hard not to take the pandemic personally . . . it was easy to overlook the fact that March was Women's History Month. However, it just stands out to me as an acute shame that women had their moment stolen and will likely not get it back. There's no space for women to express their disappointment about not receiving the recognition that all the amazing female athletes deserve for their efforts in championing women's equality.

As someone who worked in college athletics until COVID-19 put me out of a job, I am particularly interested in what is unfolding in terms of college athletic ability, in the wake of the cancellation of the spring athletic semester. . . . For example, the Saint Mary's softball team had a whopping 28 games left on the slate, just over half the season. My point is that female athletes, particularly softball, seem to be talked about disproportionately less in the wake of the NCAA's decision. For athletes such as USWNT star Alex Morgan, who timed her pregnancy so that she would be capable of competing in the 2020 games, plans that were dependent on the birth of her child have now dramatically shifted. Not only will she

be giving birth to her child during the largest pandemic since the Span-
ish flu; she will be forced to get her body back in shape during that same
time period. . . . I think this entire situation will redefine the resiliency
and strength of not just women, but of all people who have the capacity
to balance the different facets of life.

Some will claim that the pandemic is the reason so many people
watched this year's WNBA draft. This goes back to what I said in my last
journal entry—that women and their accomplishments will disproportionately be undervalued given the current circumstances.

When it comes to women's sports and advocacy for women in sports,
their battles and their voices will be drowned out on the grounds that
other battles are more important now. While this may be true, it doesn't
have to serve as an excuse to silence women who are calling for equality
and equity in sports.

In reviewing my students' thoughtful chronicles of an extraordinary
time, I found that nearly all were cognizant of the different financial
rewards reserved for female athletes, the struggle to gain critical public
attention and funding in the best of times, and the obvious setback of a
year with neither guaranteed income nor visibility. These themes appear
over and over in women's sports history, and perhaps 2020 is simply the
latest version. However, several students offered truly cutting-edge critiques: If, in normal times, women are kept out of certain athletic events
based on concerns for female health or fragility, why do we accept that
a low-paid nurse corps of women should labor 24-7 in poor PPE gear?
When are women allowed to risk their bodies for society? And to spark
sponsors' donations and audience attention, will we need to sexualize
women's sports again once live coverage resumes? Students reflected
on the balancing act for women who are both mothers and athletes and
whose careers are carefully timed with pauses for pregnancy. And they
were very aware that unlike World War I and World War II, our national
crisis of 2020 did not advance women's rights. Instead, the social scarcity of live sports centered on losses men experienced and the task of
rebuilding swiftly for male athletes and fans. Many Americans longed
for the "return to normal" symbolized by football; there didn't seem to
be a women's sport with the same seasonal hallmark, and there was no
call from the US president to restore live women's sports with all deliberate speed. However, the problematic link among live events, football,

and the spread of the coronavirus could be seen as Notre Dame's own college president returned from a White House event testing positive for COVID-19, as well as in a wire photo of unmasked Notre Dame students pouring onto the field after a football victory.

I sent our collected class writings to the NCAA, to the Women's Sports Foundation, and to the National Women's History Museum for its pandemic journals project. I was delighted that one good thing could emerge from our lockdown time, and a student wrote this to me: "Despite having the one class I was most intrigued to take being shifted online, you have allowed me to view this pandemic through different perspectives. Instead of just focusing on my own experience with Covid-19, I was challenged to consider how it affects athletes, the future of women in sport, and women in general. This unique change in perspective is something not every Saint Mary's student got this semester—so, thank you!"

In the very earliest months of the pandemic, another perspective came from Mayor Randy Johnson of Santa Cruz, the California town where I was sheltering in place. He addressed the loss of live sports as a particular communication challenge for men, whose friendships and conversations, he felt, were more limited than women's: "We men have friend-groups, but they are strictly minor-league compared to women's. The cadence and measure and flow of women's conversations are diverse and layered. Men, not so much. And we are finding out that during the COVID-19 crisis, one of our most cherished topics of conversation is in the toilet. I speak of sports. March Madness? Sorry. Baseball and opening day? Forget it. NBA Finals? Adieu. Masters? Uh uh. We can't watch them; we can't attend them; we can't even talk about them except as wistful memories."[6] Even his editorial used a baseball metaphor: "minor league."

As 2020 dragged on, every political crisis in Washington was expressed on the evening news in athletic game language, right through the contested presidential election in November. We regularly examined sports slang and sports lingo in class each year, but in the 2020 election year, American sports language seemed to be everywhere in American politics. Any sports metaphor I failed to catch in the evening news was texted to me instantly by the excited students I'd turned into eagle-eyed media critics. From the rancorous presidential debate during which Donald Trump bragged, "I'm the one that brought back football, by the way. I brought back Big Ten football. It was me, and I'm very happy to do it," to election week itself, nearly every news anchor or guest journalist on TV used sports language to express an opinion:

- September 16: He's got the ball, and he kept a hammerlock on the investigation.[7]

- September 16: That was a layup shot and a fumble on the one-yard line![8]

- September 30: The president didn't just miss the layup. We found out he's playing for the other team.[9]

- October 1: She may bob and weave at the confirmation hearings.[10]

- October 2: An already chaotic year has thrown us a curve-ball.[11]

- October 4: This is about shirts versus skins.[12]

- October 7: Did you leave it all on the field?[13]

- October 22: He boxed smartly.[14]

- November 2: It's hard to bring western and eastern Pennsylvania together, but the Eagles and the Steelers both won last night, so everybody's happy.[15]

- November 3: It's always good when your opponent telegraphs their plays ahead of time.[16]

- November 3: Georgia is a total jump ball.[17]

- November 5: The party did very well blocking and tackling in 2018.[18]

- November 5: If he wins in Pennsylvania, that is the whole ball game.[19]

- November 5: We are in for some rough sledding.[20]

- December 3: We need a full-court press on the vaccine.[21]

The rhetoric continued well into 2021, in response to the drama of President Biden's election certification and the January 6 attack on the US Capitol: "If this investigation were a football game, we'd still be in the first quarter," FBI agent Steven D'Antuono told MSNBC on January

15, and that same evening, MSNBC's Jeremy Bash described another political development as "basically a Heisman Trophy to the president." Ultimately, former director of National Intelligence James Clapper advised President Biden to "Take the gloves off" in foreign policy.[22] At one of the most critical moments in US history, nearly every comment presumed the viewing audience's expertise in male sports culture. Several of my past students wrote me to say that these examples took them back to our very first class discussion, on whether, where, and when girls are introduced to the sports talk males utilize over a lifetime of business and political conversations. Not every woman in America was literate in boxing and football terminology, and not all men were either. My own mother, intently following the political coverage, asked me to explain what *bob and weave*, *jump ball*, *whiff*, and *full-court press* meant and exactly how they applied to an election count. Nothing could better illustrate the influence of men's sports in halls of power and leadership and the subsequent marginalization of the female voter.

For the rest of 2020, a focus on decentering Whiteness and White privilege also loomed large in the news as athletes affirmed the Black Lives Matter movement with boycotts, walkouts, and strikes. The Women's Sports Foundation awarded the WNBA with their Wilma Rudolph Courage Award "for their bold courage and unity in the face of some of the most turbulent times in this country's history." Accepting the award was WNBA All-Star and Cal alum Layshia Clarendon, who only nine months before had been the guest speaker in my class at Berkeley. She and others were active in constructing a WNBA justice movement and Social Justice Council, linked to the Say Her Name campaign in honor of murdered African American woman Breonna Taylor. While some Americans were cool to the walkouts and activism of athletes bringing attention to Black Lives Matter, a *Washington Post* poll suggested that most Americans supported anthem protests and activism on the part of athletes.[23] The Women's Sports Foundation noted that Black women athletes were moving to the front and center of sports activism even as Black women remained hugely underrepresented (3 percent) in NCAA women's coaching positions.[24] My former student and three-time Olympic bobsled medalist Elana Meyers Taylor wrote movingly of her own experiences with racial profiling, in an essay for TeamUSA.org entitled "Even Olympic Medals Can't Save You" (June 26, 2020). Players in the WNBA were vocal and visible, particularly in response to remarks by Senator Kelly Loeffler, co-owner of the Atlanta Dream; Loeffler, later defeated in her bid for reelection by Raphael Warnock, had criticized the league for its social justice stance, insisting that the Black Lives Matter movement "promoted violence and destruction across the country."[25]

All the issues raised in my class were intersecting daily in public debate and policy. Thus, even as sports events were canceled or played before cutout audience photo boards, even as UC Berkeley's campus remained shut down in the pandemic, my students stayed active with topical projects. One of the most thoughtful and wise students from my fall 2019 class, Desi Carrasco, pursued a follow-up interview with Layshia Clarendon for the Cal Athletics website, successfully publishing an article that highlighted the progress of Black and LGBTQ women athletes.

> Leaving UC Berkeley with a bachelor's degree in American Studies and the record for fourth all-time scorer (1,820 points), Clarendon realized her WNBA dream as the 9th overall pick to the Indiana Fever in the 2013 WNBA Draft. Bringing the lessons in leadership she learned at Cal to professional women's basketball, Clarendon became a WNBA All-Star in 2017. Currently playing on the New York Liberty, Clarendon's contributions to the league have extended far beyond the court. Beginning as a team representative, she now serves as Vice President to the WNBA Players Association (WNBPA). Clarendon uses her leadership in the WNBA as a platform to advance economic justice by advocating for equity in wages, travel, and maternity policies, to name but a few areas of her activism.[26]

Over and over, my students have impressed me and challenged me with their own leadership. The question remains whether our society can commit to bringing American women and girls to the policy table as leaders—medical, political, and educational—making decisions on athletics.[27] What will the next year or two bring us? What will the future look like postpandemic? All these questions, I hope, will continue to be tackled by the next round of students I work with, especially as in-person teaching resumes. To quote my own favorite teacher from middle school, Henry Walker, "I still feel called by the kids I haven't met yet." Yes, I want the ones I haven't met yet to know the key events that transformed or suppressed women's sports opportunities, the turning points, the talking points, from the causes to the clauses, from Peanut Johnson to Title IX to today's platforms for calling out racism in sports. Whether I'm walking the canal trail from GWU to Georgetown or driving up Pacific Coast Highway to Berkeley, glancing leftward into the ocean that rocked me to sleep on three Semester at Sea voyages, you will find me with a syllabus in my backpack and a schedule of my college athletes' games. Looking back over twenty-five years, I see the faces of every student I had the privilege to know. As a professor, as a women's sports historian, I never tire of teaching this class. In fact, I'm just warming up for many more years to come in the classroom and beyond.

Game on.

Fig. C.2 Megan Rapinoe jersey, 2019. Both men and women cheered the US Women's National Team when they won the Women's World Cup in 2019. Confident and outspoken player Megan Rapinoe, openly lesbian, became a new kind of sports icon for fans and players alike. *Photo by the author.*

CRITICAL THINKING RESOURCES

For Chapter 1

- What is your earliest memory of a favorite childhood game? Were you a leader? Were you good? Who did you play with?

- Women: What is your first memory of being told you shouldn't play with boys or play boys' games?

- Men: When did you first become aware that certain games or toys were just for girls?

- Name the first female athlete you knew about or admired.

- Interview your mother, grandmother, or an older female relative. What sports opportunities did she have? What was physical education like in her day?

- Read John Tunis, "Women and the Sport Business," *Harper's Magazine*, July 1929. Why did sports authorities recommend limits on women's participation in the Olympics? How did society strive to protect even competitive, elite female athletes from possible overexertion?

- Read Tony Horwitz, "The Woman Who (Maybe) Struck Out Babe Ruth and Lou Gehrig," *Smithsonian*, July 2013. Do we believe that women can strike out men? Do we assume chivalrous males will throw such a contest and allow women to prevail?

- How does a political climate eliminate top athletes from competition?

- How many outstanding women athletes are unknown to us today because, due to race or ethnicity, their names were kept out of national records?

- What other sportswear and sports fads resulted from wartime?

For Chapter 2

- What do you notice about the ways female athletes are portrayed in the news, sports magazines, and film?

- What attracts fans to certain women's sports and not others? Do fans ignore or enjoy specific male sports for similar reasons?

- Read "Female Athletes Guard Figures, Complexions," *Durham Morning Herald*, August 9, 1974. How does the author present the concerns and interests of the featured female athletes? What role does beauty play in attracting both male and female reporters to women's sports?

- Read Bill Gilbert and Nancy Williamson, "Sports Is Unfair to Women," *Sports Illustrated*, May 28, 1973. Does it surprise you to see a thorough analysis of sex discrimination in sport appearing in a 1974 issue of *Sports Illustrated*? What do you think of the authors' depiction of women athletes as "second-class citizens"?

- Read Paul Farhi and Frank Ahrens, "Advertisers Pull Out of Imus Show," *Washington Post*, April 11, 2007, and Robert Smith, "CBS Radio Fires Don Imus in Fallout Over Remarks," NPR, April 12, 2007. Don Imus was not the first critic to imply that athletic women may win as a team but fail to appear attractive to men. Where else is that message reinforced? Why did this specific defamation of young African American college women create a national outcry? Are Americans more likely to confront racism when it incorporates sexism?

- Read Dave Sheinin, "Romanian Mother, 38, Takes Gold in Marathon," *Washington Post*, August 16, 2008. How often do we see a headline that identifies a male athlete first as a father? In what ways are we socialized to think of mothers as nonathletes?

- Read Jack Ross, "Lisa Saxon, the Woman Who Helped Change Sports Writing Forever," VICE Sports, November 17, 2014. Should women be sent inside men's team clubhouses as credentialed journalists? Is the sexual harassment of women sportswriters comparable to the hazing of other women entering a traditionally male profession?

For Chapter 3

- Did adults try steering you to specific sports? Were the activities expected of you tied to your being male or female?

- Were male and female athletes treated differently at your middle school or high school? How?

- In what ways are female athletes pressured to look or behave in ways society identifies as "feminine"? Do you think women can have big muscles and be beautiful? How big is too big?

- Has American culture allowed men to move beyond traditionally male activities into some sports or activities once seen as "female"?

- Does the American public still reject big muscles on women? After enduring mixed reactions to her appearance, how did Bev Francis change her looks?

- Read Frank Deford, "The Women of Atlanta," *Newsweek*, June 10, 1996. Deford suggests that women aren't yet big fans of women's sports and that it's mostly men who promote talented female athletes. Do you agree? Discuss Deford's comment "Most girls do not need superstars to look up to." Is he suggesting that it's difficult to market athletic women as role models for young girls?

- Read Elizabeth Merrill, "Kansas Religious-Based School Called Out for Removing Female Ref," ESPN, February 21, 2008. In what ways do schools use freedom of religion to limit women's athletic roles? Should boys gain experience with female officials so long as girls' games are officiated by men?

- Read Ruth Padawer, "The Humiliating Practice of Sex-Testing Female Athletes," *New York Times Magazine*, June 28, 2016. To what degree are atypical/intersex genitalia or chromosomes a specifically *athletic* "advantage" for women? Would Caster Semenya be treated differently if she were not African?

For Chapter 4

- How would you enforce or interpret a law like Title IX?

- As women grow stronger and set new sports records, do you think they will "catch up" to men? Is there a natural limit to women's athletic ability?

- We see more men coaching women than women coaching men. Will this change over time? In your experience, do you think men and women coach differently?

- Which aspect of Title IX law seems to be the most confusing, debatable, or open to misinterpretation?

- Why have so many colleges elected to drop men's sports rather than add women's?

- When does fifty-fifty come to be seen as unfair? Do you agree that equality may be perceived as a loss or as reverse discrimination?

- Do you think most women on average are less interested in sports than most men?

- Read Erik Brady, "Why All the Fuss When a Woman Beats a Man?" *USA Today*, May 23–26, 2003. Is it easier to accept a woman's athletic superiority in an individual sport, such as golf?

- Read J. Robinson, Peg Bradley-Doppes, Charles M. Neinas, John R. Thelin, Christine A. Plonsky, and Michael A. Messner, "Gender Equity in College Sports: 6 Views," *Chronicle of Higher Education*, December 6, 2002. Which writer did you find most convincing? Why?

- Read Ray Glier, "After Making the Team, She Is Making History," *Washington Post*, August 31, 2001. "I'm not trying to break a barrier—I just want to play a game." Can a woman in a traditionally masculine sport avoid being cast as a radical role model?

- Read Ellen Nakashima, "Girls Getting a New Hold on an Old Sport," *Washington Post*, February 24, 1999. Are authorities more concerned about the possibility of sexual contact between young people or the possibility of a male wrestler being defeated by a female?

- Read Carol Hutchins, Edniesha Curry, and Meredith Flaherty, "Where Are All the Women Coaches?," *New York Times*, December 31, 2019. These authors argue, "Girls and boys grow up being led by men. Guess who they come to believe are the real leaders?" How do we increase the numbers and visibility of women in coaching and sports management roles?

For Chapter 5

- Read Amir Vahdat and Mehdi Fattahi, "Iran Women Attend FIFA Soccer Game for First Time in Decades," Associated Press, October 11, 2019. Compared with boys and men, how are girls and women encouraged or forbidden to attend sports events?

- Read Bill Plaschke, "She Lost, but She's a Hero," *Los Angeles Times*, August 4, 2012. Consider the author's phrases "This giant symbol was really just a frightened, lost little girl" and "Mojica . . . appeared to look at her with a sort of maternal kindness." How does this reporting differ from the way male athletes are described?

For Chapter 6

• Read My-Ly Nguyen Sperry, "$60M Gift to Fund Baseball Complex," *Binghamton University Magazine*, Spring 2020. Who will help fund women's sports programs or women's studies departments? Do women support women's initiatives?

THE COURSE ASSIGNMENTS

First Sports Paper

Where do you see bias in sports coverage?

Your first paper should be about three pages long. First, find sources you can discuss (that are not already in our assigned class readings). Attitudes about athletes and certain sports appear in every newspaper, in magazine articles, in commercial images selling products, in television—everywhere, there are presentations of or images associated with sports, fitness, the idealized American body, and advice on athletic health. Food, toys, and beauty products also use images of athletes. Please find a short article or ad in a newspaper or magazine. (Please do not use a friend's blog, a homemade YouTube video, or a Wikipedia entry.)

In your paper, please explain why, *in your opinion*, your source relies on certain biases or stereotypes about men or women in sports. What ongoing assumptions about sex, gender, race, or ethnicity did you find? Were you surprised?

You have plenty of choices! Newspapers and magazines are bursting with articles on sports celebrities, scandals, training, school PE classes, weight-loss workouts, competitive youth, injuries, and fitness culture. Please make sure your sources are current. Beware of online material that is merely a fan's post and not actual published work. Choose sources where an author is identified.

Once you have a sample (or two) and are ready to write, look for the assumptions about gender, race, and sports performance. Who is the intended audience? Are there mixed messages or contradictions? What do these sources imply about athletes or sports? Does the author or art editor mean to provoke? What satisfies our cultural ideals about men and women as heroic or beautiful, tough, or ugly?

For this assignment, I am looking for strong writing and smart insights. Keep your tone professional, not too informal or conversational, and proofread your words carefully for spelling, punctuation, and grammar. The most commonly misspelled words in this course are *woman* (do you mean one woman or more than two women?) and *lose* (not *loose*, please). I can help you, and so can the writing center, which has daily walk-in hours.

No late papers! Plan now to submit the assignment the day it is due. That means handed in when you arrive at class—and stapled or clipped, please, not held together with a hairpin. Thank you!

Sample Midterm Exam

Please answer any *three* essays from this list. You have enough time to spend at least thirty minutes on each response. Take longer if you need to.

Draw on what you've learned from the readings, films, or any class handouts. A few double-spaced pages (two to three) per answer is about right.

- How did concerns about women's health limit their athletic opportunities over time? What kind of exercise was allowed in the past, and which women were already using their muscles? Give *specific* historical examples.

- How did race and class identities affect athletic participation in the past?

- Discuss international politics and sport in the twentieth century. Which political moments made it possible for sports heroes or heroines to gain visibility?

- Compare the shaping or production of women's bodies in the two films *Pumping Iron II* and *Doping for Gold*. How do these films capture beliefs about the "normal" female body and what it is capable of? (Hint: Your essay must go beyond merely *describing* these films. Analyze the issues raised!)

- Discuss some of the factors that made the All-American Girls Professional Baseball League a success from 1943 to 1954. What led to the end of the league?

Semester at Sea Final Exam Excerpt, Spring 2019

1. How does *climate change* impact sports? List two examples.
2. What history-making sports event took place in South Africa on June 24, 1995?
3. What is the burkini?
4. Name two countries that boycotted specific Olympic Games in certain years.
5. Who is Caster Semenya?
6. What year did FIFA agree to allow women to compete wearing headscarves?
7. At which Olympics did Saudi Arabia finally send a female athletic competitor?
8. What is a soccer hooligan?
9. Why are ice-skating rinks popping up in China?
10. New popular awareness of staying hydrated with sports drinks and water has contributed to which global issue?
11. What is the haka?
12. Who is Nawal El Moutawakel?
13. In what year were the "Nazi Olympics" held?
14. What are two raw materials used to make sports gear or toys we have seen?
15. Nike-brand products are manufactured in factory areas heavily concentrated in which two countries on our voyage?
16. What are some advantages and disadvantages of being selected for a state-run sports academy?
17. Who is the first African woman to win an Olympic gold medal?
18. For many years, segregation laws made it difficult for Black and White sports teams to play against each other—in both South Africa and the United States. Name three specific challenges for athletes trying to meet on the playing field.
19. Guards at South Africa's Robben Island prison introduced two sports for their own off-hours recreation time. What were they?
20. Which state in the United States produced the first sumo wrestling champion outside Japan?

Three Versions of the Syllabus

ATHLETICS AND GENDER

George Washington University Fall 2002 M/W 2–3:15
Instructor: Bonnie J. Morris Office hours: T/Th 10–2

Welcome! This course is one of the few undergraduate seminars in the country to explore the history of sex-role stereotyping in modern sports. How do our attitudes about male and female athletes reflect cultural beliefs? How are men and women socialized to think about competition, winning, and performance? Has Title IX made any significant impact on equality of opportunity? Why have so many male sports heroes been linked to violent crime and sexual abuse? How does our American media play a role in constructing stereotypes about winners and losers, masculinity and femininity?

Required textbooks:

Susan Birrell and Mary G. McDonald, *Reading Sport.*
Susan Cahn, *Coming On Strong.*
Sara Corbett, *Venus to the Hoop.*
Pat Griffin, *Strong Women, Deep Closets.*
Allen Guttmann, *A Whole New Ball Game.*
Mariah Burton Nelson, *The Stronger Women Get, the More Men Love Football.*
Joan Ryan, *Little Girls in Pretty Boxes.*
Lissa Smith, *Nike Is a Goddess.*

Through readings, films, guest speakers, and class discussions, we will explore the politics of athletics and gender—at our own campus, in larger society, and cross-culturally. You must ATTEND CLASS and come prepared to discuss the readings assigned for that day. Your first written assignment is a short analysis of recent media coverage of women's sports. There will be a midterm in class and a final paper on the subject of Title IX, 7–10 pages.

Finally, all students are required to keep a "sports journal" throughout the semester, in which you may note your responses to athletes in the news, any sports events you attend, conversations you notice, or other personal or media attitudes you observe concerning sex roles and sports. You are welcome to share these journal notes in class, but the journal does not have to be handed in to me until the end of the term (you'll get it back). This is an informal, though important, assignment, meaning your journal may be handwritten on loose sheets or in a spiral notepad—and you may include news clippings and magazine ads, as well as your own comments.

W, 9/4: First class: introduction to the course. Prepare an informal list of your own childhood playground games.

M, 9/9: American manhood: initiation rites through sport in early American history. READ: *A Whole New Ball Game*, chapters 3–6; *Reading Sport*, ch. 1.

W, 9/11: Ideals of American womanhood: health and proper behavior in the nineteenth century. READ: *Coming On Strong*, intro and ch. 1.

M, 9/16: Women competing in the early twentieth century: public issues, class issues. READ: *Coming On Strong*, ch. 2–4.

W, 9/18: World War II and sport: Jesse Owens versus the Nazis, and the All-American Girls Professional Baseball League. READ: *Coming On Strong*, ch. 6.

M, 9/23: Film: *When Diamonds Were a Girl's Best Friend*, dir. Janis Taylor. Interviews with former AAGPBL players. First papers are due in class today. READ: *Nike Is a Goddess*, "Baseball and Softball" chapter.

W, 9/25: Postwar tensions of race and sexuality: segregation and sex roles in the Cold War years. READ: *A Whole New Ball Game*, ch. 9; *Coming On Strong*, ch. 5 and 7; *Nike Is a Goddess*, "Track and Field" chapter.

M, 9/30: The 1960s: Olympic "femininity testing" begins. How real a woman are you? READ: *Coming On Strong*, ch. 9; *The Stronger Women Get . . .*, ch. 4; *Nike Is a Goddess*, "Swimming" chapter.

W, 10/2: Film: *Pumping Iron II*, dir. George Butler. The competitive aesthetics of the female body. READ: "The Strongest Woman in the World," by Gloria Steinem, from *Moving Beyond Words*; "Scary Monsters," by Louis Theroux, in *FHM*, January/February 2001.

M, 10/7: The destruction of the body in athletics: from playing hurt to playing high. READ: *A Whole New Ball Game*, ch. 11, "The Men in the Mirror," *Chronicle of Higher Education*, September 27, 2002; "The Truth about Women's Bodies," *Time*, March 8, 1999; "Drugs and Sports," *Newsweek*, February 15, 1999.

W, 10/9: Fitness for women and schoolchildren: Empowerment or social control? READ: *The Stronger Women Get . . .*, ch. 2–3; *A Whole New Ball Game*, ch. 7; "For French Girls, Playing Soccer Is a Tough Goal," by Elaine Sciolino, *New York Times International*, September 16, 2002.

M, 10/14: The emergence of Title IX during 1970s feminism. READ: *A Whole New Ball Game*, ch. 10; *Coming On Strong*, ch. 10; *Nike Is a Goddess*, "Tennis" and "Conclusion" chapters. You will also receive a packet of articles as a Title IX guide: "Title IX at 30: Athletics Receive C+," prepared by the Women's Sports Foundation, June 2002; "Athletics and Equality" series in the *Chronicle of Higher Education*, December 6, 1996.

W, 10/16: Midterm exam in class.

M, 10/21: Athletics and the university: school spirit versus school scandal. READ: *A Whole New Ball Game*, ch. 8; handouts: "More Schools Laying Down the Law," by Steve Wieberg, *USA Today*, September 18, 1998; "Colleges Must Act Decisively When Scholarship Athletes Run Afoul of the Law," by Jeffrey Benedict, *Chronicle of Higher Education*, May 9, 1997; "Crime and Punishment," by Gary Smith.

W, 10/23: Sexual assault in the athletic community and problematic relationships between players and coaches. READ: *The Stronger Women Get . . .*, ch. 7–8; "Growth in Women's Sports Stirs Harassment Issue," by Robin Finn, *New York Times*, March 7, 1999; "Female Athletes Face a Culture of Sexual Harassment," by Leslie Heywood, *Chronicle of Higher Education*, January 8, 1999; "GW Prospect Apologizes to Victim," by Mark Asher, *Washington Post*, June 16, 1996.

M, 10/28: Sports and sexuality today. READ: *The Stronger Women Get . . .*, ch. 1, 5, 6; *Reading Sport*, ch. 3, 9, 10.

W, 10/30: Homophobia and lesbian baiting in women's sports. READ: all of *Strong Women, Deep Closets*; *Coming On Strong*, ch. 8; "Final Frontiers," by Patricia Nell Warren, in *Out*, October 2002; "Reflections of a Gay Athletics Director," by Michael Muska, *Chronicle of Higher Education*, October 13, 2000; "Fair Game," by Liz Galst, *Out*, November 1997.

M, 11/4: Media coverage. How are male and female athletes portrayed today? What are some obvious differences? Are women visible as sports journalists and television commentators? READ: *The Stronger Women Get . . .*, ch. 9 and 19; *Reading Sport*, ch. 4; "Finding a New Gloss," by Gwen Knapp, *San Francisco Chronicle*, December 31, 2000; "Women in Locker Rooms," by Reggie White, *Asian Wall Street Journal*, April 12, 1999.

W, 11/6: Staying pretty, staying small: recent concerns in female performance athletics like gymnastics. READ: all of *Little Girls in Pretty Boxes*; *Nike Is a Goddess*, "Gymnastics" and "Figure Skating" chapters.

M, 11/11: Eating disorders and weight control. Film: *Frontline* special "Fat."

W, 11/13: Racism and racial representations in sports today. READ: *Reading Sport*, ch. 2, 5, 6; "At T.C. Williams, Separate Fields of Play," by Patrick Welsh, *Washington Post*, October 22, 2000; "A Professor Explores Americans' Reverence for Black Sports Stars," by Christopher Shea, *Chronicle of Higher Education*, March 7, 1997.

M, 11/18: The present controversy over sports teams using Native American names and symbols. Film: *In Whose Honor?* READ: "What's in a Name?" issue of the *Chronicle of Higher Education*, February 23, 2001; "Playing Indian: Why Native American Mascots Must End," by Charles F. Springwood and C. Richard King, in the *Chronicle of Higher Education*, November 9, 2001.

W, 11/20: The ethics of sports marketing, from Olympic scandals and cereal boxes to Nike logo endorsements and sweatshop manufacture of sports gear. READ: *No Logo*, by Naomi Klein; "To Market, to Market," by Thomas Heath, *Washington Post*, April 1, 2001; "Three Years after the Sit-In," by Dave Kelly, *Georgetown Voice*, November 7, 2001.

M, 11/25: Special guest speaker: referee Dorothy Hirsch.

W, 11/27: No class—Thanksgiving break begins. Read *Venus to the Hoop* over vacation!

M, 12/2: The future of competition: More pro teams for women? Better pay parity? Or . . . more sports-bra images? READ: finish *Venus to the Hoop*; *Nike Is a Goddess*, "Golf," "Soccer," "Ice Hockey," and "Basketball" chapters.

W, 12/4: Last class meets today. Turn in sports journals. Title IX papers are due in my box by MONDAY, December 9.

Semester at Sea Course Syllabus (Colorado State University)

Voyage: Spring 2019
Discipline: Sociology
Course Number and Title: S343 Sport and Society
Division: Upper
Faculty Name: Bonnie J. Morris
Semester Credit Hours: 3
Prerequisites: None

COURSE DESCRIPTION

This course offers a compelling look at how men and women fit into national sports culture, particularly where athletes are pressured to model ideological and political beliefs through their bodies. How are men and women differently socialized, from very early ages, in terms of healthful exercise and competitive games? How do media in different cultures construct images of winners and losers, ideal bodies, masculinity, and femininity? We'll explore the history of racially segregated athletes, Olympic controversy, fan violence, homophobia, and cultural beliefs about strength, training foods, and injury. In each port, you'll have ample opportunity to observe or even join in local sport activities and games and to consider the gendered aspects of recreation, sneakers, sportswear, sports heroes, and national victory.

Thought for the Voyage:

Sport is still a male-only preserve in many ports where the female body is considered shameful and its public display banned, yet in much of East and South Asia, women and girls manufacture the sports clothing and gear worn by Western female champions.

Learning Objectives:

1. Understand the politics of gender and sport in our own schools, in public life, and in global cross-cultural contexts.
2. Know the various customs, rationalizations, and social codes restricting female sports participation.
3. Demonstrate familiarity with the athletes and educators who are working to change biased attitudes and to create more opportunities for all.
4. Evaluate the limits and possibilities for sports to bring together regional enemies and/or break down barriers between political opponents.

Textbooks:

AUTHOR: Susan Cahn
TITLE: *Coming On Strong*
PUBLISHER: University of Illinois
DATE/EDITION: 2015
AUTHOR: Niko Besnier, Susan Brownell, and Thomas Carter
TITLE: *The Anthropology of Sport: Bodies, Borders, Biopolitics*
PUBLISHER: University of California
DATE/EDITION: 2018

Course Outline:

Depart Ensenada, Mexico—January 5

A1—January 7: Children's games, playtime, and sports leisure in global context. READINGS: *Anthropology of Sport*, intro.

A2—January 9: Manhood as sport ritual and performance; from the early Olympics to modern competition. READINGS: *Anthropology*, ch. 1.

A3—January 11: Ideals of women's health, fragility, and sexuality in the debate over female sports participation. READINGS: Cahn, ch. 1–3.

Honolulu, Hawaii—January 12

A4—January 14: Sport, the body, and religion. READINGS: Nigel Barker, "Is Sport a Religion?," *Psychology Today*, November 11, 2009; Rory McCarthy, "Afghan Applause Just Isn't Cricket," *Guardian*, May 18, 2001.

January 16—international date line crossing (lost day)

A5—January 17: Sport and class: games of wealthy and poor, and the construction of country clubs / free facilities. READINGS: *Anthropology*, ch. 2; Cahn, ch. 4.

January 19—study day (no class)

A6—January 20: Racial segregation in American sports history. READINGS: Cahn, ch. 5; *Anthropology*, ch. 4.

A7—January 22: The political Olympiad, from the Nazi era to regional and country boycotts. READINGS: *Anthropology*, ch. 6.

Kobe, Japan—January 24–28

A8—January 29: The state system of training champions: from East to West. READINGS: *Anthropology*, ch. 7.

Shanghai, China—January 31–February 1

February 2–3—in transit

Hong Kong, SAR—February 4–5

A9—February 6: The politics of sportswear production in South Asia. READINGS: Cynthia Enloe, "The Globetrotting Sneaker," in *Ms.*, March/April 1995.

Ho Chi Minh City, Vietnam—February 8–13

A10—February 14: Cold War–era sports culture and the issue of homophobia. READINGS: Cahn, ch. 6–8.

February 16—study day (no class)

A11—February 17: Destruction versus development of the body as a virtue. READINGS: *Anthropology*, ch. 3; FILM: *Girl Unbound*.

Yangon, Myanmar—February 19–23

A12—February 24: Review session. FILM: *Chak De! India*.

A13—February 26: MIDTERM.

Cochin, India—February 28–March 5

A14—March 6: FILM: *Offside* (Iran). READINGS: Summer Wood, "Scenes from the Axis of Evil," *Bitch* magazine, Fall 2003.

March 7—study day (no class)

A15—March 9: Islam, the Taliban ban on sport, and Sports for Peace clinics/initiatives. READINGS: *Anthropology*, ch. 8.

Port Louis, Mauritius—March 11

A16—March 12: Empowering African women through sport. FILM: *Zanzibar Soccer Queens*. READINGS: "In Nigeria, Sponsors Avoid Funding Women's Sports," BBC, June 16, 2016.

A17—March 14: Beyond *Invictus*: the apartheid era in South African sport. READINGS: on reserve, *Arms Linked*, poetry from the Springbok Tour boycott.

A18—March 16: FILM: *Alive and Kicking: Soccer Grannies of South Africa*.

Cape Town, South Africa—March 18–23

A19—March 24: Caster Semenya, femininity testing, and the future for trans athletes. READINGS: Ariel Levy, "Either/Or: Sports, Sex, and the Case of Caster Semenya," *New Yorker*, November 30, 2009; *Anthropology*, ch. 5; Cahn, ch. 9–10.

A20—March 26: Sports marketing and the emergence of the burkini. READINGS: Aheda Zanetti, "I Created the Burkini," *Guardian*, August 24, 2016; Amy Taxin, "Arab Mascot at Coachella Valley High," *Huffpost Los Angeles*, December 4, 2013.

A21—March 28: White control of Black talent in sport, "soccer hooligans" and racism in European soccer. READINGS: George Vecsey, "England Battles Racism Infecting Soccer," *New York Times*, February 2, 2003; Keith Richburg, "Fans' Racist Taunts Rattle European Soccer," *Washington Post*, December 13, 2004; "Racism and Football Fans," Social Issues Research Centre (UK).

Tema, Ghana—March 30–April 1

Takoradi, Ghana—April 2–3

A22—April 4: Bodies, food, and eating disorders: What's a sport food? READINGS: Elaheh Nozari, "The Truth about Asian Women and Eating Disorders," *Cosmopolitan*, February 19, 2016.

A23—April 6: Sport in the Western world order: opponents and the shaping of bodies. FILM: *Doping for Gold*.

April 8—study day (no class)

A24—April 9: Last class: approaches to expanding opportunities for
women athletes in North Africa and beyond.
Casablanca, Morocco—April 11–14
A25—April 15: FINAL EXAM.

FIELDWORK

Semester at Sea field experiences allow for an unparalleled opportunity
to compare, contrast, and synthesize the different cultures and countries encountered over the course of the voyage. In addition to the one
field class, students will complete independent field assignments that
span multiple countries.

Field Class and Assignment:

Field class attendance is mandatory for all students enrolled in this
course. Do not book individual travel plans or a Semester at Sea–
sponsored trip on the day of your field class. Field classes constitute at
least 20% of the contact hours for each course and are developed and
led by the instructor.

1) South African Sport, Pre- and Postapartheid

We will tour the Cape Town District Six Museum *Fields of Play* exhibit,
with its history of Coloured club teams and sport life under apartheid,
meeting some veteran athletes from the segregated clubs; afterward,
travel to a township to enjoy a pickup soccer game with kids. Get your
history and your game on!

Objectives: to look beyond the hopeful imagery of a unified South Africa (projected in the film *Invictus*) to learn about the challenges for non-
White athletes under apartheid. How did segregated sports teams and
clubs compare to the Negro League ball clubs and other Black-owned enterprises in the United States under Jim Crow law? How are the histories
of marginalized communities taught (or not) in mainstream overviews
of national sports records?

2) Athletes and Athletic Brands, China

International rivalries have long been acted out on the playing field,
as we see during both Summer and Winter Olympic Games. Unlike the
United States, most socialist states (including China) identify gifted athletes as children and enroll them in national sports academies. We will
tour a top-level sports academy, such as SECA Academy or Shanghai
University of Sport, observing (where permitted) the facilities and ideology for molding national sports champions. Ideally, we will also see a

demonstration by female martial-arts students. If possible, we will tour Nike's Asia-Pacific Headquarters and discuss the local manufacture of brand-name sports gear intended for the West. (You are also encouraged to tour a Nike factory when we reach Vietnam.)

Objectives: compare China's approach to producing elite athletes with American systems, and gain eyewitness knowledge of the environment in which Chinese women produce US athletic brands.

METHODS OF EVALUATION

Port reports: 40%
Field class: 20%
Midterm: 20%
Final exam: 20%

University of California at Berkeley
100AC: Sports and Gender in US History

Fall 2019. Class # 31604; 4 units.
Dwinelle 145, Tu/Th 3:30–4:59 p.m.
Instructor: Bonnie J. Morris
Office hours: T/Th 2–3:20 pm. and over coffee after class by sign-up.
This course satisfies the American Cultures Requirement.

Welcome, all! This class invites you to examine the history of sex roles, race, and culture in American sport, with a special emphasis on where and how women have entered full (or limited) athletic participation. Sports events, as public and televised spectacles, reinforce a range of intended politics: community pride, international competition, the ranking of public bodies, symbolic warfare, the exploitation of Black talent by White ownership, the reinforcement of rewards for male strength, and female marketability. In US society, high school and college sports have also served as access to education and social mobility while reinforcing stereotypes about race, gender, and "natural" ability. Across history, we find athletes pressured to model society's ideological and political beliefs through their very bodies, and though the "best" bodies may set world records in an event, the winner frequently returns to a society where he or she is a second-class citizen at best.

How do our attitudes about both male and female athletes reflect learned cultural biases and expectations? How are men and women, boys and girls, trained to think about health, performance, and victory in athletics? What role has our media played in constructing winners and losers, idealized fitness, masculinity, and femininity? And how do these questions of boundaried athleticism intersect with shifting racial codes—and women's emergence into full public and political representation?

In line with the American Cultures mission to desegregate the history curriculum and examine the lived experiences of all communities represented at Cal, we will:

1. analyze the ways schools and state interests have used sport to perpetuate and exaggerate both racial difference and gendered reproductive roles. We'll move from sacred games and the colonization of bodies in early America to the emergence of scientific racism in nineteenth-century fitness culture and the construction of segregated recreation facilities through Jim Crow law.

2. apply the contexts of medical and anthropological race and health classifications to fitness and eugenics narratives, examining immigrant sports leagues and sport at historically Black universities and colleges (HBUCs) as sites of resistance. We'll also interrogate health advisories to map women's entry into formerly male-only spheres of play.

3. follow where and how marginalized groups of male and female athletes enter the mainstream based on government needs; we'll see approaches of normalizing the segregation of Native Americans, Japanese Americans, Jews, and African Americans through wartime sport, Negro League, and exhibition games. With the rise of Cold War–era homophobia, we'll also examine the intersection of sport as heterosexism, the Olympics as a global stage for acting out notions of equal opportunity, and the narratives of closeted LGBTQ athletes before Stonewall.

4. inquire about double standards for sports violence and injury, as well as for criminalizing athletes (or bringing sexual predators to justice), and ways that gendered and racialized aspects of sport are reinforced through profitable material culture: clothing brands, action toys, health foods, sneakers, and uniform logos.

Conceptually, in each period of history, we'll incorporate the journeys of African American, Native American, immigrant, and LGBTQ athletes in the following ways: as producers for White consumers of sports entertainment; as independent actors, coaches, and managers for community-run sport programs; as communities of resistance against imposed race laws; as role models for other aspiring athletes; as public speakers using the sports platform to advocate civil rights reforms and boycotts; and as stereotyped images appearing on toy and food brands, as team mascots, and in cultural messages about "normal" male and female traits. It should be implicit in the syllabus that each day will include integrated material in reference to diverse groups, with certain specific topics highlighted or dominant for the day.

LEARNING OBJECTIVES/OUTCOMES

Each class will combine equal parts lecture and discussion to allow for diverse perspectives: you are encouraged to reference your own experiences with gender and sport in education, recreation, public life, and globally. During this semester, you'll also be asked to:

- know the various codes and customs restricting female and minority access to sports participation in US history

- demonstrate familiarity with athletes and educators who helped change attitudes, laws, and opportunities

- identify the intersection of race, class, and gender in the construction of sports participation and facilities in the United States

- analyze the evolving nature of the Olympics as a global geopolitical event with overlapping ideological narratives

- identify biases and themes in media coverage of men's and women's athletics

- compare restricted country-club sports and other membership-based facilities with public courts, YMCA and YMHA recreation, open versus segregated parks and pools, and street ball

- understand and address the background of Title IX law and its ongoing applications

- analyze aspects of social diversity (ethnicity, race, socio-economic status, gender, sexual orientation, age, ability, etc.) and how they affect American sports training

- explain how social categories and structures of power may affect human athletic potential

- articulate a critical account of double standards in health and fitness history

- demonstrate your familiarity with the readings and other course content through exams and short papers

TEXTBOOKS

Susan Cahn, *Coming On Strong*. University of Illinois Press, 2015. A full accounting of twentieth-century women's sports progress and backlash, including analyses of class, race, and homophobia in the promotion and rules governing women's events.

Mary Corey and Mark Harnischfeger, *Before Jackie: The Negro Leagues, Civil Rights and the American Dream*. Paramount Market Publishing, 2014. Approaches to the legacies of Negro League baseball in terms of Black management and community autonomy, with critical attention to the women of the leagues and issues of travel in the Jim Crow South.

Harry Edwards, *The Revolt of the Black Athlete*. University of Illinois Press, 2018. Fiftieth anniversary edition of this work by a legendary UC Berkeley professor; examines racism and economic injustice in sport.

John Hoberman, *Darwin's Athletes*. Houghton Mifflin, 1997. A critical overview of scientific myths surrounding Black athleticism.

Caitlin Murray, *The National Team*. Abrams Press, 2019. A backstory of the US women's national soccer team and their struggle for equal pay, visibility, and fair treatment by media.

Suggested further reading:

Niko Besnier, Susan Brownell, and Thomas F. Carter, *The Anthropology of Sport*. University of California Press, 2018.

Sarah Fields, *Female Gladiators*. University of Illinois Press, 2008.

Ken Mochizuki, *Baseball Saved Us*. Lee & Low Books, 1995.

Nina Revoyr, *The Necessary Hunger*. Simon & Schuster, 1997.

William Rhoden, *$40 Million Slaves*. Random House, 2007.

Dave Zirin, *What's My Name, Fool?* Haymarket, 2005

FILMS

Dare to Compete: The Struggle for Women in Sports
Doping for Gold
In Whose Honor? Native American Mascots
The Manzanar Fishermen's Club
Playing for the World
Pumping Iron II
Unforgivable Blackness: The Rise and Fall of Jack Johnson
When Diamonds Were a Girl's Best Friend

COURSEWORK AND EXPECTATIONS

Please arrive on time, having read the material assigned for that day; attendance is factored into your overall grade. Your grade will begin to be affected after your third absence (exceptions will be made for athletic events). If you are a participating Cal athlete, provide a game schedule to me early on so I can assist you in making up any work missed due to travel. Accommodations for students with disabilities will be made on an individual basis. For other personal concerns not covered by the syllabus, please see me at the start of the semester; I am also happy to meet at times beyond the designated office hours. Written assignments must be completed on schedule: no late work!

1. The first paper is a short analysis of intersectional race and gender bias in sports media.
2. There will be an in-class midterm. It is closed book and closed note, covering the readings and historical material from the first month of class, with an emphasis on body classifications, wartime sport, and racial exhibition games. There will be a review in class prior to the exam.
3. A final exam will cover your familiarity with the following: Title IX, the globalization of sports culture, the state's political investment in fitness, and race and sex codes embedded in sports marketing.

Final grades are calculated with the first paper weighing 20% and the midterm and final paper 40% each. You will be evaluated on your ability to write at college level, with proper citations and sources. Please familiarize yourself with the university code of academic integrity: copying from the internet, utilizing another student's paper as your own, or other violations will result in failure of the assignment. In all assignments, "I" statements are fine where appropriate, while a conversational or sarcastic tone should be saved for lively class discussion.

A+ 99–100 A 94–98

A- 90–93 B+ 87–89

B 84–86 B- 80–83

C+ 77–79 C 74–76

C- 70–73 D+ 67–69

D 64–66 D- 60–63

F below 60

Nondiscrimination Statement

The classroom is a diverse and inclusive community. The University of California, in accordance with applicable federal and state law and university policy, prohibits discrimination against any member of the school's community on the basis of race, color, religion, national origin, sex, sexual orientation, citizenship, age, gender identity, pregnancy, ancestry, marital status, medical condition, physical or mental disability, or military service. This nondiscrimination policy covers admission, access, and treatment in all university programs and activities.

On Sexual Harassment

No form of harassment will be tolerated in our classroom. As UC employees, all instructors are Responsible Employees required to report incidents of sexual violence, sexual harassment, or other conduct prohibited by university policy to the Title IX officer. To report sex discrimination or sexual harassment, contact the Title IX Office. Confidential resources available to students include the CARE Advocate Office, which serves survivors of sexual violence and sexual harassment.

Students who need accommodation will work with the Disabled Students Program to make the official designation and associated accommodations. If you have a letter of accommodation, you are responsible for sharing it with instructors in order to get the help you need, such as extended exam time and/or note-taking assistance. Requests for midterm proctoring are due in September.

Use of a personal laptop for note-taking purposes is acceptable. To avoid distraction to your colleagues, yourself, and your professor, do not use your cell phone during class. You are welcome to email me: just include a proper greeting ("Hello, Dr. Bon" is fine) and do consider what you've written before you hit Send. I may not respond instantly, but I'll reply within twenty-four hours.

Readings and Class Topics by Calendar Date

PART I: Sacred games and colonized bodies: historical anchors of race, class, and gender.

Th, 8/29: First class: introduction to the subject. The US women's soccer team commands our attention, but what's the long American history behind more-recent female achievement? Make an informal list of your favorite childhood or playground games. How do we learn who is "naturally" good at which sports? What are some ways schools influence or are influenced by athletic talent as a path to popularity, favoritism, or success?

Tue, 9/3: American manhood: body attitudes in American history, from Puritan encounters with Indigenous games to the "muscular Christianity" of the nineteenth century. READ: Nigel Barker, "Is Sport a Religion?," *Psychology Today*, November 11, 2009.

Th, 9/5: Ideals of American womanhood: racial and religious roles of the "good" woman, and medical and class attitudes toward female health and behavior across the centuries, including the double standards for maternal health of White women and enslaved Black women. READ: *Coming On Strong*, intro–ch. 1.

Tue, 9/10: (AC presentation.) Racial classification, immigration, and the eugenics movement in the early twentieth century. READ: *Darwin's Athletes*, intro–ch. 1, 6, and 13; Christopher Reardon, "American Gothic," *Teaching Tolerance*.

Th, 9/12: The anthropological display of the "savage" Indigenous body: from Native American sports performance at the World's Fair to the exhibit of the living man Ota Benga in the Bronx Zoo. Film in class, *Playing for the World*. READ: Geoffrey Ward, "The Man in the Zoo," *American Heritage*, October 1992.

Tue, 9/17: Women competing in public: class issues, colleges, beauty queens, and the start of basketball. READ: *Coming On Strong*, ch. 2–3.

Th, 9/19: The development of racial codes in Jim Crow sport and in twentieth-century media. Film, *Unforgivable Blackness: The Rise and Fall of Jack Johnson*. READ: *Darwin's Athletes*, ch. 2–3; *Before Jackie*, ch. 1–3; *Revolt of the Black Athlete*, introduction, foreword, preface, and ch. 1.

PART II: Turning points for inclusion, exclusion, and "othering" in sports.

Tue, 9/24: World War II: from Nazi politics at the Berlin Olympics to the internment of Japanese Americans. READ: handouts; *Coming On Strong*, ch. 4 and 6; *Baseball Saved Us*; and Ira Berkow, "Long Overdue, Germany Recognizes a Champion," *New York Times*, October 28, 2002. Recommended film: *The Manzanar Fishermen's Club*.

Th, 9/26: The All-American Girls Professional Baseball League. Film: *When Diamonds Were a Girl's Best Friend*, directed by Janis Taylor (interviews with past AAGPBL players). No readings. First paper due in class today.

Tue, 10/1: Postwar tensions of race and sexuality: segregation and sex roles during the Cold War era, with a focus on the Tennessee State Tigerbelles and the role of Negro Leagues baseball. READ: *Coming On Strong*, ch. 5 and 7; *Before Jackie*, ch. 4–8; *Revolt of the Black Athlete*, ch. 2–3.

Th, 10/3: Contesting womanhood in elite sports, from 1960s "femininity testing" and the East German scandals to trans athletes today. Film: *Doping for Gold*. READ: *Coming On Strong*, ch. 9.

PART III: Contesting and reinforcing standards of sexuality through sports.

Tue, 10/8: Staying pretty, staying young, staying . . . White? How do performance sports, including gymnastics, ice-skating, and ballet, draw in girls? How did soccer become a game for privileged suburban youth in the United States? What are the rewards for youth sports? There will be an overview of sports literature aimed at children, including the role of patriotism and school loyalty. Film: *Kick Like a Girl*. READ: George Vecsey, "England Battles Racism Infecting Soccer," *New York Times*, February 2, 2003; Keith Richburg, "Fans' Racist Taunts Rattle European Soccer," *Washington Post*, December 13, 2004; and *The National Team*, prologue–ch. 6.

Th, 10/10: How muscular are White women permitted to be? This complicated question gets a work-over in the film *Pumping Iron II*. READ: Gloria Steinem, "The Strongest Woman in the World," *Moving beyond Words*.

Tu, 10/15: Review for midterm. Film in class, *Dare to Compete*.

Th, 10/17: MIDTERM EXAM in class.

Tue, 10/22: Title IX, Billie Jean King, and the women's revolution of the 1970s. READ: *Coming On Strong*, ch. 10. You will also receive a packet of current essays on Title IX.

Th, 10/24: The uses of sexuality: to sell, to intimidate. This class positions historic fear of Black manhood with the selling of White female sexuality in sports marketing and the media critique of Black female sexuality and power. READ: Holly Thorpe, "Using Sex to Sell"; Adam Kilgore, "For Rutgers Players, a Great Run Spoiled," *Washington Post*, April 2007; *Revolt of the Black Athlete*, ch. 4–5; and *Darwin's Athletes*, ch. 4, 5, 8–12.

Tue, 10/29: Adjusting the body for public acceptance: extreme dieting, sports food, and the history of eating disorders. READ: Sophie Gilbert, "To the Bone," *Atlantic*, July 14, 2017; R. Marie Griffith, "Apostles of Abstinence," *American Quarterly* 52, no. 4 (December 2000).

Th, 10/31: Homophobia in sports culture, from abusive coaches to school policies to the first out LGBTQ athletes and the Gay Games. Film in class: *Training Rules*. READ: Shannon Keating, "Lesbians Won the Women's World Cup," BuzzFeed News, July 8, 2019.

Tue, 11/5: Continuing focus on sports and homophobia. READ: *Coming On Strong*, ch. 8; handouts, TBA.

Th, 11/7: Anxiety about women catching up to men, then and now. Film in class: *Up to Par*. READ: Ariel Levy, "Either/Or: Sports, Sex, and the Case of Caster Semenya," *New Yorker*, November 30, 2009.

Tu, 11/12: Title IX and equity at Berkeley. How do we implement "fairness"? Readings TBA.

Th, 11/14: Special Title IX guest speaker, Denise Oldham.

PART IV: Commercialized racism in sports marketing, scandal, and media.

Tue, 11/19: Racial marketing in sports brands. How has the usage of Native American mascots made actual Native American athletes less visible? Film: *In Whose Honor?* READ: Amy Taxin, "Arab Mascot at Coachella Valley High," *HuffPost Los Angeles*, December 2, 2013; Bruce Anderson, "That Guy on the Helmet Is Not Me," *Washington Post*, 2014; Charles F. Springwood and C. Richard King, "'Playing Indian': Why Native American Mascots Must End," *Chronicle of Higher Education*, November 9, 2001.

Th, 11/21: Continued focus on sports marketing: from Olympic ads and Wheaties boxes to Nike sweatshops overseas. Who makes our sneakers? What brand names or logos were essential in your house or neighborhood? What trends do you see in brand marketing now? How has the sports market reached out to Muslim athletes? READ:

Cynthia Enloe, "The Globetrotting Sneaker," in *Ms.*, March/April 1995; Aheda Zanetti, "I Created the Burkini," *Guardian*, August 24, 2016.

Tue, 11/26: Misogyny, athletic offenders, and international conflict in our headlines. How might the media critique athletes' participation in sexual assault or violence without racializing such behavior? Where do we find female athletes criminalized? In what ways do Americans categorize opponents on the playing field now? How does taking a knee shift the focus to American racism as an enemy within society? READ: *Darwin's Athletes*, ch. 14–15; Tricia Jenkins, "Do Fans Have to Cheer for America, Too?," *Washington Post*, February 3, 2013; *Revolt of the Black Athlete*, ch. 6 and appendices.

Th, 11/28: NO CLASS: holiday break. Please finish reading *The National Team*.

Tue, 12/3: The year in review: How has the media treated athletes of 2019? What issues emerged from the women's World Cup victory? Whose stories were rediscovered? READ: Sopan Deb, "From Second Base to Center Stage," *New York Times*, June 16, 2019.

Th, 12/5: LAST DAY! How far have women (and men) come in the global acceptance of women's sports coverage and competition? What are the controversies ahead for gender parity in athletics? How have students changed their responses to those questions over the past fifteen years? READ: Andrew Zimbalist, "The NCAA's Women Problem," *New York Times*, March 26, 2016.

Reading/review week: Monday, 12/9, through Friday, 12/13. Extended office hours and study help available. Your final exam will be on Friday evening, December 20. Final course grades will be submitted by 12/24.

NOTES

INTRODUCTION

1. A discussion of young Abigail Pogrebin's challenge to the Wheaties brand may be found in David Kamp's *Sunny Days: The Children's Television Revolution That Changed America* (New York: Simon & Schuster, 2020), 244–45, 308–9.

2. Men's coach Billy Tubbs referred to women's basketball as "money down the drain." His views were supported by then Oklahoma governor Henry Bellmon, who said, "The women will still have intramurals, won't they?"

3. Jenny Lyn Bader, "Larger than Life," in *Next: Young American Writers on the New Generation*, ed. Eric Liu (New York: W.W. Norton, 1994), 8.

1. THE STRENGTH OF OUR FOREMOTHERS

1. Both quotes verbatim from MSNBC evening news, September 16, 2020.

2. See Neil Faulkner, *A Visitor's Guide to the Ancient Olympics* (New Haven: Yale University Press, 2011).

3. This 1851 speech has been reprinted in countless texts. *Narrative of Sojourner Truth: A Bondswoman of Olden Time* was published in 1878. Scholar Deborah Gray White cites the 1968 reprinting of this book in her own work *Ar'n't I a Woman?*, pointing out that in the 1878 narrative, Truth uses "arn't" rather than "ain't." White, *Ar'n't I a Woman? Female Slaves in the Plantation South* (New York: Norton, 1985), 169.

4. British physical education teacher Constance M. K. Applebee introduced field hockey in the United States in 1901.

5. Mary E. Odem, *Delinquent Daughters: Protecting and Policing Adolescent Female Sexuality in the United States, 1885–1920* (Chapel Hill: University of North Carolina Press, 1995), 13–16.

6. See, for instance, Sarah Eisenstein, *Give Us Bread but Give Us Roses: Working Women's Consciousness in the United States, 1890 to the First World*

War (London: Routledge, 1983); Alice Kessler-Harris, *Women Have Always Worked* (Urbana: University of Illinois Press, 2018) and *Out to Work* (New York, Oxford University Press, 1982); and Anzia Yezierska, *Bread Givers* (Garden City, NY: Doubleday, 1925).

7. "The First Game," 125 Stanford Stories, https://125.stanford.edu/the-first-game/.

8. Jessie Graham Flower, *Grace Harlowe's Third Year at Overton College* (Philadelphia: Altemus, 1914), 197–99.

9. Susan Cahn, *Coming On Strong: Gender and Sexuality in Women's Sport*, 2nd ed. (Urbana: University of Illinois Press, 2015), 47.

10. See www.brakettes.com for a history of this remarkable championship fast-pitch softball team.

11. Ashley Brown, "Swinging for the State Department: American Women Tennis Players in Diplomatic Goodwill Tours, 1941–59," *Journal of Sport History* 42, no. 3 (Fall 2015): 289–309.

2. HOW FEMALE ATHLETES DISAPPEAR

1. Claire Williams, Department of Kinesiology, Saint Mary's College, online forum, September 8, 2020.

2. Samuel Redman, *Bone Rooms: From Scientific Racism to Human Prehistory in Museums* (Cambridge, MA: Harvard University Press, 2016); see also Barbara King's review, "'Bone Rooms': Where Scientific Racists Stored Their 'Evidence,'" *Washington Post*, April 15, 2016, https://www.washingtonpost.com/entertainment/books/bone-rooms-where-scientific-racists-stored-their-evidence/2016/04/14/d6aeae46-eed7-11e5-a61f-e9c95c06edca_story.html.

3. Geoffrey C. Ward, "The Man in the Zoo," *American Heritage* 43, no. 6 (October 1992), https://www.americanheritage.com/man-zoo.

4. William I. Thomas, *Sex and Society: Studies in the Social Psychology of Sex* (Chicago: University of Chicago Press, 1907), quoted in Stephanie L. Twin, *Out of the Bleachers: Writings on Women and Sport* (Old Westbury, NY: Feminist, 1979), xxv.

5. See Stuart Creighton Miller, *"Benevolent Assimilation": The American Conquest of the Philippines, 1899–1903* (New Haven: Yale University Press, 1982), 134.

6. *Washington Post*, November 16, 2016.

7. See Eileen McNamara, "Uta's Victory a Female Thing," *Boston Globe*, April 16, 1996, and Lorie Conway, "It's Time to Tell the Bloody Truth," *Nieman Reports*, June 22, 1996.

8. In the 1990s, Jane Curry, who formerly played on the All-American Red Heads professional women's basketball team, began presenting a one-woman show called *Nice Girls Don't Sweat*.

9. See Jules Boykoff, "The Forgotten History of Female Athletes Who Organized Their Own Olympics," Bitch Media, March 18, 2019, https://

www.bitchmedia.org/article/forgotten-history-female-athletes-who
-organized-their-own-olympics.

10. NBC, February 17, 2006. Incidentally, the 2006 Winter Olympic Games
were the first year when women figure skaters were permitted to wear
pants.

11. Mariah Burton Nelson, *The Stronger Women Get, the More Men Love
Football: Sexism and the American Culture of Sports* (New York: Harcourt
Brace, 1994), 222–23.

12. Rosie O'Donnell, foreword to *WNBA: A Celebration: Commemorating the Birth of a League*, by Kelly Whiteside (New York: HarperHorizon,
1998), vi.

13. Pat Summitt, *Raise the Roof: The Inspiring Inside Story of the Tennessee Lady Vols' Undefeated 1997–98 Season* (New York: Broadway Books,
1998), 15–16.

14. Nelson Hernandez, "Ehrlich Is Back in Town, Back in the Game,"
Washington Post, February 6, 2003.

15. *USA Today*, May 23–26, 2003. The aforementioned threat of defeated
men having feminine hygiene products left in their lockers is a very real
phenomenon experienced by many of my male students, who shared that
in high school, their own coaches punished them for losses by filling their
lockers with tampons or forcing them to run around the bases wearing
bras. These abuses occur in the athletic programs of private parochial
schools, as well as public ones.

16. Manuel Roig-Franzia, "For Some, Protest Is a Lost Cause," *Washington Post*, April 12, 2003.

17. Eleanor Reissa, "Dreams of Augusta," *Women's Sports Experience* 12,
no. 1 (April 2003): 13.

18. Sally Jenkins, "Protest Is a Drag, among Other Things," *Washington
Post*, April 13, 2003.

19. In David Kamp, *Sunny Days: The Children's Television Revolution That
Changed America* (New York: Simon & Schuster, 2020), 244–45, 308–9.

20. March 19, 2013.

21. Taylor Craig and Emily Wang, "Title IX Examined: Investigating
Equality in Choate Athletics," *News*, Choate Academy, February 3, 2012.

22. All quotes from comments section posted March 26, 2016, in response to Andrew Zimbalist, "The NCAA's Women Problem," *New York
Times*, March 25, 2016.

23. *Washington Post*, June 10, 2011.

24. See Reggie White, "Women in Locker Rooms," *Asian Wall Street Journal*, April 12, 1999, and Lisa Disch and Mary Jo Kane, "When a Looker Is Really a Bitch: Lisa Olson, Sport, and the Heterosexual Matrix," *Signs* 21, no. 2
(Winter 1996): 278–308.

3. TOMBOY IDENTITIES, MUSCULAR IDEALS

1. Elizabeth Merrill, "Kansas Religious-Based School Called Out for Removing Female Ref," ESPN, February 21, 2008, https://www.espn.com/college-sports/highschool/news/story?id=3257427.

2. Stephen Ward, "The Superior Athlete," in *Motivations in Play, Games and Sport*, ed. Ralph Slovenko and James A. Knight (Springfield, IL: Charles C. Thomas, 1967), 311, quoted in Stephanie Twin, ed., *Out of the Bleachers: Writings on Women in Sports* (Old Westbury, NY: Feminist, 1979), xxxv.

3. "Hockey Canada Apologizes after Canada Hockey Women Party on the Ice," Metro, February 26, 2010.

4. Peter Perl, "Forward Motion," *Washington Post Magazine*, September 15, 2002, 12.

5. See Elaine Sciolino, "For French Girls, Playing Soccer Is a Tough Goal," *New York Times*, September 16, 2002.

6. Colette Dowling, *The Frailty Myth: Women Approaching Physical Equality* (New York: Random House, 2000), xxvi.

7. Dowling, 51.

8. Dowling, 64.

9. See Joan Ryan, *Little Girls in Pretty Boxes: The Making and Breaking of Elite Gymnasts and Figure Skaters* (New York: Warner Books, 2000).

10. My Georgetown student Kiran Gandhi created headlines by completing the London Marathon while visibly bleeding; see Helin Jung, "26-Year-Old Woman Free Bleeds Proudly through Her First Marathon," *Cosmopolitan*, August 6, 2015, https://www.cosmopolitan.com/health-fitness/q-and-a/a44392/free-bleeding-marathoner-kiran-gandhi/, and Radhika Sanghani, "This Woman Ran the London Marathon on Her Period without a Tampon," *Telegraph*, August 10, 2015, https://www.telegraph.co.uk/women/womens-life/11793848/Free-bleeding-This-woman-ran-the-London-Marathon-on-her-period-without-a-tampon.html.

11. Dowling, 94.

12. Dowling, 229.

13. See Hamil R. Harris, "Divas to Be Reckoned With," *Washington Post*, June 11, 2003.

14. Megan Krug, "Powder Puff Game Challenges Gender Roles." *Hoya*, November 12, 2002.

15. See also Ann Pellegrini, *Performance Anxieties: Staging Psychoanalysis, Staging Race* (New York: Routledge, 1997), 165–70.

16. For a list of colleges and universities that ban LGBT students from enrolling, such as Liberty University, consult GLSEN (https://www.glsen.org) and Outsports (https://www.outsports.com/).

17. Begin your search with J. D. Doyle's Queer Music Heritage website, https://www.queermusicheritage.org. Women's music is available online and through Goldenrod Distribution.

18. Rosemary Auchmuty, *A World of Girls* (London: Women's Press, 1992), 60.

19. Auchmuty, 142–43.

20. See Susan Cahn, *Coming On Strong: Gender and Sexuality in Women's Sport*, 2nd ed. (Urbana: University of Illinois Press, 2015), 262–65.

21. Jane Trahey, *Life with Mother Superior* (New York: Farrar, Straus and Cudahy, 1962), 172.

22. October 13, 2000. See also the *Chronicle of Higher Education* feature "The Loneliest Athletes," November 1, 2002.

23. Donald Padgett, "Out on the Field," *Out*, February/March 2021, 46–47.

24. Peter Perl, "The Incredible Shrinking Duyers," *Washington Post Magazine*, March 30, 2003, 10.

25. Throughout this book, champion musher Susan Butcher, a frequent winner of the Alaskan Iditarod, is referred to as "the Butch" by her male competitors.

26. Cahn, *Coming On Strong*, 66.

27. Cahn, 64.

28. Dowling, 32.

29. Cahn, 62.

30. An excellent source is Celia Brackenridge and Kari Fasting, eds., *Sexual Harassment and Abuse in Sport: International Research and Policy Perspectives* (London: Whiting & Birch, 2002), particularly Sandra Kirby and Glen Winthrup, "Running the Gauntlet: An Examination of Initiation/ Hazing and Sexual Abuse in Sport," 65–90.

31. Warren Casey, quoted in Boze Hadleigh, *In or Out? Gay and Straight Celebrities Talk about Themselves and Each Other* (New York: Barricade Books, 2000), 227.

32. Dave McKenna, "Pro Football, Pro Bono," *City Paper*, May 30, 2003, https://washingtoncitypaper.com/article/253668/pro-football-pro-bono/. Though the Divas advanced to the playoffs, publicity waned; I had to tune into the 1:00 a.m. radio program hosted by WPFW's late-night host Lady E to hear an ad for the championship game.

4. FROM HALF-COURT TO FEDERAL COURT

1. Sally Jenkins, "Government Should Leave Title IX Alone," *Washington Post*, January 25, 2002.

2. Ryan Winn, "Why Title IX Is Bad for Georgetown," *Georgetown Academy*, February 2005.

3. Meredith McCloskey, "On a Level Playing Field," *Hoya*, January 23, 2001.

4. Alex Lau, "Title IX's Beneficial Intent Becoming Discriminatory," *Hoya*, October 1, 2010.

5. Matt Emch, "Title IX Causes Inequity," *Hoya*, October 28, 2011.

6. Grant Teaff, "Not All Sports Are Equal," *USA Today*, November 8, 1995.

7. Welch Suggs, "Wrestling Complaints Denied in Title IX Ruling," *Chronicle of Higher Education*, June 20, 2003.

8. Frank Rienzo, "Title IX: An Examination of Georgetown University's Department of Athletics, Revised July 15, 1976," 19, quoted in Elizabeth Bent, "Women in Sports and Title IX at Georgetown University" (senior thesis, May 1999), 16.

9. "Title IX and Race in Intercollegiate Sports," Women's Sports Foundation, 2003. See also Marilyn Yarbrough, "A Sporting Chance: The Intersection of Race and Gender," *Texas Law Review*, 1997.

10. In *Ms.*, December 2002/January 2003.

11. "Now She's Got Game," *Time*, March 3, 2003, 58.

12. December 31, 2019. Article by Lindsay Crouse featured in Equal Play video series by Carol Hutchins, Edniesha Curry, and Meredith Flaherty.

5. GLOBAL ENCOUNTERS WITH WOMEN'S SPORTS

1. CNN, April 21, 2010.

2. *Sabah*, Turkish press, August 8, 2012.

3. BBC, June 16, 2016.

4. See Amy Taxin, "'Arab' Mascot at Coachella Valley High School Sparks Debate about Ethnic Caricatures," Associated Press, December 2, 2013.

5. Rama Lakshmi, *Washington Post*, August 21, 2016.

6. CHALLENGES FOR A WOMEN'S SPORTS PROFESSOR

1. This scandal resulted in an intensive study by Harvard's athletics department on ways to improve the climate for female athletes. I had the privilege of being approached as a consultant.

2. See the Raliance report "Athletic Trainers as Leaders in Sexual Violence Prevention," February 17, 2021; contact info@raliance.org.

3. Frank O'Brien, "To the Editor," *Metro Weekly*, January 23, 2003.

4. Cynthia Pemberton, *More Than a Game: One Woman's Fight for Gender Equity in Sport* (Boston: Northeastern University Press, 2002), 238–39.

5. Andrea Stover, in *Public Works: Student Writing as Public Text*, ed. Emily Isaacs and Phoebe Jackson (Portsmouth, NH: Boynton/Cook, 2001), 1.

6. Angela Hewett and Robert McRuer, "Composing Student Activists," in Isaacs and Jackson, *Public Works*, 100–101.

7. Zach Schonfeld, "Swain Withdraws Communications VP Offer Following Criticism for Role in Nassar Case," *GW Hatchet*, August 15, 2020.

8. Becca Rothfeld, "At-Will Employment Is the Real 'Cancel Culture,'" *Jacobin*, October 2020.

9. Kevin Blackstone, "It's Time . . . Long Overdue, in Fact . . . to Put an End to the Student-Athlete Charade," *Washington Post*, May 24, 2015.

10. Marianna Brady, "Megan Rapinoe: Why Is America's Newest Hero So Polarizing?," BBC News, July 14, 2019.

11. Celia Brackenridge and Kari Fasting, eds., *Sexual Harassment and Abuse in Sport: International Research and Policy Perspectives* (London: Whiting & Birch, 2002), 5.

12. Associated Press, May 23, 2003. From the online *Women's Sports Weekly*, May 29, 2003.

13. Nancy Dunne, "The Women Leading the Field in Business," *Financial Times*, March 28, 2003.

14. See Richard Rothstein, "Lessons—Are the Three R's Crowding Out P.E.?," *New York Times*, November 29, 2000.

15. John Gerdy, in *College Board Review*, no. 198 (Winter 2003): 31.

CONCLUSION

1. Nancy Gillen, Inside the Games, September 25, 2020.

2. Jessica Luther, NBC News, May 11, 2020.

3. Juliet Macur, *New York Times*, March 21, 2020.

4. Ben Pickman, *Sports Illustrated*, March 26, 2020.

5. Melanie Fine, *Forbes*, April 29, 2020.

6. Randy Johnson, "A Loss of Conversation in Sports," *Santa Cruz Sentinel*, April 4, 2020.

7. Bob Woodward, MSNBC, September 16, 2020.

8. Brian Williams, MSNBC, September 16, 2020.

9. Anti-Defamation League chief executive Jonathan Greenblatt, *Washington Post*, September 30, 2020.

10. Bill Svelmoe, professor of history at Notre Dame University, MSNBC, October 1, 2020.

11. NPR, October 2, 2020.

12. Dana Bash, CNN, October 4, 2020.

13. Brian Williams, MSNBC, after the vice-presidential debates, October 7, 2020.

14. Jake Tapper, CNN, October 22, 2020.

15. Joe Biden, in his final campaign speech before the national election, November 2, 2020.

16. David Plouffe, MSNBC, November 3, 2020.

17. Former Missouri senator Claire McCaskill, MSNBC, November 3, 2020.

18. James Carville, MSNBC, November 5, 2020.

19. Chris Hayes, MSNBC, November 5, 2020.

20. Rep. James Clyburn, CNN, November 5, 2020.

21. Dr. Anthony Fauci, CNN, December 3, 2020.

22. CNN, March 19, 2021.

23. Rick Maese and Emily Guskin, "Most Americans Support Athletes Speaking Out, Say Anthem Protests Are Appropriate," *Washington Post*, September 9, 2020.

24. See Yvette Lynne Bonaparte, "Meeting the Moment: Black Lives Matter, Racial Inequality, Corporate Messaging, and Rebranding," *Advertising and Society Quarterly* 21, no. 3 (Fall 2020).

25. See Sopan Deb and Kevin Draper, "Exploring What's Next for Loeffler and the W.N.B.A.," *New York Times*, January 7, 2021.

26. Desi Carrasco, "150W at Cal: Layshia Clarendon," Cal Athletics, October 9, 2020, https://calbears.com/sports/2020/10/9/150w-at-cal-layshia-clarendon.

27. See also Sally Jenkins, "College Sports Embraced Reckless Greed. With the Coronavirus Crisis, the Bill Has Come Due," *Washington Post*, August 7, 2020, and Sally Jenkins, "NCAA's Message to Women's Basketball Players: You're Worth Less," *Washington Post*, March 19, 2021.

BIBLIOGRAPHY

Ardell, Jean Hastings. *Breaking into Baseball: Women and the National Pastime*. Carbondale: Southern Illinois University Press, 2005.

Awkward, Michael. *Burying Don Imus: Anatomy of a Scapegoat*. Minneapolis: University of Minnesota, 2009.

Baughman, Cynthia, ed. *Women on Ice: Feminist Essays on the Tonya Harding / Nancy Kerrigan Spectacle*. New York: Routledge, 1995.

Benedict, Jeff. *Out of Bounds: Inside the NBA's Culture of Rape, Violence, and Crime*. New York: HarperCollins, 2004.

———. *Public Heroes, Private Felons: Athletes and Crimes against Women*. Boston: Northeastern University Press, 1997.

Berlage, Gai Ingham. *Women in Baseball: The Forgotten History*. Westport, CT: Praeger, 1994.

Besnier, Niko, Susan Brownell, and Thomas F. Carter. *The Anthropology of Sport: Bodies, Borders, Biopolitics*. Oakland: University of California Press, 2018.

Birrell, Susan, and Mary G. McDonald. *Reading Sport: Critical Essays on Power and Representation*. Boston: Northeastern University Press, 2000.

Blais, Madeleine. *In These Girls, Hope Is a Muscle*. New York: Atlantic Monthly, 1995.

Bledsoe, Lucy Jane. *No Stopping Us Now*. New York: Three Rooms Press, 2022.

Blum, Arlene. *Annapurna, a Woman's Place*. San Francisco: Sierra Club Books, 1980.

Blumenthal, Karen. *Let Me Play: The Story of Title IX*. New York: Atheneum, 2005.

Bolin, Anne, and Jane Granskog, eds. *Athletic Intruders: Ethnographic Research on Women, Culture, and Exercise*. Albany: State University of New York Press, 2003.

Bond, Marybeth, ed. *A Woman's World: True Stories of World Travel*. San Francisco: Travelers' Tales, 2003.

Boschert, Sherry. *37 Words: Title IX and Fifty Years of Fighting Sex Discrimination*. New York: New Press, 2022.

Boyne, Daniel J. *The Red Rose Crew: A True Story of Women, Winning, and the Water*. New York: Hyperion, 2000.

Brackenridge, Celia, and Kari Fausting, eds. *Sexual Harassment and Abuse in Sport: International Research and Policy Perspectives*. London: Whiting & Birch, 2002.

Brooks, Geraldine. *Nine Parts of Desire: The Hidden World of Islamic Women*. New York: Anchor Books, 1995.

Brown, Rita Mae. *Sudden Death*. New York: Bantam, 1983.

Brownell, Susan. *Training the Body for China: Sports in the Moral Order of the People's Republic*. Chicago: University of Chicago Press, 1995.

Brumberg, Joan Jacobs. *The Body Project: An Intimate History of American Girls*. New York: Random House, 1997.

Buren, Jodi. *Superwomen: 100 Women, 100 Sports*. New York: Bullfinch, 2004.

Burns, Robin. *Just Tell Them I Survived! Women in Antarctica*. Crows Nest, Australia: Allen & Unwin, 2001.

Cadogan, Mary, and Patricia Craig. *You're a Brick, Angela! A New Look at Girls' Fiction from 1839 to 1975*. London: Gollancz, 1976.

Cahn, Susan. *Coming On Strong: Gender and Sexuality in Women's Sport*. 2nd ed. Urbana: University of Illinois Press, 2015.

Cayleff, Susan E. *Babe: The Life and Legend of Babe Didrikson Zaharias*. Urbana: University of Illinois Press, 1995.

Cleary, Beverly. *My Own Two Feet: A Memoir*. New York: Morrow Junior Books, 1995.

Corbett, Sara. *Venus to the Hoop: A Gold-Medal Year in Women's Basketball*. New York: Doubleday, 1997.

Corey, Mary, and Mark Harnischfeger. *Before Jackie: The Negro Leagues, Civil Rights and the American Dream*. Ithaca, NY: Paramount Market, 2014.

Costa, D. Margaret, and Sharon R. Guthrie, eds. *Women and Sport: Interdisciplinary Perspectives*. Champaign, IL: Human Kinetics, 1994.

Creedon, Pamela, ed. *Women, Media, and Sport: Challenging Gender Values*. Thousand Oaks, CA: Sage, 1994.

Daddario, Gina. *Women's Sport and Spectacle: Gendered Television Coverage and the Olympic Games*. Westport, CT: Praeger, 1998.

Daniels, Dayna. *Polygendered and Ponytailed: The Dilemma of Femininity and the Female Athlete*. Toronto: Women's, 2009.

Davis, Laurel. *The Swimsuit Issue and Sport: Hegemonic Masculinity in Sports Illustrated*. Albany: State University of New York Press, 1997.

Demers, Guylaine, Lorraine Greaves, Sandra Kirby, and Marion Lay, eds. *Playing It Forward: 50 Years of Women and Sport in Canada*. Ottawa: Feminist History Society, 2013.

Dowling, Colette. *The Frailty Myth: Women Approaching Physical Equality.* New York: Random House, 2000.

Edwards, Harry. *The Revolt of the Black Athlete.* 50th anniversary ed. Urbana: University of Illinois Press, 2017.

Fausto-Sterling, Anne. *Myths of Gender: Biological Theories about Women and Men.* 2nd ed. New York: Basic Books, 1992.

Festle, Mary Jo. *Playing Nice: Politics and Apologies in Women's Sports.* New York: Columbia University Press, 1996.

Fields, Sarah. *Female Gladiators: Gender, Law, and Contact Sport in America.* Urbana: University of Illinois Press, 2005.

Gavora, Jessica. *Tilting the Playing Field: Schools, Sports, Sex, and Title IX.* San Francisco: Encounter Books, 2002.

Gori, Gigliola. *Italian Fascism and the Female Body: Sport, Submissive Women and Strong Women.* London: Routledge, 2004.

Gottesman, Jane. *Game Face: What Does a Female Athlete Look Like?* New York: Random House, 2001.

Griffin, Pat. *Strong Women, Deep Closets: Lesbians and Homophobia in Sport.* Champaign, IL: Human Kinetics, 1998.

Griffith, R. Marie. *Born Again Bodies: Flesh and Spirit in American Christianity.* Berkeley: University of California Press, 2004.

Grundy, Pamela. *Learning to Win: Sports, Education, and Social Change in Twentieth-Century North Carolina.* Chapel Hill: University of North Carolina Press, 2001.

Grundy, Pamela, and Susan Shackelford. *Shattering the Glass: The Remarkable History of Women's Basketball.* New York: New Press, 2005.

Guttmann, Allen. *A Whole New Ball Game: An Interpretation of American Sports.* Chapel Hill: University of North Carolina Press, 1988.

———. *Women's Sports: A History.* New York: Columbia University Press, 1991.

Hanson, Katherine, Vivian Guilfoy, and Sarita Pillai. *More Than Title IX: How Equity in Education Has Shaped the Nation.* Lanham, MD: Roman & Littlefield, 2009.

Hargreaves, Jennifer. *Sporting Females: Critical Issues in the History and Sociology of Women's Sports.* London: Routledge, 1994.

Heywood, Leslie, and Shari Dworkin. *Built to Win: The Female Athlete as Cultural Icon.* Minneapolis: University of Minnesota Press, 2003.

Hoberman, John. *Darwin's Athletes: How Sport Has Damaged Black America and Preserved the Myth of Race.* Boston: Houghton Mifflin, 1997.

Hong, Fan. *Footbinding, Feminism, and Freedom: The Liberation of Women's Bodies in Modern China.* London: F. Cass, 1997.

Hult, Joan, and Marianna Trekell, eds. *A Century of Women's Basketball: From Frailty to Final Four.* Reston, VA: National Association for Girls and Women in Sport, 1991.

Jay, Kathryn. *More Than Just a Game: Sports in American Life since 1945.* New York: Columbia University Press, 2004.

Jinxia, Dong. *Women, Sport, and Society in Modern China: Holding Up More Than Half the Sky*. London: F. Cass, 2003.

Kessler, Lauren. *Full Court Press: A Season in the Life of a Winning Basketball Team and the Women Who Made It Happen*. New York: Dutton, 1997.

King, Billie Jean. *Billie Jean*. New York: Viking, 1982.

King, Billie Jean, with Johnette Howard and Maryanne Vollers. *All In: An Autobiography*. New York: Knopf, 2021.

Kirk, David. *Schooling Bodies: School Practice and Public Discourse, 1880-1950*. London: Leicester University Press, 1998.

Knudson, R. R. *Zanballer*. New York: Delacorte, 1972.

LaBastille, Anne. *Woodswoman*. New York: E.P. Dutton, 1976.

Large, David Clay. *Nazi Games: The Olympics of 1936*. New York: W.W. Norton, 2007.

Lawler, Jennifer. *Punch! Why Women Participate in Violent Sports*. Terre Haute, IN: Wish, 2002.

Leder, Jane. *Grace and Glory: A Century of Women in the Olympics*. Chicago: Triumph Books, 1996.

Lessa, Christina. *Women Who Win*. New York: Universe, 1998.

Littman, Jonathan. *The Beautiful Game: Sixteen Girls and the Soccer Season That Changed Everything*. New York: Avon Books, 1999.

Lomax, Michael E., ed. *Sports and the Racial Divide: African American and Latino Experience in an Era of Change*. Jackson: University Press of Mississippi, 2008.

Longman, Jere. *The Girls of Summer: The U.S. Women's Soccer Team and How It Changed the World*. New York: HarperCollins, 2000.

Louganis, Greg. *Breaking the Surface*. New York: Random House, 1995.

Louv, Richard. *Last Child in the Woods: Saving Our Children from Nature-Deficit Disorder*. Chapel Hill, NC: Algonquin Books, 2005.

Luther, Jessica. *Unsportsmanlike Conduct: College Football and the Politics of Rape*. New York: Akashic Books, 2016

Macy, Sue. *Winning Ways: A Photohistory of American Women in Sports*. New York: Henry Holt, 1996.

———. *A Whole New Ball Game: The Story of the All-American Girls Professional Baseball League*. New York: Henry Holt, 1993.

Magdalinksi, Tara, and Timothy J. L. Chandler, eds. *With God on Their Side: Sport in the Service of Religion*. New York: Routledge, 2002.

Margolick, David. *Beyond Glory: Joe Louis vs. Max Schmeling and a World on the Brink*. New York: Knopf, 2005.

Mazo, Joseph. *Dance Is a Contact Sport*. New York: Saturday Review, 1974.

McDonagh, Eileen, and Laura Pappano. *Playing with the Boys: Why Separate Is Not Equal in Sports*. Oxford: Oxford University Press, 2008.

McElroy, James. *We've Got Spirit: The Life and Times of America's Greatest Cheerleading Team*. New York: Simon & Schuster, 1999.

Messner, Michael. *Out of Play: Critical Essays on Gender and Sport*. Albany: State University of New York Press, 2007.

———. *Taking the Field: Women, Men, and Sports*. Minneapolis: University of Minnesota Press, 2002.

Messner, Michael, and Donald Sabo. *Sex, Violence & Power in Sports: Rethinking Masculinity*. Freedom, CA: Crossing, 1994.

Murray, Caitlin. *The National Team: The Inside Story of the Women Who Changed Soccer*. New York: Abrams, 2019.

Navratilova, Martina. *Martina*. New York: Knopf, 1985.

Nelson, Mariah Burton. *Are We Winning Yet? How Women Are Changing Sports and Sports Are Changing Women*. New York: Random House, 1991.

———. *Embracing Victory: Life Lessons in Competition and Compassion*. New York: Morrow, 1998.

———. *The Stronger Women Get, the More Men Love Football: Sexism and the American Culture of Sports*. New York: Harcourt Brace, 1994.

———. *We Are All Athletes: Bringing Courage, Confidence, and Peak Performance into Our Everyday Lives*. Kitty Hawk, NC: Dare, 2002.

Nyad, Diana. *Find a Way*. New York: Knopf, 2015.

Oglesby, Carole, ed. *Encyclopedia of Women and Sport in America*. Phoenix: Oryx, 1998.

O'Reilly, Jean, and Susan Cahn, eds. *Women and Sports in the United States: A Documentary Reader*. Boston: Northeastern University Press, 2007.

Parker, Kate T. *Strong Is the New Pretty: A Celebration of Girls Being Themselves*. New York: Workman, 2017.

Pemberton, Cynthia. *More Than a Game: One Woman's Fight for Gender Equity in Sport*. Boston: Northeastern University Press, 2002.

Pope, Harrison G., Katharine Phillips, and Roberto Olivardia. *The Adonis Complex: The Secret Crisis of Male Body Obsession*. New York: Free Press, 2000.

Revoyr, Nina. *The Necessary Hunger*. New York: Simon & Schuster, 1997.

Rhoden, William C. *Forty Million Dollar Slaves: The Rise, Fall, and Redemption of the Black Athlete*. New York: Crown, 2006.

Ring, Jennifer. *Stolen Bases: Why American Girls Don't Play Baseball*. Urbana: University of Illinois Press, 2009.

Roberts, Randy, and James Olson. *Winning Is the Only Thing: Sports in America since 1945*. Baltimore: Johns Hopkins University Press, 1989.

Ross, Cindy. *Journey on the Crest: Walking 2,600 Miles from Mexico to Canada*. Seattle: Mountaineers, 1987.

Roxxie, ed. *Girljock: The Book*. New York: St. Martin's, 1998.

Ryan, Joan. *Little Girls in Pretty Boxes: The Making and Breaking of Elite Gymnasts and Figure Skaters*. New York: Warner Books, 2000.

Salter, David. *Crashing the Old Boys' Network: The Tragedies and Triumphs of Girls and Women in Sports*. Westport, CT: Praeger, 1996.

Schiot, Molly. *Game Changers: The Unsung Heroines of Sports History*. New York: Simon & Schuster, 2016.

Schultz, Jaime. *Women's Sports: What Everyone Needs to Know*. New York: Oxford University Press, 2018.

Silby, Caroline. *Games Girls Play: Understanding and Guiding Young Female Athletes*. New York: St. Martin's, 2000.

Smith, Lissa, ed. *Nike Is a Goddess: The History of Women in Sports*. New York: Atlantic Monthly, 1998.

Staurowsky, Ellen, ed. *Women and Sport: Continuing a Journey of Liberation and Celebration*. Champaign, IL: Human Kinetics, 2016.

Staurowsky, Ellen, and Allen Sack. *College Athletes for Hire: The Evolution and Legacy of the NCAA's Amateur Myth*. Westport, CT: Praeger, 1998.

Steinem, Gloria. *Moving beyond Words*. New York: Simon & Schuster, 1994.

Stratford, Trisha. *Guts, Tears and Glory*. Auckland, New Zealand: New Women's, 1988.

Summitt, Pat. *Raise the Roof: The Inspiring Inside Story of the Tennessee Lady Vols' Undefeated 1997–98 Season*. New York: Broadway Books, 1998.

———. *Sum It Up: 1,098 Victories, a Couple of Irrelevant Losses, and a Life in Perspective*. New York: Crown Archetype, 2013.

Switzer, Kathrine. *Marathon Woman: Running the Race to Revolutionize Women's Sports*. New York: Carroll & Graf, 2007.

Talley, Jeannine. *Women at the Helm*. Racine, WI: Mother Courage, 1990.

Twin, Stephanie, ed. *Out of the Bleachers: Writings on Women and Sport*. Old Westbury, NY: Feminist, 1979.

Turco, Mary. *Crashing the Net: The U.S. Women's Olympic Ice Hockey Team and the Road to Gold*. New York: HarperCollins, 1999.

Tyus, Wyomia, and Elizabeth Terzakis. *Tigerbelle: The Wyomia Tyus Story*. New York: Edge of Sports, 2020.

VanDerveer, Tara. *Shooting from the Outside: How a Coach and Her Olympic Team Transformed Women's Basketball*. New York: Avon Books, 1997.

Ware, Susan. *Title IX: A Brief History with Documents*. Boston: Bedford, 2007.

Whiteside, Kelly. *WNBA: A Celebration: Commemorating the Birth of a League*. New York: HarperHorizon, 1998.

Willard, Frances. *How I Learned to Ride the Bicycle: Reflections of an Influential 19th Century Woman*. Sunnyvale, CA: Fair Oaks, 1991.

Woolum, Janet. *Outstanding Women Athletes: Who They Are and How They Influenced Sports in America*. 2nd ed. Phoenix: Oryx, 1998.

Wushanley, Ying. *Playing Nice and Losing: The Struggle for Control of Women's Intercollegiate Athletics, 1960–2000*. Syracuse: Syracuse University Press, 2004.

Zang, David. *SportsWars: Athletes in the Age of Aquarius*. Fayetteville: University of Arkansas Press, 2001.

Zimmerman, Jean, and Gil Reavill. *Raising Our Athletic Daughters: How Sports Can Build Self-Esteem and Save Girls' Lives*. New York: Doubleday, 1998.

Zirin, Dave. *What's My Name, Fool? Sports and Resistance in the United States*. Chicago: Haymarket Books, 2005.

INDEX

Bonnie J. Morris, PhD, has been teaching women's sports history for more than twenty-five years, becoming Professor of the Year and emeritus professor at George Washington University, Silver Vicennial Medalist at Georgetown, and a nominee for the American Cultures Excellence in Teaching Award at UC Berkeley. The author of nineteen books and a member of the Authors Guild, she is a scholarly adviser to the National Women's History Museum, a history consultant to Disney, and the archivist for Olivia Records, as well as three-time faculty for the global Semester at Sea program. Morris is currently a lecturer in history at the University of California at Berkeley. Find her talks on C-SPAN and her writing at www.bonniejmorris.com.